African Writing Today

ᘓᔍ

A Literary Review Book

ANGOFF, Charles and John Povey, sels. and eds. **African writing today; Ethiopia, Ghana, Kenya, Nigeria, Sierra Leone, Uganda, Zambia. Manyland Books, 84–39 90th St., Woodhaven, New York 11421, 1970 (c1969). 304p il bibl 71-108630. 6.95**
John Povey is the real editor of this volume, having solicited the stories and poems himself for original publication in the literary review. His introductory essay makes the point that patronizing whites "appreciate" African literature because it is quaintly primitive, while in reality it has become mature by our own standards. Compared with other collections, this book has several characteristics: First, it is written in English only. Second, it taps the post-colonial writing of English speaking Africans, as opposed to those writing in French, Arabic, or other African languages. Third, it is contemporary in orientation rather than ethnographic or archaic. Fourth, it is not generally political, ideological, polemical, or racist anti-white — unlike much African French writing. Fifth, it is sub-Saharan. Many of the stories and some of the poems are quite moving or entertaining and should be enjoyed by students or the general public. The editor himself clearly denigrates, however, the solitary Ethiopian contribution, a poem in Eliot's style by Solomon Deresse, which seems to show English poetic sophistication as well as personal agony.

CHOICE   *MAY '71*

Language & Literature

Other

ETHIOPIA

GHANA

KENYA

NIGERIA

SIERRA LEONE

UGANDA

ZAMBIA

AFRICAN WRITING TODAY

Selected and Edited by

CHARLES ANGOFF
Fairleigh Dickinson University

JOHN POVEY
University of California, Los Angeles

MANYLAND BOOKS • NEW YORK

AFRICAN WRITING TODAY
Copyright 1969, by The Literary Review

MANYLAND BOOKS, INC.
84-39 90th Street
Woodhaven, N.Y. 11421

Library of Congress Catalogue Card No. 71-108630
SBN: 87141

MANUFACTURED IN THE UNITED STATES OF AMERICA

African Writing Today

Table of Contents

Table of Contents Arranged by States

Foreword

My part in the preparation of the present volume is both integral and peripheral. The bulk of the contents comprised the Africa number of *The Literary Review*, of which I am editor, and for which I assumed ultimate responsibility. At the same time, the bulk of the actual compiling and editing was done by the guest editor, Dr. John Povey.

It would be presumptuous of me to add anything to his learned essay on "African Writing Today." What little I know of the subject I have learned to a great extent from him. At the same time, I do feel I can say something about the purely literary aspects of the contents. What stays in the mind is the deep involvement of the African writers in the folklore of their people, as is especially evident in the haunting novella, *Under the Iroko Tree*. This African folklore appears to have much in common with Hebrew folklore: it is mystical, sorrowful, lyrical, in intimate contact with divinity—and there hovers over it the threnody of the fragile place of woman in this earthly life, as well as of the haven of strength she is. The last three lines of the novella echo this intertwined concern: "I'll be back home soon, Mama. Much sooner than I thought. And you will wait for me, Mama. You promised you'd wait. You'll wait, Mama, won't you?"

There is also the lovely innocence of childhood, its bedazzlement with the unending miracle of the life burgeoning before it almost hourly. "The Child and the Water-Tap," by Sadru Kassam, is a case in point. It is brief, sharp, soft, lovely, and haunting. What takes place? Nothing— and everything. It begins: "The naked child stood there in the scullery in front of the tap, staring intently at the water dripping in a little tin." The child looked piercingly, as children do. "Time dripped on." Then the child, with the aid of a toy, knocked the head of the tap, and a revelation burst forth: "There was a sudden gush of water as the head loosened and the child screamed with joy as if spurting forth his own energy. Slowly, holding the toy in his lap, almost hugging it, he sat down, cross-legged, under the tap, smiling, just smiling, while the water flowed over him and the warm beam of sunlight settled on his navel."

Only one and a half pages long is this story, yet it's sheer magic.

It's the poetry that, to me, is the most striking aspect of African literature. It is often soft and lush and sensuous, but more often than not, apparently, this softness and lushness and sensuousness are nature-directed rather than man-directed. Consider the first stanza of "The First Yam of the Year," by R. N. Egudu:

> "I have dug it fresh,
> this boneless flesh
> of air, earth, warmth
> and water, this
> life out of the heart
> of death;
> its cap of fibre
> will mail the elder's
> head against grey rain,
> and its body proof his
> to spite time's arrows."

As with the Jews, the Africans are on close terms with God, almost in partnership with Him, and they relate Him to both death and birth. "The Image of God," by John M. Ruganda, illustrates this:

> "It is the sweet death
> Of The God who dies
> In Man's birth,
> That is the spring of Kato's freedom,
> Alike in vanity and divinity;
> And it is the victory
> Of the God who is
> When man dies
> That impels Kato
> Not to want heaven,
> But the eternal form of pleasure:
> For God is
> Because man lives."

It is difficult to resist the temptation to point out how much richer, as sheer literary art, African writing is than so much of the blatant black writing in the United States today. The American black poets and fiction writers have more than a little to learn from the Africans.

CHARLES ANGOFF
Fairleigh Dickinson University
Rutherford, New Jersey

John Povey

The Quality of African Writing Today

EVEN TODAY, in this era of the United Nations and TV news coverage, our image of Africa is a dark one. Some curious compendium of Stanley and Livingstone, and Saturday matinees with their Tarzan adventures, has fixed with apparently ineradicable force an American popular view of Africa which is not just outdated, but which always was absurdly inaccurate. Even the events of contemporary Africa filter through this distorted mirror of our understanding. Upon this prejudice are superimposed the attitudes of a century of missionary proselytizing for funds to help the heathen, and a recollection of bold exploring, conceived as purely geographic but resulting in occupation and exploitation. Sometimes there is hardly even this knowledge, but only a blank incomprehension, as empty as those remote white interiors on Renaissance maps of Africa which were decoratively populated with improbable legendary monsters.

What do we believe of Africa? It is the "black" continent (with all the damning connotations which that word has to pale-faced Europeans). It is populated by savages who live in twig huts and have bones through their noses. According to *New Yorker* cartoons, they exist upon a diet of stewed missionary. Most of this is an obvious joke, of course. We "know" Africa isn't the place of the Disneyland ride with head-hunters and savage beasts prowling. What then do we substitute? More importantly, what can we assert as of value to *us* in present-day Africa?

Only relatively recently have scholars been able to begin asserting a different view of Africa. In the last decade it has been possible for a Philip Curtin or a Basil Davidson to add an African dimension to a history previously seen only as a reaction to the European activities that formed the Colonial period. Until ten years ago, African history was only imperial history; and this reaction may be more widespread than we admit. After all, we still do not have a history of the United States from the standpoint of the Indians!

The major point that must be stated with all possible urgency is the difference that appears in our attitude to Africa in comparison with our feelings for most other areas of the world. In a very real sense we have despised it. In spite of a general xenophobia we have made distinctions. With every other culture, no matter how foreign and exotic, we have, with some measure of grudging space, admitted the possibility that we might gain from another indigenous yet highly different sensibility. Take China, Japan, India; we admire the beauty of their art, draw upon the experience of their civilization. In religion we bring Zen perception, Confucian sayings, Buddhist ethics, into our own moral philosophy—or at least make our interest the starting point for debate. But with Africa this is not so. The missionaries have done their work too well. The Africans are heathen, their religions are a series of blasphemies—bestial, blood-stained, black arts that must be driven out by the Holy Light. In architecture we rightly admire Angkor Wat, but after the discovery of the great Rhodesian temple of Zimbabwe we spent fifty years, not in appreciating its architectural power, but in fruitless searching for some exotic group of invaders from the East who might have built it, since it had to be taken for granted, that no African people could have been competent enough to construct its impressive, decorated walls. The pottery of China, the wood carvings of India, are deservedly renowned. The similar arts of Africa, so richly varied and sophisticated, are "primitive"; they are never to be found in a gallery of art, but are put in the ethnic museums as curious artifacts, presumed to be of some functional purpose according to anthropologists, but without any aesthetic worth.

Is this putting things too strongly? Obviously there are recent changes. There was the First World Festival of Negro art in Dakar in 1965. Collectors now avidly seek the beautiful masks of the Dan tribe which have become stylistically familiar to us through interpretations by Picasso and Modigliani, which we once assumed were individual innovations. But can we say this is yet more than the concern of a few? Our present attitude seems not dissimilar to that of the rulers of medieval China, who, we are told, saw the Europeans as barbarous and ugly invaders who could offer nothing of worth to the Sun Kingdom, which had already reached the apex of culture and knowledge.

Part of our attitude may be traced to the relatively inhospitable geography of the African continent which prevented more people from being brought to a personal experience of this culture. Yet the difficulties of intruding into the Asian continent did not so distort our attitudes there. The original source of our reaction must be traced to the appalling effects of the evil trade in slaves. Even now we are only beginning to measure the debilitating effect it had upon Africa, not only in the loss of population, but in the attendant destruction of the whole fabric of social organization. Apportioning the relative blame amongst Arab, European, and African chiefs is hardly to the point. The result was inter-tribal warfare, the disintegration of family structure and the break-down of that continuity of administration which is the stuff of social existence. These effects were only compounded when Africans reached the other side of the Atlantic. The concept of slavery destroyed the willingness to accept African humanity. If there was no sense of equality, if the whole system was geared to establish continuously the inevitability of inferiority, what else could result? What residue remained upon which to assert that the African way might have its own dignity and value? When these unfortunate slaves reached America, any remaining cohesion was eliminated by deliberately conceived policy. Families were separated, tribes mixed, to destroy the elementary cohesion that derives from a shared language. From being Africans they were made slaves without the dignity of cutural association and continuity. They were sold the tag ends of the Western system in a manner designed to destroy their own inherited cultural tradition. So effectively did the system deny the creation of any substitute cultural allegiance that even now the search for cultural roots is a heart-felt urgency for many Negroes. This can be seen in sources as widely separated as the poetry of the French West Indian Aime Cesaire and the self-investigation of Ellison's *Invisible Man*.

Such slaveowner attitudes received their justification from Christian philosophy. The monolithic power of Catholicism had largely inspired the early slave raiding along the Isle of Gorée off the coast of

present-day Senegal. Bringing the light to the heathen was the pro-
fessed reason as it had been the cloaking justification of South American conquest, where fierce Spaniards had attacked the barbarous
native in the name of the Cross. The coming of Protestantism did
nothing to ease the Africans' lot. Protest they might at the apparent
abberations in Catholic belief; but towards Africa, Protestant theology incorporated the same attitude. Although elements in the
church early in the 19th century must be given credit for their involvement in the campaign for abolition, the firm ring of the chapel
hymns remained into the period of my own contemporary memory
as we lustily sang at school: "From Greenland's icy mountains and
India's coral strands / they call us to deliver their minds from
heathen chains." I doubt that Europe awaited any such specific "call,"
for empires were being founded upon missionary expeditions; but
the attitude of the verse was symptomatic. The Africans had to be
freed from their heathen ways and liberated into a new concept of
existence which would, by definition of its desirability, be Western.
This attitude is just as persistent in our own day, even though we
now substitute not the largely ignored missionary groups, but the
new technocratic theology which takes the efficiency of industrial
economics as the new learning that must be demonstrated to the
backward Africans for their greater good and our own advantage.

II

An introduction such as that above is probably doomed to failure
in that it is simultaneously both too long and too short. It is too short
to document effectively the very broad assertions of attitude which
have been made, but perhaps already too long to retain the interest
of readers who want to know about African literature. What have
slavery and missionaries to do with prose and poetry? There is justification in this discursive attempt, however, if we can learn through
it to re-examine accepted prejudice, and thus start with an attitude
of intelligent receptiveness to the unexpected. The thought of "literature from Africa" inevitably creates in a new audience a sense of
amazement and an anticipation of something very different than the
writings which will be found in this collection. It was essential to

speculate upon the unwarranted basis for our surprise. Pre-judgments might expect some translations of oral epic or perhaps traditional tales; a recently discovered Swahili Beowulf or a new, indigenous Congolese Uncle Remus. Such items can be found. But if in an introduction one wishes to assert both generally and with supporting evidence from this present collection that there is a literature being produced in present-day Africa which is contemporary and available to us, in the same way in which the literature of France or Russia is a relevant part of our world culture, one must begin by making sure that some very old myths are properly moribund. This contemporary African writing is good writing. That is why it has to interest us. It is not interesting merely because it is written by Africans. It is not to be judged useful for the light it may throw upon a different continent. It is simply and demonstrably worthy of reading by all the critical standards we have so carefully established for our own literature. If it does not achieve that enrichment of our perception, that extension of our sensibility which is the reason for all our literary study, then it would have no right to justify itself on the specious appeal to other elements of curiosity, social or anthropological. The African writer asks only to be read with understanding—without patronage. He will stand the judgment of honest evaluation in such a light. He is a writer, not an eccentricity of our age; an artist, not the odd foreign phenomenon our ignorance may expect.

III

The most significant quality that differentiates the new African literature from most other national literatures is that it is written in a second language. Most African writers do not at present use their mother tongue. (The few exceptions such as Duro Ladipo, the Yoruba dramatist, may reach us in translation.) The Colonial rulers wove their languages deeply into the intellectual and social fabric of the countries which they administered. Education, except for the very elementary stages, was in English and French (and to some extent in Portuguese). Government was conducted in these languages. The preamble to the recent new constitution of Uganda is typical. It states quite directly: "The national language of Uganda shall be English." There are several reasons for this decision. The historical reason alone would be enough. The nations of present-day Africa were created as the result of greedy competition between the expansionist European powers, armed with inadequate maps and ignorant of locale. There is often little logical coherence in the countries which have achieved their independence in the last decade—a fact which is at the base of much of the unrest and dissension exhibited by recent African events. Boundaries, externally established, cut across all the natural African tribal and linguistic groups that might have made for national cohesion and removed the main centralizing force that a common language can give to the unity of a country. If one observes how the mere bilingualism of Canada creates a dissident element in such an "advanced" country, one can better imagine how difficult it is to bring the infinitely fragmented linguistic areas within the boundaries of many African countries into cohesion. Separate languages are inevitably centrifugal in their pulls. Nigeria, one is told authoritatively, has more than two hundred individual languages within its borders. Hence the new Africa is the continent of the European language. French and English are utilized not as a reluctantly remaindered residue of Colonialism, but as a tool of independence that creates nations out of separatist elements. It grants them an international device that opens to them the world of economic and technical advance and permits their connection with the worldwide concern of their political appeals. The usefulness of such a language is evident and for a writer the use of an international tongue not only offers a tempting extension of audience in Africa and outside that continent, but also expands the possibilities of publication in Europe; for Africa, as yet, has few presses for book-printing. Writers have welcomed the chance to address the world and expose the nature of their African experience without the necessity of an intermediary translating linguist.

But a language cannot exist by sudden fiat. It is the gradually evolving expression of a national or racial group. The English or French which the African writer borrows cannot be taken like a screwdriver and employed without reference to the culture that has sustained and shaped its development. The issue of the degree to which language is "culture-tied," is a complex one. Clearly the English language has had a long tradition of being "internationalized." English has been made American in both the verbal and cultural sense in this country. The English of Australia in both speech and vocabulary, is increasingly differentiated from the British English. Much more will these changes occur when the borrowed language must stand against the more familiar and constantly utilized mother tongue of the speaker. His own first language will press its intrusive syntax and pronunciation patterns upon the second language—English. This produces the odd forms that are the butt of the foreign-speaker jokes. The Chinese do not in fact say "flied lice." The apparent sound results from the linguistic fact that the Asiatic does not distinguish between our "r" and "l" sounds (which are similar), but utilizes a middle form that the undiscriminating ear of the English speaker tries to make either one or the other familiar sound.

More significant than minor matters of speech is that question of culture. English began as the vehicle for the expression of the Anglo-cultural context. It has expanded to become the tool to record the new interpretation of the American, Canadian, and Australian landscape and in doing so has extended its vitality beyond the geographic limitations of its origin. But it must be remembered that those adaptations are made by English speakers who remain completely comprehensible to one another. Now the Africans and Indians who use this language must adapt it to a much more foreign environment, in a context which includes other languages. Today, as African writers seek a cultural nationhood, they use a borrowed foreign tongue. They must make this language shape itself to concepts and issues far removed from its origin, and mould it to the new spirit of their countries and their times.

For them there will always be a battle. For though they may welcome the opportunity to become international, they must at the same time remain fundamentally African if their writing is to have roots. To seek that cosmopolitan audience and escape from the inherent limitation of their small mother-tongue readership is a challenge. Yet they must also remain true to their own African experience and reflect a sensibility which may often be at odds with the language which they are using, and a mystery to the readers they have gained. There is another issue to be stressed. Not only their language and the location of their publication, but their entire out-look emphasizes the internationalism of these writers. These men are not the simple tellers of folk tales. They know, of course, the oral epics and stories of their ancestry; yet they are sophisticated men, educated in universities which in English and French-speaking Africa are modeled on the metropolitan equivalent. A writer like Wole Soyinka has learned in the academic sense the whole range of the English "Great Tradition" that F. R. Leavis has described. He has learned his literature from English expatriate lecturers, teaching an English university syllabus for exams set and graded in London with no concessions made to African elements. Such a writer knows that in using English he draws upon a thousand years of literary tradition. This influences his choice of *genre* and his sense of structure and tone in many ways. Such observations could be made even more strongly for the French writers educated in an even more rigorous system.

How then does an African assert his Africanness in the face of the multiple pressures that he become "international" in the bad, lowest denominator kind of way? How can he resist assimilation when foreign language, audience, publication, and alien literary traditions push him towards being a mere adjunct of some wider concept of literature in the English language? How did English literature in America become American literature? The French-speaking writers have indicated one way. You establish a philosophy that asserts an aggressive totality of Africanness, albeit in the language and perhaps even in the philosophical spirit of the rejected imperial power. This is *negritude*. The concept derives its emotive power from the deliberately chosen word. *Negre* in French does not mean Negro but is nearer the emotive equivalent of "nigger." So the African deliberately takes upon himself the stigma of the colonialists' rejection and returns it as a proud declamation of honor. "Yes," the French poets, Senghor and Diop cry, in their rhetorical verse, "we are niggers. We have suffered the penalties and stigma of that role."

"In those days
When civilization kicked us in the face
When holy water slapped our cringing brows

The vultures built in the shadow of their talons
The bloodstained monument of tutelage
In those days ..."

(David Diop, *The Vultures*)

These despised men are the "niggers" of the colonialists. "They call us cotton heads, and coffee men, and oily men, they call us men of death," says Senghor. But these wretched people have something vital to offer the world, for they have retained the humanity and warmth that has been deliberately excluded from the Western ways which emphasize sterile intellectualism. Senghor asks the rhetorical question in his famous poem "Prayer to Masks": "For who else would teach rhythm to the world that has died of machines and cannons?" This theme is developed most effectively in the poem he wrote to *New York*. Here the sneers against white Manhattan are set against too fulsome praise for Harlem and a resulting assertion justifies what the Negro can offer the Western world where control and logic are built up into a social system that denies feeling. Scorning "nylon legs. Legs and breasts that have no sweat nor smell. / No tender word for there are no lips," he turns to find in Harlem, "pavements ploughed by the naked feet of dancers / Bottoms waves of silk and sword-blade breasts, water-lily ballets and fabulous masks." But his final words bring a new union to the dissident elements. He begs New York to allow Negro life to bring back sensuousness into its cold existence:

"New York! I say to you: New York let black blood flow into
    your blood
That it may rub the rust from your steel joints, like an oil of life,
That it may give to your bridges the bend of buttocks and the
    suppleness of creepers ..."

Here is an African asserting the validity of his culture to a world which has rejected it across three centuries.

There are varied interpretations of the degree to which a similar philosophy can be found in English language writing. "African Personality," their equivalent concept, sounds suspiciously similar,

and verses can be found which echo the mood. The ironic prayer of
Francis Parkes from Ghana appeals:

> "Give me black souls,
> Let them be black
> Or chocolate brown
> Or make them the
> Colour of dust—
> Dustlike,
> Browner than sand.
> But if you can
> Please keep them black,
> Black."

Yet the oft quoted statement of Wole Soyinka sounds a contradictory
note. "A tiger," he explained with ironic dismissal, "does not have to
proclaim his tigritude." Perhaps also the English-speaking Africans
inherited the rather pragmatic common-sense of the British approach
which takes pride in being beyond foreign "isms." It is not accidental
that like so many other French artistic cults, negritude was formu-
lated in discussion in the Monmartre cafes of Paris. It was a thesis
asserted by those intellectuals of Africa whom French colonial policy
had most effectively moulded as Black Frenchmen who were worthy
of assimilation into the French cultural community. It had been the
very success of this policy that had made such men the people who
most had to establish an alternative to their Frenchness if they were
to obtain any individuality.

But if the British colonials did not accept such a simplistic philosophy of rejection of Europe, they had their own intellectual problems. They did not really face assimilation, yet they realized that
they stood at the intersection of two traditions assuming a dual heritage. It is from this recognition that the concept of "culture conflict"
has been derived. Perhaps this issue has been overstressed in modern
Africa, and certainly it has been the source of too much plot motivation in African literature in English. Yet some element of its significance must be acknowledged. There are two worlds that meet in the
educated African. He is an heir to his own tradition, which is, by
nature and circumstance, conservative, static, and continuously back-

ward-looking. Yet he is invited to share the impact of Western culture, which is dynamic, contemporary, and inherently destructive to all such tradition by making change the single legitimate purpose of education.

This whole division is set up within the opening lines of the long religious poem of Christopher Okigbo, "Heavensgate." It begins with a simple dedication to the Igbo mother goddess, but within the space of a few lines his dedication has changed to a completely different source and the Christian memory echoes in the latter lines:

"Before you, mother Idoto,
naked I stand,
before your watery presence,
a prodigal,

leaning on an oil bean,
lost in your legend ...

Under your power wait I
    on barefoot,
watchman for the watchword
    at heavensgate;

out of the depths my cry
give ear and hearken."

With similar effect, but after a more specific analysis, the same intellectual division is found in Gabriel Okara's revealing poem, "Piano and Drums." The first stanza describes the African drums and how they affect him. "My blood ripples, turns torrent / topples the years," so that he returns to an awareness of his childhood, which is simultaneously his racial past. Then in the second stanza, "I hear a wailing piano / solo speaking of complex ways ... of far away lands / and new horizons." This is his present, created by his Western education. He is unable to resolve this discrepancy, and the last stanza significantly sees him poised between the two worlds of which he is the troubled heir.

"And I, lost in the morning mist
of an age, at a riverside, keep

wandering in the mystic rhythm
of jungle drums and the concerto."

IV

From this double heritage African writers have begun in the
last decade and a half to create a new literature. They have learned
from the pioneering French African writing, which has its roots
some thirty years earlier, but their backgrounds have led them into
different channels. They are citizens of nations which became independent without the intellectual self-questioning imposed by the
French policy of *assimilation*, for the British always worked through
the Africans when imposing their administration and did not attempt to acculturate Africans to their ways. These Africans have
inherited a language infinitely more flexible than French, for it does
not pretend to legislate against modernizing change in the manner of
the restrictive French Academy. English has discovered through centuries the reciprocity of foreign borrowing and adaptation that has
made it the major instrument of world communication today. These
writers inherit a thousand years of impressive and varied literature,
marked more by rebel experiment than by restraining academic
theory. But they remain proudly African, drawing at the same time
upon a heritage that is theirs by birth and from the significant tradition of their race. It is compromise they achieve as they work; not
disdaining the language of their creativity, rather rejoicing in its
strength and extent. They forge from it a new idiom which will
record an experience that the language has never before undertaken
to describe.

African literature in English began with an unexpected varia-
tion; the work of that much-criticized figure Amos Tutuola. His
eccentric English, heavily modified by his mother-tongue vernacular,
was published in London in a form that carefully retained the aberrations of his inaccuracies without editorial correction. Africans were
dismayed by this device, claiming that it was patronizing; deliberately confirming the image of the quaintly primitive African. Yet
Dylan Thomas was also right when he called it a "thronged, grisly
and bewitching story written in young English." And the *New*

Yorker reviewer emphasized that quality. "Mr. Tutuola tells his story as if nothing like it had ever been written down before." The opening lines have all the confident ease of the natural story teller:

"I was a palm-wine drunkard since I was a boy of ten years of age. I had no other work more than to drink palm wine in my life. . . ."

The story in this collection by Mr. R. A. Freeman has something of this legendary quality of theme and a similar moulding of English syntax by the attendant vernacular, as he takes us into a weird world of folk fancy.

There have been few who have attempted this stylistic adaptation: merging the old oral style—the stories of ghosts and demons, with the new language. The majority of the writers use the conventional genres of novel, poem, and play with little apparent African modification, though we might, in fact, occasionally miss this evidence out of limited knowledge. It is this formal literature which is the concern of the editor and which makes the material for the present selection.

To a dramatic extent African literature in English—at least till a year or two ago—was concentrated in Nigeria and South Africa. South African writing has a very long tradition of vernacular printing and an extensive present day publication of dissident writers, both black and white, who often have chosen exile in protest against the apartheid regime of their country. The tender poetry of Dennis Brutus and the angry descriptions of Alex La Guma deserve to be better known in this country. But their concerns in all their political anguish set them apart from the tone of writers in independent African to the north and would better make a separate study. The writing of the great middle belt of West and East and Central Africa offer a sufficiently broad canvas of expressive and varied writing. There seems to be no easy explanation for the fact that Nigeria was the center from which the spark that ignited African literature was born. One can, especially at present, make no assumptions about the connection between that country's literary and social development. It is fascinating to discover that the four major writers of contemporary Africa, Wole Soyinka, Chinua Achebe, J. Pepper Clark and Christopher Okigbo happened to be at Ibadan University together, and to speculate what strange catalytic effect this joining might have had upon their individual capacities.

The fact remains that for the present, estimation of the quality of African writing in English must stand or fall upon the published work of these four, no matter what significant potential we may detect in a handful of younger writers. There is exciting promise in several recent African novels but nothing yet to equal the monumental tetralogy of Chinua Achebe who traces the social history of Nigeria in this century through a series which reaches full tragic import: *Things Fall Apart, No Longer at Ease, Arrow of God, Man of the People.* Beginning from the first impact of those improbable white invaders, he traces the disintegration of a traditional system. In *Arrow of God,* the most powerful novel, the honorable old priest clashes with the new British administrator, himself a man of great personal integrity. But circumstances are too destructive for honor to control events. Both men are destroyed, and the victors are the quislings who batten on the country as lackeys of the imperialists. The two novels on the contemporary period are less profound, perhaps, for modern life may lack the stuff of heroics. But they assert the same irony inherent when men live optimistically with only day-to-day pragmatism to sustain them. The old gods are dead, and no new belief is available to guide those who live after the deluge. Individual greed becomes the most essential motivation of a social era. The last novel, *Man of the People,* ironically concluded with a climactic military coup that anticipated, by a few days, the same inevitable event in graft-ridden Nigeria.

The plays of Wole Soyinka have an artistic sophistication that have made them box office successes wherever they have been produced; most recently off Broadway. His range is immense, from the Jonsonian comedy of *Brother Jero,* rogue in *The Alchemist* tradition, to the neat reversal of the clicheic progressive theme in *Lion and the Jewel* which concludes with the young beauty rejecting her progressive and educated lover for the strength of the polygamous old chief. There are the powerful attacks on dark superstition in *The Strong Breed* and *The Swamp Dwellers,* and the sardonic rejection of the false ideals of national pride in *Dance of the*

Forest, which dares to ridicule the too easy optimism of African independence. Always in a tone supremely sophisticated, ironically searching, Soyinka casts his witty, acid, yet poetic eye upon his characters and the society they inhabit.

The poems of J. P. Clark are available through London publication in *Reed in the Tide,* and he has also published three plays which attempt to recreate the Greek tragic concept in an African setting. The first play, called *Song of a Goat,* reminds us of the origin of the very word "tragedy," and he sustains this connection in impassioned poetry. The concluding lines of the chorus figure have that controlled tranquility that terminates great tragedy:

> "You may well cry. But it is nothing
> To beat your breasts. It was how
> We all began and will end. A child
> Once out of the womb will shout . . ."

Clark can occasionally be irascible, as his sardonic scholarship diary *America Their America* can unkindly demonstrate. But he is by nature a poet of supreme tenderness and intimacy, sustaining through sincerity an occasional otherwise lush excess.

Christopher Okigbo, a more cerebral poet, has not yet been published in full outside of Africa, although in this country, Northwestern University Press distributes the two slim African-printed volumes which were the promised beginning of a major work. Although he brings into African poetry an intellectualized style owing much to Ezra Pound, he wrote lines which flash with the more vivid sensuality when read amongst his spare intelligent lines. The most famous image in modern African poetry is his, in its evocative visual flamboyance.

> "Bright
> with the armpit dazzle of a lioness,
> she answers,
>
> wearing white light about her;
> and the waves escort her
> my lioness,
> crowned with moonlight."

What a tragic comment upon Africa today it is, that of these four, only J. P. Clark is permitted an artistic existence; and even he is silenced by despair. Christopher Okigbo is as dead as Major Okigbo of the Biafran army. We have been out of touch with Achebe for months and the London *Times* has announced his death. Wole Soyinka is again in jail charged with high treason against the new military regime.

During 1966 there were six major English language African novels published, and three of these were by Nigerians—a large, but diminishing, proportion. What is happening in African writing at present is a series of extensions. The most obvious extension is geographic. There are now novels from Kenya, Cameroons, Malawi, Rhodesia, Sierra Leone, Ghana, Gambia. There is also an increasing variety of works. No longer is the novel the most accepted form; there are long poems in the epic tradition, reworkings of ancient myth into drama, stories which have more in common with the old tales than with Somerset Maugham. And writers are looking not only back, but more widely outwards: in the drama, to Brecht, and the Japanese *Noh* as well as to Pinter and the English stage.

There are stylistic changes, most dramatically in the extraordinary experiment of Gabriel Okara in his novel *The Voice*, which seeks to represent the rhythm and intonation of his native Ijaw tongue into the idiom he forces upon his English style. Changing too are the themes. The old often repeated semi-autobiographical plot in which the young hero copes with the culture conflict of his daily life that too exactly mirrors the author's own, are being superseded by broader, more literary concerns. Novels such as Wole Soyinka's *The Interpreters* or Mbella Dipoko's *A Few Nights and Days* show a sophistication that takes their very subject matter into a wider dimension than Africa. It is not an accident that the first African novel written by a woman, *Efuru* by Flora Nwapa, did not present any whites to indicate a counter-force to the tradition she so intimately records.

V

To date, the most influential magazine from English-speaking

Africa has been *Black Orpheus*. Conceived by Ulli Beier and supported by a committee which includes all the major published writers, this magazine was a project of the Ibadan Mbari Writers' Club. This journal was fundamental in the initiation and development of African writing in English. Last year Ulli Beier left Nigeria for Papua, and the magazine has apparently died with his departure for all the vague discussion of its continuance. The end of this publication is the end of a particular period in African literature; for its sad demise, even at a time when it has been argued that it has achieved what it set out to perform, is a point of significant change. Recently, even while it was at the height of its influence, there had been some complaint that it had become a clique magazine for certain writers; that it had begun to take on that merely cult appeal that had done so much to invalidate lately the originally impressive work achieved by the French journal *Presence Africain*. A journal that is not eclectic will miss much in a rapidly changing literary scene.

That criticism is debatable and it is not my immediate concern. I wish merely to indicate to those who may know of *Black Orpheus* that the present collection is not its continuance, nor the residue of its material, but evidence of a new start in African writing. We might have liked to publish the work of those highly professional writers such as Wole Soyinka. But such writers are becoming known through international publication. To print more of their work might have given a false picture of stasis in the field of African literature; for we would be harking back to the established names, not looking forward to what is really happening. There is now already a new generation of African writers with new ideas and ambitious plans. Young men and women, many still students, gifted, capable people—these will be the writers of Africa in the next decade. Such is the absurd speed of change that as Senghor repudiated the old French elite and Achebe repudiated the corruption in the new African elite that took the place of the colonials, so new writers are reacting too against some aspects of the presently successful authors. They reject the limitation of their subject matter. They reject the social commitment they make as artists, and seek a more literary experience for their own work. In choosing to move beyond the fields staked out by these earlier writers they do not cease to ad-

mire the skill of the major names. They recognize that without
their publication the whole battle for the legitimate beginnings of
an African writing would have to be fought now in the literary
markets of the world. But like all younger groups, they consider
that they have something new to say. They speak for their own generation. And this is not a generation which is the product of a single
country or a single tribe, but is stretched across a continent that is
itself in a state of flux. They live in an Africa where pragmatic governments negotiate their deals with the external pressures and internal difficulties that comprise the data with which all African
leaders must work as they seek to transform poverty and backward-
ness without that attendant dangerous paternalism that has accompanied assistance in the past.

Our range here is a wide one. Christina Aidoo from Ghana has
written a sad, wry little story. Joe Okpaku of Nigeria has contributed
the haunting and powerful novella. The poets range across the traditions. But this is young Africa speaking. There is no simple common
denominator; no general form to observe. The range is as wide as
the vastness of their own gigantic continent. They seek to be read
because they speak of new ideas and the changing visions of their
new nations. Yet they ask no critical indulgence. The patronizing
attitude of "Remarkable, considering it is by an African," is resented
as the last antagonism of a foreign superiority. This is writing that
demands our respect for what it attempts. It is an early stage of a
new literature that should interest and concern us all as it finds its
channel of continuance among the necessary experiment. The range
of this collection might have been wider, but the inevitable impedi-
ments occurred. In spite of two trips across Africa the editor suffered
the frustration of inadequate posts, of indifference to concepts of
time. Pieces offered for printing were withdrawn for earlier publication elsewhere while he attempted to gather sufficient other items
that would range representatively across the scene of African writing. More seriously outbreaks of civil violence, if they did no worse,
took thoughts away from creativity to deal with more immediately
pressing social problems. As this collection goes to press one has to
offer the usual editorial qualifications. If only I could have got a
piece from that poet in Dar Es Salaam. If only that a Malawan author

whose writing was so good had not decided to support a local publication with his latest piece. My frustrations, in fact, are so trivial in the balance that they should hardly be mentioned as one considers the problems in present-day Africa for the budding writer. This collection must stand as best it may as the result of two years of pleas, of gains and losses, of sifting and discovery. Whatever quality it has is a commendation of the virility and talent of African writing today. The omissions are the fault of editorial limitations.

The difference between the ideal concept and the reality must always be something of a disappointment. But I am proud of many of these pieces and impressed by their caliber. I am grateful for the willingness of these young writers to contribute, and the result seems to me worthy of our attention. These people speak of a new Africa, and their voices should be heard in this country.

MALE STATUETTE

BAGO TRIBE OF GUINEA

R. Sarif Easmon

The Human Touch

THE BARRISTER-AUTHOR, Garvin Smith, knew the irresistible force of his wit had encountered *the* immovable object in
the person of the man born without a sense of humour, when he
received this letter from the Prime Minister's Office:

"Sir,

"The Prime Minister and the Foreign Minister would like
to see you in this office at 10 a.m., Tuesday the 20th. instant.

"2. I am to say that His Excellency M. Pierre Chardin, Ambassador of France, will be at the interview.

"Your obedient Servant,
"R. Scott
"Secretary to the Prime Minister."

Garvin grinned from ear to ear. His eyes, twinkling with mischief, rested on the name of the diplomat, Chardin.

"Ass!" he murmured, going upstairs from his office to his living
quarters on the first floor. "How the devil can one take an ass seriously because he is an ambassador?"

He was just going into his study when his wife, beautiful as
women can be in Luawaland, came into the dining-room from her
kitchen.

"Garvie," she moved over to him, the smile in her face changing
into a look of worry ,"what mischief are you up to now?"

Garvin's eyebrow arched in a look of hurt innocence: *Me?*"

"I know that look too well, Garvie," she retorted, following him
into the study.

"It's the look I wear," he smiled, sitting in the chair at his desk
and waving her to the armchair at the window opposite, "when
mischief is up to me."

Do what she would, he wielded such charm over her that her eyes were soon replying to the merriment that danced in his.

"An *official* envelope!" she laughed. "Let me guess. His Excellency Monsieur—"

"The Ass."

"—Chardin has taken your quarrel to ministerial level."

Garvin's grin broadened: "To the P.M. himself."

"Good Heavens! Has the man lost his senses?"

"Darling, how much sense has an ass to lose? Look!"

Handing her the new letter, he moved to the steel filing-cabinet to the right of his desk. He took out one of many files in the top-drawer and handed it to her.

The top drawer belonged to Garvin's second profession as an author, and had nothing to do with what he now called the drudgery of the Law. The study gave proof of the dichotomy of its owner's character: the right half was dignified, lined with bookcases groaning under the weight of Law books bound in Buckram. The other half, untidy, a third Bohemian, a third raffish, a third serious, was devoted to Literature of all sorts, and in three languages: English mostly, French, a few books in Italian, including Boccaccio's *Decameron*.

Opening the file on her lap, Esther gasped as she read the letter her husband sent the Ambassador two days before:

"Your Excellency,

"I cannot thank you for your letter of even date. I feel compelled, however, to quote Your Excellency the Duke of Wellington's famous note when, like me, a correspondent had exhausted his stock of politeness: 'Sir, This correspondence must now cease.'

"I am,
"Your Excellency,
"Yours faithfully,
"Garvin Smith."

She read through the letters in the file, and, with a smile of mystification, handed it back to her husband.

"Why's Chardin making all this fuss?" she asked. "After all, the story you wrote from your Holiday diary was perfectly true."

"Ah, but it is also funny. Chardin cannot believe a man can be funny, French, and a diplomat all at the same time. That's what makes the whole thing so explosively laughable."

On the 20th, fifteen minutes before the Ambassador and Garvin Smith were expected, the Prime Minister and the Foreign Minister were sitting over a file in the former's sumptuous office. The file was dedicated to what had begun to be called *L'affaire Chardin-Smith*. Its contents mystified the Prime Minister and the Foreign Minister even more than it had done Garvin's wife.

"Ronny," the P.M. asked in a rather harrassed voice, turning to his Secretary in the chair to the left of the big Mahogany desk, "do you think we can get your friend to apologise to his Excellency?"

Before Scott could reply the Foreign Minister asked:

"Excuse me, P.M., *what* should Garvin apologise for?"

"Damn if I know!" the P.M. growled. "I want the Genema Dam completed. Ronny, you and Garvin were schoolmates. I hope you've convinced him that, lawyer and writer though he is, he can never get half a million pounds anywhere for writing the three words 'I am sorry.' That's the free grant from France we're likely to lose with this his silly quarrel with Chardin."

Still puzzled, the Foreign Secretary suggested they go over the correspondence again to see if they could winkle out a cause for apology.

The trouble started when the Secretary of the Bar Association received the following letter:

"AMBASSADE DE FRANCE EN LUAWALAND.
"*L'Ambassadeur.*

"Dear Mr. Seisay,

"You have no doubt read, in the programme which was distributed to all persons attending the Ball of the Bar Association on the 11th instant, the article signed by MR. GARVIN SMITH. This story covers a certain French diplomat with ridicule.

"I am somewhat surprised that the organisers of an evening to which, French and diplomat, I had been invited to attend, had accepted to publish in a booklet intended to be read by hundreds of people, an article so offensive to myself and my country.

"I have written to MR. GARVIN SMITH asking him for all details regarding the Frenchman whose conversation he is supposedly relating, to enable me to check, if this is possible, the truth of the allegations in this article.

"Yours sincerely,
"G. Chardin."

The Ambassador's two letters got a "retort courteous" from Garvin:

"His Excellency, The Ambassador of France,
"Luawa.

"Your Excellency,

"I received yesterday the letter you were good enough to address me regarding my story in the souvenir programme of the Bar Association Ball. Our Association Secretary has also shown me the letter you sent him.

"Your Excellency has missed the point of my story. Its hero is only *incidentally* a Frenchman: having the human touch, he could have come from any part of the world. He did, in fact, come from France, as my story happens to be a true one. I know his name. But I do not see I am under any obligation to divulge it to Your Execllency.

"I regret that in the penultimate paragraph of your letter to my Association's Secretary you say you think my story offensive. I do not agree with you. But in this imperfect world it would be too much to expect writers to know all the vagaries of the diplomat's mind, or for diplomats to understand the nuances of good writing. On the question of taste, I must remind Your Excellency that *Chacqun à son goût.*

"However, I take strong exception to the last paragraph of your letter to our Association's Secretary. I would, therefore, like Your Excellency's assurance in writing that you do not mean it as a reflection on my veracity. If I do not receive that assurance soon, I shall instruct my solicitor to communicate with Your Excellency on the subject.

"Yours faithfully,
"Garvin Smith."

The Ministers had got so far when the Secretary at the French Embassy telephoned the P.M.'s Secretary: Monsieur L'Ambassadeur was indisposed and, with all regrets to the Prime Minister, could not come to the interview, and was calling off the affair with Garvin Smith.

At sharp ten o'clock Garvin was announced.

"Now Garvin," said the P.M., as he and the Foreign Minister rose to greet the most brilliant barrister in the country, "what have you done to His Excellency to give him cold feet this morning?"

"I knew he wouldn't come," Garvin grinned, taking one of the two chairs across the desk. He handed the P.M. a copy of his letter with the Duke of Wellington quote.

"But how did it all start?" the P.M. asked, laughing more loudly than all the rest at Garvin's coup de grace.

"It needn't have started, Sir, if Chardin were not a typical product of the French Colonial Service. That type of bureaucrat is not merely unendurable in independent Africa, but should be eliminated with rat poison."

"Hi-hi!" P.M. strove to keep laughter out of his voice. "We have to keep on the right side of de Gaulle, Garvin."

"Well, this is what started it, Prime Minister."

He handed over the brochure the Bar Association had printed for its centenary Ball, and Ronald Smith read out:

HOLIDAY DIARY

Wednesday, 22nd August.

SIGNORA TAGLIATI lives in a beautiful modern flat high on the Janiculum with a superb view over Rome. The décor and some of the paintings in the flat were done by her artist daughter. The signora is handsome, middle aged. Her hair is worn in a coiffure displaying just that carelessness so attractive in a woman when she begins to suspect that youth, like time, does not dally. But I remem-

ber her best because, though she spoke very good English, now and
again she was tripped up by the idiom. She pluralised abstract nouns,
and pronounced the *ed* in all her past tenses. She accented the Ed
with a kind of affection, as though Ed were a young man she loved
when young, and had not since forgotten.

The signora had invited my wife, Esther, and me to dinner.

Eight of us sat at the table, including Signor Tagliati, a handsome appendage to his spouse. An English cadet officer sat opposite
Esther. An Argentinian lady—who had so fallen in love with Italy
that she had decided to make it her home—faced me across the
table. Our end of the table, with the Signora at the head, spoke
English. The other half spoke Italian, the Signora now and then
bridging the heritage of Babel between us.

One of the guests was an Italian-speaking Frenchman, an original if ever there was one. When, in reply to Signor Tagliati, I said I
came from Luawaland, the Frenchman proceeded to tell them how
small my country was. I caught the word *piccole* and understood his
drift. Signor Tagliati explained to me in English, haltingly. I suggested Monsieur was mistaken.

"I'm not," our Frenchman said. "I know that part of Africa
well. Luawaland is near the Cote d'Ivoire."

"Out by a thousand miles!" I laughed. "We are neighbours to
Liberia and Guinea."

"Guinea I know, of course," the Frenchman continued, un-
ruffled, startling everybody with the irrelevance of his digression,
"We French are happy now we have no colonies. *Grace à Dieu*,
even l'Algerie is off our hands. Talking of Algerie puts me in mind
of Nigeria."

"You're not suggesting," I smiled sideways to him, sure he was
unaware of the existence of the Sahara Desert, "that Nigeria has a
common boundary with Algeria?"

To my astonishment he threw up his hands. He was a small
man with greying hair, attractive manner and very alert eyes.

"N-no," he said, obviously not sure of himself. "But there is a
small country in West Africa. I should know, because it is British,
and I was in Senegal."

"Monsieur, you *must* mean the Gambia!" Esther laughed.

"C'est vrai!" Monsieur's eyes twinkled. He had the rare gift of enjoying a joke against himself. *"Mon dieu, chère Madame,* how did I forget that?"

"Monsieur's geography," I commented, "is rather confused."

"Is that so strange?" Signora Tagliati's eyes sparkled with laughter and mischief. "Monsieur works in an Embassy."

"No wonder," the Prime Minister roared with laughter as Scott came to the end of the piece, "Chardin is so mad at you, Garvin. This fellow-diplomat and countryman of his must have cut a ridiculous figure."

"On the contrary, P.M.," Garvin spoke with warmth, "my wife and I found him one of the most charming people we ever met. We saw much of him during the fortnight we spent in Rome. The only thing I've since found to his discredit is that he is Chardin's compatriot."

R. Sarif Easmon

Knave of Diamonds

NATURALLY, THE DOCTOR was not a diamond digger or trafficker himself.

No. He had no need to be. At least, living in a country which the maddest of diamond booms had for years stood on its head, that was what he would tell himself when his fainting moral insight gained the upper hand of that cupidity which—as he knew very well himself—was inherent in human nature. But he handled at second hand the people who dealt, uninhibitedly and even flamboyantly, in the stuff. He was, in fact, a medical practitioner engaged in medical practice in the capital of Sierra Leone, Freetown. And though in that super-boom year Hausas and Mandingoes would come to his Surgery and offer him gem-stones by the cigarette-cupful at a third of their illicit market value, the Doctor would not "take."

"You see," he would tell these well-wishers, "I come of a family of doctors—father, grandfather, the whole damn lot. And that kind of family breeds a species of ass whose hereditary burden is respectability." Always he would say this with a kind of bravado, and hope he was creating an impression on those who heard him. But in his heart he would curse himself for the fact that, deep down, he was not really respectable at all: he only feared the jail that would follow if he was caught with the stuff on him.

For this congenital kink which made it impossible for him to make a quick thousand—and a quick penny in the boom could as likely have been a quick thousand—the Doctor was to be found every day, except Sunday, digging an ever deeper trough in his gastric ulcer by worrying over the ailments of the scores of fellow-Africans who flocked to his Surgery to consult him.

One afternoon of one such busy day, he was sitting in the

consulting room of his Surgery. A patient had just left and passed
through the communicating door into the waiting-room. The Doctor had just raised his hand to the bell-push on the wall to summon
his dispenser when a young man burst in upon him from the
waiting-room.

"What the devil do you mean rushing in like this?"

"Sorry, Doc. . . ."

"Don't *"Doc"* me. Go out and wait your turn."

"Sorry—but it's urgent, Doc."

"Christ! How I *hate* that word, *Doc*! Now get out and . . ."

"I mustn't, Doc—I mean Doctor! Alhaj'll probably be dead if
you don't come at once."

The Doctor ground his teeth as he looked the intruder up and
down. Instead of counting ten, he slipped a couple of antacid
tablets into his mouth and chewed them to coax his ulcer. At that
time of day, every week day, his energies were generally approaching the point of exhaustion. He was in need of a holiday. Hence
he was never ever-patient with matters or people who wasted his
time.

"Being a Hausa you're a liar, Allie" he growled at the young
man in *Khaftan* and a fez cap. "You people are just as bad as the
Mandingoes. You think because your damn diamonds enable you to
pay cash down . . ."

"I've got the cash right here, Doc!"

"Don't *Doc* me, you young fool!"

"Sorry, Doc—I mean Doctor! But you must come at once. Alhaj
asked me to pay ten guineas. . . ."

"Ten guineas?" the Doctor asked in surprise and exasperation.
Everyone knew the fee was only two guineas.

"*He* said you wouldn't come if I didn't bring your fee. . . ."

"What a scandalous thing to say about me!" the Doctor exploded.

"*I* didn't say it, Doc—sorry, *Doctor.*" Allie grinned with embarrassment. "I'm only repeating what Alhaj Mohammed said."

"It's Mohammed, eh?" the Doctor could not help smiling.
"The old rogue! There's a bill of fifteen guineas outstanding against
him—and that for six months! He sends ten pounds . . ."

"*Guineas*, Doc—I mean Doctor!"

. . . and he expects to get his consultation on tick! What if I say I'm not budging?"

"Then," Allie smiled slyly, reaching into his pocket, "Alhaj said I was to pay you the remaining five guineas as well as the two guineas for the consultation."

While the Doctor looked up the Alhaj's card, Allie doled out the seventeen guineas on the table. As he studied the records the Doctor was vaguely conscious of the Hausa's perfume. But even though for the moment he was not looking at Allie's face, he could not forget its expression: the triumphant cockiness that radiated from the round, black face proclaimed Allie from the housetops a diamond trafficker. It was a look the Doctor never got used to; and, when it was extreme, it sometimes made him regret he was a physician and not a hangman. At twenty-two years Allie already had the hard, brazen look of wealth too easily come by; wealth ready to pay instantly for everything—from a reluctant girl's virginity downward.

"I suppose," said the Doctor looking up with a smile at Allie, "Mohammed has been over-eating again?"

For answer the young man stepped briskly to the communicating-door and closed it. When he came back towards the Doctor's desk his face was transformed with a tremendous grin of mischief and merriment.

For a messenger sent by that skinflint, Mohammed, allegedly to call him "urgently," the Allie's behaviour was so strange that the Doctor asked what he only too truly feared:

"Are you mad?"

Allie whipped out his handkerchief and stuffed it into his mouth. The Doctor heard the muffled roar of his laughter jammed against the back of his throat. The chap's eyes were running with tears."

"What the devil's the matter with you?" the Doctor burst out angrily.

Allie uncorked himself.

"Sorry, Doc—that is to say *Doctor*." He swallowed hard and

managed to control himself. "No, it's not the old belly this time. He's not had this complaint before."

"What is it, then?"

"Its— its— its, er—woman palaver, Doctor."

The Doctor's eyes pierced Allie through and through. Allie squirmed under the torture. But the Doctor asked him no more questions about the patient. *He* felt a pang of delicacy—for Alhaj Mohammed was old enough to be Allie's father. He would have liked to think Mohammed was past that sort of thing. But he suddenly remembered that fine old polygamist, Sulyman—Mohammed's eighty-five-year-old father. Every other year the old warhorse took a young girl in marriage—and every year, one of his women bore him a child that was the very spirit-likeness of him.

"What could Mohammed have got up to now?" he asked, having lost the gift of being astonished by anything these amazing Hausas did.

"Its a *different* kind of woman palaver, Doc—Doctor I mean." The ghost of a smile twitched at the corners of Allie's mouth. "You see, its the *husband* Alhaj has with him in the bedroom."

"Now I *know* you are crazy."

"Then come and see for yourself, Doc—sorry, Doctor. Do *hurry!*"

II

Allie picked up the Doctor's bag and led him through the crowded, frowning waiting-room, to a new Chevrolet in the street. With more dash than good sense—several times he brought the Doctor's heart to his mouth by taking curves too fast or by reckless overtaking—he drove to Alhaj Mohammed's half a mile away at Sackville Street.

He managed to squeeze the Chev between a Chrysler and a Mercedes Benz. Both sides of Goderich Street and the nearby sidestreets were parked with large cars, all relatively new, all more or less battered—and all illegitimate offsprings of the diamond racket. The Doctor was not the least surprised by this, for he knew the area to be the stronghold of the Hausas, and that these diamond barons would sooner buy a new car than repair a damaged one.

Carrying the medical bag Allie hurried into the big paved yard upon which both the front and back doors of Mohammed's house opened. The Doctor was quite used to the menage. The Hausas, he knew, had blended their acquired Moslem religion with their old tribal genius for living communally. Hence Mohammed's house was a warren occupied by himself and wives, his father and his brothers, cousins and their offsprings, etc. In fact, other houses opened into the great backyard.

Along the muddy yard the Doctor picked his way through a host of small children all looking healthy and filthy, living in harmony and understanding with dirt. Several Hausa women, some with tribal markings, were moving about the place—three in the kitchen to one side of the yard. One five-gallon Negro-pot brimful of rice was boiling on stones at the centre of the compound. The Doctor caught himself worrying that some of the toddlers might fall into the open fire. . . .

Meantime Allie had vanished by the back door. The Doctor hurried up the concrete steps to the front. As he paused on the landing waiting for the door to be opened, a beautiful cultured voice called from the far side of the yard:

"Allo, Doctor! Comment ça va?"

"Ma chere Mariama!" the Doctor waved back to the woman. She was standing at the entrance to a small house. Around her the tide of dirt in the yard appeared to have been magically halted. *Her* house was freshly painted, spick and span, clean to the *nth* degree. She was so elegantly turned out in her Susu clothes she looked alien to her surroundings. *"N'ma -ah kalohn . . .* I did not know, Mariama," the Doctor continued in the Susu tongue, though he spoke French fairly well, "you'd returned from your holiday in Guinea. I hope you left our people well?"

"EE-yo, Docteur! . . . Yes, Doctor." Her teeth flashed in the sunshine. She belonged to both the Susu and Mandingo tribes; this, along with her French background, made her the last word in native sophistication. "And they all ask to be remembered."

It gave the Doctor great physical pleasure to see Mariama and talk to her in their native tongue instead of the *lingua franca*, Creole. He was beginning to enjoy himself when the front door swung inward and half a dozen Hausa men cried in unison:

"*Bismillah*—you're here, Doctor!"

The Doctor allowed them to lead him into the chaos of the sitting-room. By the street a large, new, and extremely expensive radiogram was playing "Pops" from the B.B.C. The usual "lovey-dovey" music made a startling contrast to the expressions the Doctor observed in the faces around him. The owners, of course, were inured to the noise, and even in normal circumstances would not have been listening at all.

"For God's sake," the Doctor cried, "switch that damn set off!"

The oldest and gravest of the turbaned figures carried out the order and came back worriedly to the Doctor.

"Doctor," he spoke with gravity through the copious greying beard that framed his face beneath the Fez, "you're the only person in the world who has any influence on the young devil. Do get him to open the door."

"And you, Musa, being the only sensible soul in Sackville Street," the Doctor retorted, "ought to know I have dealings with devils, real or imaginary."

"Oh yes, Doctor, you have." Musa led him across the room. The house, owning many mistresses, was apparently cared for by none: all over the cream paints of the sitting-room carried dirty finger marks; not one of the settees or armchairs was set straight; dirty dishes and cups lay everywhere; and chaos became perfect when two mangy dogs engaged in single combat in the very middle of the room. The Hausas paid them no attention whatever—till the victor chased the vanquished out of the house. . . .

"It's your friend Sheikh, Doctor," Musa found himself taking very loudly in the quiet that followed the dog's exit. Cars were speeding up Goderich Street. "He's in there with Alhaj."

"Oh—*he*!" The Doctor could not help a tone of laughter creeping into his voice. To call Sheikh a devil seemed, to say the least, an unwarranted understatement. Sheikh was, by universal consent, the most resourceful and dangerous diamond-runner in the country. "What the deuce is he up to now?"

By now they had approached the bedroom door, to which two other Hausas held their ears worriedly; one of them proceeded to

twist and untwist the door knob in a rather frenzied and unreward-
ing manner.

"*I* don't know, Doctor" a very scared voice issued from behind
the panels. An uncanny situation, thought the Doctor. "But its
a mercy he's not killed me yet."

"*Kill you*, Mohammed?" the Doctor cried in bewilderment.
"What you people want is the Police—not a doctor."

"If you call the police" a very powerful voice, rasping with
anger, called aggressively from inside the room, "I promise you I'll
leave them a hell of a mess to clear up!"

"For Allah's sake," Mohammed choked and whimpered, "don't
call the police, Musa. Doctor, do tell Sheikh to open the door."

"*Sheikh!*" the Doctor called in exasperation.

"Yes, Doc?"

"Damn you—don't *Doc* me! Open the door at once!"

"Very well, Doctor. But you must come in alone. And," he
ended with a lugubrious chuckle, "I don't think you need your bag."

The door opened just wide enough for the Doctor to squeeze
in and was immediately banged to and locked from inside the
room.

The Doctor had been in the room before, so the chronic un-
tidiness made no impact on him. But the chaos of the place was
heightened by the drama in the large, four-poster iron bedstead.

Naked down to his waist, a fat Hausa man was lying on his
back. His fat but powerfully built torso was glistening with sweat.
His eyes popped wildly as he stared up at the Doctor. A long
and very tough leather thong with a buckle was looped round his
throat—and Sheikh was holding grimly, tautly to its free end—
while Alhaj Mohammed had managed to slip his fingers of his
right hand under the leather loop, and was pulling at it with a
desperate urgency to release the pressure on his throat.

"My God—Sheikh, are you mad?" the Doctor cried almost in
stupefaction. "Let go at once!"

Instantly Sheikh released the strap, slipped his fingers under
the loop and drew the buckle with the whole strap from his victim's
neck. With a flick of the wrist he cracked the strap like a pistol
shot across the room.

The Doctor backed away from the bed, and surveyed the young and the middle-aged Hausas with a blend of anger and amazement.

"Will you two lunatics tell me what fun you get playing at murder?"

"You may well call *him* mad, Doctor." Mohammed spoke in a small, almost womanish voice. Understandably, he didn't sound very pleased. He sat up rubbing his throat with one hand, while he reached for a towel with the other and began to wipe the sweat off his face and body. "He's quite rabid with jealousy. One would thing he's the only man in the world with a pretty wife."

"I'm mad, eh?" Sheikh cried aggressively, cracking the strap to and fro. "Damn it—you'll be telling me next I'm blind and deaf as well."

Shocked to hear a young African addressing an older man in such rude tones, the Doctor protested: "That's no way to talk to an Alhaj, Sheikh."

"*He* an Alhaj!" Sheikh's face twisted up with contempt. "Of course, its true his money has taken him to Mecca three times. But the Pilgrimage has done his soul no good. If he has a soul, he probably left it back here in the dustbin! He thinks he can buy his way to Heaven. Allah can let him. But *I* won't let him buy his way into Mariama's bed."

The Doctor queried weakly: "Mariama?"

"Yes," Sheikh retorted with resentment. "My wife Mariama."

"*Toujours cherchez la femme!*" the Doctor murmured to himself. Aloud he observed: "I see she's come back from her trip to Guinea."

"Aye," said Mohammed lugubriously. "And she's come back with all the old confusion and mischief that always seem to surround her wherever she goes. I bet they were not sorry to have her leave Conakry!"

"There'd be no confusion," cried Shiekh, practising musketry rounds with the thong, "if men would let her alone."

The Doctor smiled at the simplicity of the type of man that generally gets itself enmeshed with the Mariama type of woman. For Mariama was born with that fatal charm which men were not designed to leave alone any more than bees were designed to leave honeysuckle flowers alone.

"But Sheikh," he said with the mildness of a peace-maker, "as her husband, you should be used to this Mariama's built-in confusion by now, My friend, you must not take it that a woman necessarily has any use for every man who smiles or makes eyes at her."

"Of course not, Doctor," Sheikh returned reasonably enough. "But this time as well as confusion there'll be murder too if Alhaj doesn't stop it."

"Be reasonable, man!" Mohammed cried with some heat. He was still rubbing his throat. "What wrong was there in my giving her £100 when she was going on her holiday? Your last journey to Bo had brought me quite a packet. So why cut up rough over a mere hundred pounds?"

"The first hundred was alright, Doctor." Sheikh, the Doctor observed, was struggling valiantly to keep calm. "At least, I was fool enough to believe so. You see, Doc—alright, Doctor—he gave it to her in my presence. But *why* give her another hundred pounds when she returned home? And WHY behind my back? Tell me that, Doctor! How would *you* like some old devil to be slipping a hundred quid into your wife's hand without your knowing about it?"

The Doctor glanced warily in Mohammed's direction. Of course, the old dog, that was the weak point in his case. With such a wife as Mariama, any gift, however kindly-meant, must necessarily take on a Grecian character in the husband's eyes. . . . Besides, whatever Mohammed's intentions towards Sheikh's wife, his ancestry was decidedly against him. Mohammed, in short, could not live down the enormous virility of his own Father. . . .

"Ah, Allah!" cried he with a piousness that the Doctor thought rather hollow, "This fellow condemns me for the very charity that the Prophet enjoined as a virtue."

"And where," Shiekh demanded, "did the Prophet say you were to give a woman £100 behind her husband's back?"

Mohammed, taking the question as both rhetorical and irrelevant, did not bother to reply.

"Keep your charity from Mariama" Shiekh stormed at him.

"That's all I ask of you." He reached a hand into the pocket of his shirting tunic, tore out four wads of notes from it, and tossed them down on the bed. "There's your filthy two hundred quid back. And I'll get even with you for this Alhaj. By the way," his throat swelled with vengefulness, "I'h NOT going up to Bo on Tuesday."

"*La-illah-il- Allah*! SHEIKH!" the man on the bed yelped like the money-grabber that he was. "Doctor—why, this *is* getting serious. But Sheikh, my boy," gone were his fear, his wounded vanity: money-making was the hub of his life, the centre of his pleasures, all in all to him. "Do you want to ruin us all?"

Sheikh's long face shortened and appeared to concentrate his bitterness and determination in a smaller, more rascally-looking area: "I mean what I say."

"*Now* I know you're crazy."

"Not at all. When you lose thousands of pounds every time I know you to be itching to get into bed with Mariama, you'll try and behave less like your father's son."

"But Shiekh . . ."

"I swear by the Prophet, Alhaj: I DO mean what I say."

With that Sheikh stalked away from the bed, unlocked the door—and stormed out of the room.

The Doctor closed the door again, returned into the room stroking his chin.

Mohammed rose from the bed, and, with what dignity he could muster, began to slip a pale, indigoed gown over his head.

"I just *can't* believe," said the Doctor bluntly, speaking low so that the others outside should not hear, "that, at your age, Mohammed, you have designs on young Mariama."

"What do you mean—*my* age?" Mohammed retorted very sharply. He darted an angry look at his friend, while his head remained half-stuck out of the gown—like a tortoise peeping out of its carapace. "Even Dad has been making passes at her!"

The laugh burst uncontrollably out of the Doctor's belly.

"Sorry," he said, genuinely apologetic, for he realized that it was too much to expect Mohammed to see the funny side in two men, whose combined ages must be approaching a century and a half, making sheep's eyes at a woman in her twenties—particularly as he was so ludicrously involved himself. "But you Hausas are beyond my comprehension."

"Nonsense!" Mohammed moulded the folds of the gown over his shoulders. "Of course, you're a doctor—and we all, including Mariama, are your patients. But surely, it's not natural for a black man to follow a profession that makes an impotent of him." And then, surveying his friend across the room, he chuckled till the eyes disappeared in the fatness of his face. "Or have you, *too*, been having a go at the little witch?"

The Doctor laughed and told him he thanked God he wasn't a Hausa, and Mariama and her like were safe with him.

Mohammed only sniffed and growled: "I tell you it's not natural, man!"

"What's not natural," the Doctor said, "is your present relation with Sheikh. If you *must* make passes at his wife, then in the name of sanity dismiss the chap from your service."

"*Li-illah!* Dismiss Sheikh? NO!" Mohammed shook his head till his cheeks wobbled like custard. "Why, my friend, the chap's worth ten of the best of my other workers. Dismiss *him*! You may as well tell me to shut my business down."

"It's your pigeon, Mohammed. I'm your doctor, not your business advisor. Think over the suggestion, though. If not," with a grim smile, "the next time I may be too late to get Sheikh to remove his dog-collar from that your rogue's neck."

Mohammed's belly undulated jovially. Really, he could not look on the serious side of life for long.

"I'll think it over, Doc."

"Damn it—don't *you* start Doc-ing me!"

III

For six weeks after that only toddlers were brought from Sackville Street to consult the Doctor.

Then one night, the front door bell buzzed viciously and long.

The Doctor woke up, squinted at the luminous dial of his wrist-watch. Two o'clock in the morning! He swore profusely and lay still.

The bell rang again, and continued to ring as though whoever had his finger on the push had ambitions on Eternity. The Doctor got up, slipped on his dressing gown. His slippers raised echoes through the three stories of the house as he hurried to the front door to let the patient in.

Crouching angrily over the desk in the consulting-room, the Doctor barked: "I suppose, Mohammed, you've been over-eating again!"

Under the flourescent lamp Mohammed's complexion—and Sheikh's too—had turned an unnegroid colour God never intended. Apart from that, however, Mohammed looked both sick and worried.

"I am sick," he groaned. "But it's Sheikh who has the symptoms."

The Doctor glared at him and bit his lip.

Then he turned to the lean man in the *khaftan*. Sheikh's long, and usually devil-may-care face, registered the distraught expression of one suffering acutely from dysentery.

"Doctor," he mumbled in sepulchral tones, "warn Alhaj Mohammed he must give me no more Castor Oil. A pint of it he's forced down my throat these last two days."

More bewildered than ever, the Doctor ran his fingers through his hair and ground his teeth. He opened a drawer in his desk, took out two antacid tablets to cool his stomach. Then he growled at Mohammed:

"Every minute you keep me down here at this god-forsaken hour of the morning will cost you four guineas. Are you ill or is he?"

"Of course I'm sick" Mohammed's voice rose in pitch like an angry woman's. "You'd be sick, Doctor, if £4,000 of your money were locked up in another man's belly and you couldn't get it out. Alright!" observing that the Doctor's brow had clouded like thunder. "Alright! Shiekh, tell him what happened."

"It happened at Bo" Sheikh began, talking more loudly than was his custom, to drown the Castor oil noises inside him. "The Lebanese Khalil met me buying diamonds from Pah Demba. Wanted to cut me out. But Pah Demba has an understanding with

Alhaj here. He wouldn't sell to Khalil. Later he sold me five stones. Khalil must have informed the police against me. I have no license, you see. Next morning, as I was sneaking out of Bo in one of Alhaj's lorries, the police gave chase. They caught up with us towards Bumpe. To save any trouble I—I—I" he gulped at the unpleasant memory, "I swallowed the diamonds."

"Well done! Well done!" Mohammed nodded encouragingly. "But Sheikh my friend, when a diamond goes in, it must come out again."

Sheikh did not quite see the logic of this—at any rate not in regard to his own circumstances:

But a whole pint of Castor oil, Alhaj!" he protested with feeling. "Did *I* tell the diamond to anchor up in my gizzard? Doctor," turning appealingly to their elected Solomon across the table, "Alhaj has purged four of the stones out of me. But the fifth, why," gripping his belly, "it hurts he here," tapping, "and here," tapping another spot. "It's cutting my inside like glass. But it *"won't* come out, never mind the pint of Castor oil."

By now the Doctor was struggling manfully to keep the grin of a lifetime out of his face. He felt like a god on Olympus surveying the follies of men—here indeed, he thought, was a situation for a company of gods to split their sides on. The joke was too much for one man to bear it. If only he could have had the Commissioner of Police present in an unofficial capacity his pleasure would have been rounded off, though not quite complete. All he said, however, was:

"How big was the diamond?"

"*La-il-Allah*, Doctor!" exclaimed Sheikh. "It was *very* big." He slid the thumb and index finger of his left hand as a ring up and down the thumb of the right. Apparently he could trust neither his own judgment nor the Doctor's credulity to fix on the size of the solitaire. So he fixed the Doctor with a rather dead eye and threw out more emphatically than ever: "It was VERY BIG, Doctor!"

"Very fishy," thought the physician. "All right," aloud, "go "go behind the screen and undress, Sheikh."

He followed the patient behind the screen and began to prod his belly as he lay on the examination couch.

"Ouch!" Sheikh yelped as the Doctor's fingers pressed in.

"Does it hurt here?"

"Ouch—yes!"

"And here?"

"OOH—yes!"

"Here too?"

"Ouch—OOH—Ouch! Yes!"

The Doctor grinned. "Where does it hurt most?"

Sheikh spied slyly up at him, passed his hand all over his abdomen, and finally rested his fingers accusingly on a spot low on the left side.

"Very well, Sheikh. Dress up."

The Doctor returned to his desk, made a few notes. As the patient came round the screen be barked out suddenly:

"Of course, Mohammed, as the diamond has stuck in there for three whole days, I'll just have to admit Sheikh into hospital for an operation."

Sheikh's face, already long, grew an inch downwards. He gaped two or three times before he shaped the words:

"Al-Alhaj, I—I—I don't mind—taking a little more—Castor oil."

The Doctor eyed his sternly. "Go and wait in the car," he ordered.

Hearing the front door close on Sheikh, the Doctor smiled to Mohammed and queried:

"Are you *sure* he swallowed that diamond?"

Mohamed's eyes dilated with horror.

"What d'you mean, Doctor."

"Well, my friend," as usual with doctors, he tried to hedge: for there's no mathematical certainty in Medicine. "There are a few places in a man's guts where a very large diamond *might* stick. But the large intestine isn't one of them! Do you *trust* this man?"

At once Mohammed began to sweat. He wiped the moisture off his brow. His features were twitching. The Doctor, knowing that diamonds are not a good breeder of honesty in men, felt sorry for him. He guessed that Mohammed's faith in his fellow trafficker and smuggler was—nil. And so when the Hausa spoke again, the Doctor understood perfectly that, though they rang with emphasis, his words were to be taken as a capitalist's prayer for the soundness of his investment:

"Trust Shiekh? Like my own Father, Doctor."

The Doctor did not expatiate further on Shiekh's trustworthiness.

"There's no cause for worry, then. And I'm glad to see you've made it over Mariama."

"Certainly," Mohammed returned, rising to leave. "As a matter of fact, she's since become one of my agents. She flew down to Lagos for me a fortnight ago. She took an eight thousand pound packet for me. . . ."

"She *what?*"

"That's nothing, my friend!" Mohammed laughed good-humouredly. "As Sheikh said, Mariama has only to smile at Customs and Security—and she can get away with hell itself!"

"Was it Sheikh, then," the Doctor asked with misgiving, "who recommended Mariama as an agent?"

"Yes—isn't he clever!"

"Very!" said the Doctor dryly, leading the way to the front door. "Good night, Mohammed. Let me know how the mighty diamond fares. . . ."

IV

The denouement came four afternoons later when Mohammed burst into the Doctor's over-crowded Surgery.

"What the hell—"the Doctor protested when the Hausa man ran unannounced into the consulting-room.

"Quick, Doctor—something to steady and strengthen my nerves!" Mohammed screeched hysterically, throwing himself into the settee in front of the Doctor's desk.

The Doctor swallowed his anger along with two antacid tablets, and waited for his friend to calm down.

"Feel a little better now," Mohammed croaked after a minute or so. "Look, Doctor—LOOK!"

The Doctor leaned over the desk and took the letter from the Hausa's trembling hand:

I hope Sheikh delivered the diamonds safely. Khalil doublecrossed us, but I'm sure Sheikh is clever enough to have got clean away from the police. The big fellow weighs forty carats. Sheikh left an I.O.U. in your name for it for £4,000.

Yours,
(Sgd.) J. Demba

"Good Lord!" the Doctor cried in horror. He was truly sorry for the old skinflint across the desk. "I'm sorry for this, Mohammed. Or," he added without any hope really, "did Sheikh pass the stone out?"

"Pass out? Pass out!' Mohammed began to breathe very hard. "It's I who'll pass out, my friend! OHHH!" He groaned and beat his head with his fists. "Doctor," hopelessly, "Can you help me to *dispose* of a young woman and a three-year-old child? No? . . ."

"Talk sense, man," the Doctor expostulated.

"I'm talking sense, Doctor. They're all I've got for my money. They're Sheikh's wife and child . . . OOOHHH!"

"Shiekh's wife! Then at last Mariama has come back from Lagos . . ."

"Damn Mariama!" Mohammed blazed, shaking his fists at High Heaven. "If you're my friend you must never mention her name in my hearing. I'm talking of Sheikh's first wife. *She* has a squint like a tailor's shears. OH! OH! . . . Mariama runs away with £8,000 and her air fare . . ."

"The hell she has!" the Doctor cried, angry on his friend's account, as well as at the young people's duplicity. "All you have to do then, Mohammed, is to squeeze Sheikh—squeeze him as hard as hell, man."

"I can't my friend—I CAN'T . . . OOOH—OOOH! . . ." Sweat of agony was pouring out of every pore in his face. "Can't you see? Sheikh—damn him!—yesterday—Sheikh absconded by air—to Lagos! OOOOHHHH!!!!"

"Towards Christmas"—Hezbon Edward Owiti

Steven P. C. Mayo

"No Short Cut"– an epic poem

Yapulula, Robiswayo, Mika and Webbeie halt to listen
About that sweetest, longest, saddest land voyage
For which fate gained the plunder in vain.
When productive NyaPhiri served, worked, wrought by love for
    her progeny
At that time, in that honest spell, how opportune
When our ancestors, our dead-living masters
Poured a single battalion of misfortunes . . .
Drought and plague and hunger and hate and rebellion and war
Then when I, effeminate and budding as I was
Held once by a lanky masculine-like Black belle
NyaPhiri
Chosen to sacrifice even a life of innocence
Sacrifice to appease the dead, the dead-living
For the continued existence of our clan, our race, our humanity;

This prodigy fell in that 'ere' of the severest war served
War of spitfires, gas and gun, then
When my mother and I in her womb laboured 'gainst the chilly
    tropical night;

And thus my mother and I sat by a glowing fire,
As she glared and then fondled, as she set to
Narrating her declaration:
        "Never to wed again;
        Never to bear again!"
But at this my eyes ran with water
For young as I was, and never born before
And since nourished with Negro mother's-milk . . . I
Did passionately thus cry—"No! Never throw

Never throw bearing power for the ngwee's sake
Never disloyal to the integrity and life
Of our culture, our heritage and religion
Of our whole humanity, un-vacuum of hermits, exploiters, or
        cannibals;
Better be tortured, scorched alive, or be a target for a fire-squad
Or hang in public
Better insulted, spat on, or lie outstretched
Nude in the market-square
Than lose your hard won liberty,
Better so
Than forsake your principles, your core, your Self . . .
Never in word of mouth or act of beck
Nor thus even spurious be":

But the belle was the stouter and grimmer
And in melic retorted, narrating how
She rescued humanity from ancestral wrath 'n ferocity. . . .

For so long had the three years gone past
The equatorial thicket never rain-embargoed before
Now in this year, fourth, aridity had fully set in. . . .
The first of this period was served with a shower
And that was the Alpha 'n Omega of water from heaven,
Year two came, but never tasted a drop
Save the dew that fell on the ground;
Humanity was the hardest hit . . .
Shrubs, undergrowth, trees all queued for the guillotine
And the third year celebrated the fall of life, as
Man's old experience broke away from course;
I, the belle's first son caught drought-fever
And was immuned
Yet the first born could not survive,
And so was the second,
And the third until I, born after the curse;
As many mounds visioned, two-fold so of the once-famished dead
        ones
For two or more lay in one tomb, under one mound

Token of the curse from the ancestors
And now many more longed for death
Expectancy was computed by circumstance
Life was at stake, in danger of extinction
Green tarnished to maize while dust and whirlwind
Played the tune, as drought regally walked in to accomplish
Work begun, work that apparently was never to cease
For it was penalty for decadence
When the opulent at the pauper frowned
And held him unreal as on movie-screen;
This was the act that beckoned the pour of misfortunes
One that provoked the tranquility of the masks of the grave and hut;

And the palm-tall Black woman of the mountain forest
Lofty as the cattle Watutsi
Stood
And in tangible penetrating voice cried, "Leap
And leave for our abode of origin with all zest."
But at this a man black even in the ear chose his own
And replied, "No woman shall lead,
And those that shall follow me straight into the Congo
On a stretched string,
Rid yourselves of those selfish babes on your backs,
Slay your babes or be slain together on this acre!"
Men many in count and loveless women responded
And Mufaya took to lead.
While the old belle, untiring cried her plea again
And at this we plagued the belle's old experience
"Why for,
And which way do you lead us?"
"Rise, rise to leave for the Congo," she rallied,
"Drought all our children shooes to the grave
While the easterners it forces to prey or plunder on us,
And verily this old ally of easterners has so abjured
Our military-pact of long standing, for foreigners,
Rise, rise, good countrymen!"
Ere had this wench stopped her innocent plea

Did a frenzied tiny NyaMbosi cry, "Hie yonder
On the mountains of the sun, the impis come,
Lo! Their assegais shine against the sun."
The easterners had drawn in, but which way, which way—
The south was full of blood-thirsty white barbarians
West we could trail, but our babes
Our babes are all meat for the friendly cannibal
That so dwell in the tropical thicket
Where the gory swelling river breaks its back six-fold;
Which way, which way, which way
Had we to hope for, which way would our
Haven, our home next be?

"To Congo all of us that adore liberty
Lift your babes, and we flee!" cried the tall one.
And those that had chose, followed her
And to the Congo they set out for;
And as for Mufaya it's only names that came back
As there they met death
Where they gained tombs, or were preyed on
So dying without tombs or mats of theirs;

The narrator with voice drowning, dropped her face,
Closed her eyes, then ope'd and closed, then
Heaved her head to let the eyelids loose
And water trailed thence down her oil-less cheeks
Like an experienced canoer in a Mweru storm
Taut in her face as though to invoke
        'God is dead' as she uttered
"O Sons of pastoralists, sons of coppersmiths
Honour your sacramental vows of the kraal—
To love and to cherish
In poverty or in wealth
In sickness or in health—
Be not a bad breed that devalues its progeny,
To the Congo let us all flee
Never without our babes."
And all those mothers 'n' fathers

That bent knees to NyaPhiri,
All by the southern route fled for the Congo
And south and south-bound they trailed
With their babes on their backs
True cases of malnutrition
And on their heads high towered pots 'n' packs of dried vegetables
Lofty on heads, yearning to touch the cloudy skies, but never
The sun
As it lay behind the mountains in the west
Some three rivulets away,
And only a stream of straight beams
Like hands of a hidden man in strict prayer for manna
Food from some hidden abode above,
The reddened rays of the sun could thus be picked
Far beyond
As they pierced callously thro' their prey,
The dying cumulus.
The people on the first day had so journeyed from noon till eve;
And the next day on trek broke out rainless,
As though in collusion with the first,
And so did the next, cloudless and bright excepting
The orange-red-mauve rainbow-striped horizon
While still the next came as if to restore sinking hope
It appeared full of clouds in the morn,
Yet by noon the meeting of the colour in the sky was over
And the day remained cloudless, rainless and enervating
And the pace of a despaired people
Dropped and turned snail-like;
In the rear distant the easterners could be heard
Panting for a fleeing plunder—ourselves, if they could,
And spitting threats and curses . . .
And forsooth what was to be had so to be,
It was all for the glory of Providence,
As in front loomed the unexpected invaders,
A whole army of bloody, fiery white barbarians
And those that were in the van of our procession
If this ever-diminishing cult could qualify to be called "procession"

They stopped and motionless plagued
The old belle's mean alleviating platitude;
They pressed on her
But the woman harassed and grey
Yet still with spirit imbued 'n' incadescent
Tho' on this fourth day since departure
Distress, despair, famine and fury mounted
And on run upon the lion from the wolf
She revealed declaring in broken voice
With full spirit and devotion:

> "Here on this bank of the Great Zambezi
> Shall we for the night lie
> To gather the lost energy when
> The men go to give sacrifice in the caves
> While the youths go picking fruits 'n' roots
> Albeit night, dear countrymen!
> We must serve if we are to save
> These our products of our drudgery."

The glowing fire was low, very low, too low
To detect the full glamour in the countenance of the narrator,
As she stood up (as though she had sensed my complaint)
And went out, coming later with firewood . . .
Mika, Yapulula, Webbie and Robiswayo sustain
To listen on
This shall in my heart always remain
Forever shall it be treasured in my memory,
This one adventure—
The saddest and the sweetest . . .
Vision of rapture begun to come back
As she put wood on fire and blew
And she blew and blew, again and again
And then continued her narration—

In the still of the night all did disperse
To gather edible fruits 'n' roots
To sacrifice to the ancestors, who
Now were years away from the descendants;

At three-hundred cubits east the men made a huge fire there
No it was no sacrifice in no cult nor esoteric
And veritable enough
This fire the old belle did condemn and praise; . . .
The firewood she had put on she exalted as
After a hut-ful of smoke gave up to blazes
And her face was naked once again; . . .
Soon all did begin to come back
And the youths brought assorted roots 'n' fruits
Poisonous and famine-crushers,
The huts were erect, all by women, but
None in them snored
And the men from sacrifice all came
And reported the failure and success of the sacrifice;
Ere had the assurance come
Did at three-hundred cubits east, at the altar
A battlefield erupt 'twixt the easterners and the barbarians
That had into this foreigner-still acre entered, and
The troops could be heard wailing and hailing
As they fought in blinded confrontation
Since the barbarians spat saliva on sight of the black easterners
And the easterners pledged like innocent dogs
In request for barter, black labour for white aid
Nshima[1] had to force the easterners relinquish liberty and
     sovereignity,
Principles and integrity . . .
At the ear of the wailing and the hailing
NyaPhiri with all stole away
And guided them to the west though
Famished 'n' worn down and weary
Carrying their fruits and roots unsorted— No more.
West and west they trailed
West and west they set their eyes upon the worst
For here was Angola
And they run upon the hyena from the lion 'n' wolf

---

[1] Nshima: Zambian dish prepared out of mealie-mealie (maize-flour).

Alas! It was land under the Portuguese
The hyenas that swore never to see a thing black
And for-sure there was no Blackman in scene . . .
But fearless, bold 'gainst all advice
NyaPhiri
Firm and mindful set to meet them;
But ere had she left
To seek passage through Angola
She
Stood and commended:

> "Time optimum sight has
> And as life must needs see head and tail wed
> So let as I traverse on this bar,
> To the grace of our fathers of old,
> Our whole ancestry,
> For the bloom of this abode-seeking people,
> And glory of the child, every child unborn,
> Have Buchizya, the child of God
> Beloved of ancestors and
> Mystagogue of the living,
> Lead,
> And in the vanguard of this civil revolution be . . . ,
> Draw out of the throng and
> This sacred spear of old accept."

As she so spoke a spirit whistled through
Blowing ungently and stealthily
And all, for fear, in silent kept unmoved,
Still unmoved in complete stillness
Until another,
Of the same sex and stance, exclaimed "Kadaleka, Chinombo,
Great Ancestors, why do you so neglect us?"
The wind blew stronger as she exclaimed the more
And the sweet chorus of the leaveless trees
And the teaming of dust whirling
And the breaking of boughs 'n' branches
And the wailing of the owl crawling into commotion, all

The order of the dry feast broke
And NyaPhiri in mystery vanished
Sinking into the underworld
Or embraced by the angry spirits
To be Companion of the gods above;
But as all mumbled in quest of the mystery
The effeminate hearts broke out lamenting loudly
So beckoning the easterners and the barbarians in connivance
Tears streamed and as streamed with same innocence as muswela
That innocent rain
"Maybe that was the only rain!" muttered my mother;

Mika, I wished you were present
And you would have heard her voice break and rise
And her face
Brighten, then sink to pale, her thick lips flatten and
Then move away suddenly to sob in private
And indeed as she growled "Maybe that was the only rain"
You could have been adorned with same pity,
Imagine,
I simply wept, thank the smoke intruding
For in me life came back, and
My mother went to fetch more firewood
Poor dead woman, she could not say a thing
'Till she was settled on her reed-mat
Staring into my face and saying:

> "Shall not cook unless the period is over;
> Shall not eat till the journey is finished
> Famine is conquered by sight of food;
> Listen!"

And at the word
She turned again to let loose
Only to me
Not you Robiswayo
Nor Mika, Webbie and Yapulula
Only to me she let loose how she disappeared
By drinking of the roots of the milky plant

So leaving the spear sacred three-fold
And never to be touched, as it stood straight there,
Never to be touched even by her priest
Who there stood knowledgeable of suspicion
But no more, yet with authority enough
Asking NyaMbosi, the pristine prayer-woman, say
Even after NyaPhiri had vanished:
"Buchizya is not in seen, mama
(As if she spoke face to face with her)
And no one here has clean knowledge of him;
Or he fled with vagary Mufaya on a stretched string into Congo
Or is one big child 'mongst the little children
In nowise insincere, tending those tiny unselfish ones,
Dying poor little things
That soonest on death to paradise justly fly
To be nurtured no more on wild fruit 'n' root or dried leaves
Nor on long forgotten negroid milk—but
The warmth and motherliness of sexless ancestors so to enjoy,"
For ancestors were now angels of God of the Sun and Life.

The journey was incomplete, and now incomplete the more;
Mama, so called for her ingenuity, courage, drive, and spirit,
Was in strain— How were her children, her followers
To go on witthout herself?
Or even her 'anointed' one?—
While the question of her disappearance remained a mystery
There she was wrangling with the men from Portugal
"I only seek passage through to the Congo," and
Before she could recompose herself
A tubby, toughy little man, newest commander, and youngest,
Retorted, "Who are you that seeks entry
In time of war, rebellion and revolution?
Are you a white man's friend or foe?"
"I am black. Indigena Africano and this Africa is my Africa
I am the daughter of Mwata Yamvu,
The Great Mwata Yamvu that never turned 'way the Portuguese
Mwata Yamvu the Great, the great son of Mwata Lusenge

Who truly founded this land, this empire
With the help of the Portuguese,
Mwata Lusenge whose great-great-grandson forgave Msidi
Who always hated the Portuguese for monopoly in an act of sin,
That slave trade for whom there is penalty in store for your ancestors
In hell,
The slave trade which never knew the realm of Cibinda Ilunga
That sage who would have built a village for Christian Portuguese
These are my great-great-great-grands
Whose generosity has never sunk before,
I am."
At the mention of "Christian," Stefanios
The young commander
In one more throe of passion and reason
Judged his best reply
"But are you not the same as Tanzania and Ghana? Who
On May 25 contemned and continue so contemning the whites
For the medicine and the education and the law,
The entire civilization that they brought to you!
For this disdain back, and return unhurt,
We welcome no spies,
Back must you!"
(Though easterners and barbarians blocked the way.)
No, she could not return without a positive reply
And so kept still, unmoved
With eyes about to let loose that rain without clouds,
And this pitied Stefanios
And memories of masterly in slave time stiffed Stefanios
Who asked if a slave-song and not a cadernata[2] could be produced
One song in which praises were given to the Portuguese
With memories of Africa in slave-centuries
And the gory battles, and the heavy wooden yoke
Balanced on neck and shoulder—about to sing
The unforgiving song,

---

[2] Cadernata: Pass or permit for moving from one district to another, commonly called
Phaso, i.e., a piece of paper.

She paused as if to say the terms were not favourable,
No,
She paused to ask if three and seventy more,
The remnants of a once-large procession,
Would on song receive passage and protection
Thro' to the border with the Congo—their abode of origin.

Waiting the issue
As she kept in good order and submissiveness
Yet perishing of desire to lead her children
Out of wilderness,
There as she stood, shameless
The owl, that bird of women, ill-omen,
With the global eyes gruesomely rotating
Panting
As if in servitude to some cruel master,
With feathers soiled same as from a wrestling-bout
On a mound
Yet with the white on head and beak—
A hope for peace 'twixt Stefanios and NyaPhiri?
But brought by a bird of ill-omen,—the milk from
Euphorbia of the graveside
Plant that harbours ghosts that never love the tomb
This home for serpents, ghosts and owls, all mysterious beings;
With brand of origin thus on beak 'n' head
The owl as one that is an outcast
Or a Kudu foal charged by an aged lion
That in stagnance roars and roars like the "Mosi-oa-Tunya"
While in desperation runs about and about
Likewise the owl came
Afloat in the air and settled on a dead branch at last
And from there gruffed
While the meeting with the eyes of NyaPhiri seemed a guerdon
to the rude creature as it seemed to narrate
"Ay, I have observed deities in that dear dwelling
In altercation
One pursuing that the journey cease

While another convulsed and cowering advocated the slaughter
Of NyaMmbosi, who now was the pale priest of mute people below
As sacrifice of human blood,
Sacrifice dearer than all beer that they pour
On mother earth to appease the dead who dwell above,
But yet another,
A ghost all in robes whitest as latex, heaved from the underworld
And though loftier to one score cubits high and strangely like pike
Spoke with a corrupted voice slashing at the injustice
Of discussing the fate of the living ones, so
Baulking honour due to these gods o' the grave
Who went away grunting to themselves, but never abandoning
The convocation on limiting their rights of the crafty art
In which Death was the supreme head."
As for NyaPhiri, since though mysterious in looks 'n' voice
Yet still all matter, a junior goddess herself,
All that the owl spoke heard with anxiety
And longed to return to her people, who
Homeless and had no food, had no proper leadership of worship
Since Mwanga pronounced a whole realm of the bard
That heirs must sing on coronation, as Buchizya remained unseen;

Forsooth the famished abode-seekers were at destruction's verge
As for NyaPhiri, to return to them or not to return
But death where to leadeth her (them);
When those with Stefanos as they compromised,
Not to yield their hunger-for-women on her
Though attractive a thing she used to be
Until this evil season,
Mooted a brainwave: "Stop!" shouted one
As NyaPhiri tried to walk away
To face the pursuing foes from that battlefield, from
The altar thence had come the wailing and the hailing
As each on recognition of the other chose
Setting their eyes upon their common foe
That was bent for the Congo
Although now held by the unforgiving Portuguese;

And as the easterners plus the southerners sighed, the commotion
    grew
And men rebelled against the women who between themselves
Tamed hate;
And verily "stop" instilled new hope, forlorn hope?
Yet not withdrawing the dilemma before NyaPhiri
... had to serve if she were to save ...

And in a wave of passion for her progeny
She stopped
Stood there
And broke in one traditional ode
In low groans sang, contemning the once slave masters
As she poured out all her genius in the song:

> "Kalelo makolo athu analikusautsidwadi
> Cifukwa ca ukapolo anagulitsidwa nsalu
>   Anali kusautsidwadi powatenga kuwao
>   Mnjiramo anali kufa n'njara, njota ndi kutopa ..."[3]

And as she loudened the song, her progeny
On run from the pursuing foes
In a rush joined in the song wailing,
Poor things, cases of malnutrition
Came to be in the care of the Portuguese,
No, it was no care
Since there was no food, no accommodation
For the procession that was on run
In search of its independence,
Political, social, or was it from hunger
And under protection of the Portuguese
Without delay
As they thought the traditional ode was

---

[3] Literally the song is:
    "In those old days our ancestors were being troubled because of slavery
    "They were sold for cloth . . .
    (chorus)
    "They're troubled when they were captured and taken away from their homes,
    "On the way they 'died' from hunger, thirst, and being tired."

A song of praise to them, so
Gave them way;

Yapulula Robiswayo, Mika and Webbie,
At this act of the Portuguese,
Our people so proceeded on to their abode,
Our abode of origin
Although that chant that saved them
Was a praise to the sturdy slaves,
Those heroes who were tortured,
Our heroes whose spirits founded us
Paved us the way to suffer for our
Heritage, religion, and liberty
Our culture, integrity, our humanity—
Thus NyaPhiri led her people, her children
Past the mouths of the wolf, the lion, and the hyena
And now they were again bent on their destination
To the Congo they faced . . .
To the Congo they advanced, but the journey was incomplete
And so they moved, walked on and on
On to the Congo . . .

Eldred Jones

Show Me First Your Penny

K UNLE'S SECRETARY HAD gone out for her lunch hour
when he returned to his office. He pushed the door open and
saw the beautifully polished brown shoes, the knife edge creases on
the trousers, a large newspaper covering the body.

"Guess who?"

It would be no one but the Minister for Air, Tom Brunswick. If
he was half as crooked as everyone thought he was, Kunle did not
see how he could survive a purge. But Tom had an extraordinary
gift for survival. His whole career had been a series of miraculous
escapes from disaster. He had been discreetly removed from school
on the advice of the headmaster when he had burgled the Latin
master's study, copied out an examination paper and done a roaring
trade selling copies at five shillings a time. But as he had already
been entered for his school certificate, he had been allowed to take
the examination. He passed in the first division, and entered the
Post Office as a third grade clerk. After three years, some very clever
forgeries involving postal orders were traced to him. He was prose-
cuted, but he got off on what the lawyers call a technicality. He
found his way to England, qualified as a lawyer and was soon on
the crest of the wave at home. His reputation as a sharp lawyer grew
rapidly. He left more scrupulous colleagues gasping as he pulled
trick after trick at the bar. The Bar Council had him up twice but
could pin nothing on him. Each time old Sir David Wren-Smith the
President of the Bar Association had given him a severe reprimand.
Tom stood for Parliament in his native village and was returned
with a large majority. He was one of the smartest men in the house
and was given the Ministry of Mines where he soon acquired the
soubriquet of "Mr. Ten-per-cent." An embarrassed Prime Minister
soon had to shunt him off to the safer Ministry of Air. But his voice

and his vote in the cabinet when large projects were discussed kept foreign contractors on his doorstep with prerequisites as before. His annual European holiday was alleged to cost him nothing, and when he stopped payment on his large powerful sports car after the first installment, the local agent made the best of a bad job and told him to forget about further payment. Old Toufic was left open mouthed when Tom thanked him and said that in that case, how about returning the first installment which he had paid before realising that the car was a friendly unsolicited gift. His gall was only matched by his devilish cleverness.

"Let me be the first to congratulate you, Mr. Sandi. For a man of your years you have a well-deserved reputation. You should have heard the P.M. talk about you in cabinet yesterday. Phew! Honesty, integrity, hard work—the lot. And very well deserved, too. I congratulate you."

"Thank you, Minister. I do my best, but I am sure you did not call on me merely to congratulate me."

"Surprising as it may seem, that was just it. I thought I'd better drop in while your praises were fresh in my mind."

"Thank you again, Mr. Minister," he fingered a file.

"I know what a busy man you are, Kunle"—he wore his most charming smile—"so I won't keep you. I want to tell you that I too feel that there is no better man in the civil service for the delicate job the P.M. has given you. I won't presume to advise you, but I think you should be careful not to play into the hands of the opposition. Not exen the P.M. would thank you for that. Besides, as you know yourself, what is at stake is the stability of the country. The country needs a good government, and no other party but ours can give it that. If you run us out of office, you will run the country into chaos. So don't rock the boat, boy; don't rock the boat."

"Mr. Minister, you flatter me. How can I bring down the government? Anyway I have my instructions, and I can assure you they are not to bring down the government."

Kunle wondered what exactly Tom Brunswick had up his sleeve. He knew the minister was only biding his time. But he too could wait. He did not want to scare him off too soon. He sat down and lit a cigarette. The minister puffed at his cigar, frowned gravely, and looking straight at Kune, asked: "What do you think is the greatest need of this country now, after independence?"

Kunle stalled. "Well, I don't know that I can give you a simple answer to that, Mr. Minister. We need a lot of things."

"Look, I can tell you. What this country needs more than anything else in the world is a moneyed middle class."

Kunle almost lost his control to counter: "What this country needs is fewer crooks like you and more men with conviction and guts," but he let the minister continue.

"It is the duty of people like you and me, men with a good education, to acquire wealth. Then we could industrialise. It was middle class capital that made all the industrial nations of Europe; made America; made Japan. The future of this country should be in the hands of people like us. We should own the mines and the beer and cigarette factories, the banana plantations. It is our *duty* to acquire wealth."

"I do not have any great desire for money myself and the government pays me reasonably well."

"For a man of your brains? Mere chicken feed! You are in a position to make money. You should make it."

"How, sir?"

"Look, I sent Schweiner to you the other day. He represents the very big European consortium which is interested in those new deposits of high grade iron ore. They are willing to pay good money to get in. They know the score. They are used to this sort of thing. They want to make sure that their offer is *very carefully* considered. Your Ministry of Commercial Exploration will have to make the final recommendation. The fellow told me he was amazed at your attitude."

"I told him, Mr. Minister, that he would get every consideration along with the other companies."

"Yes, but he wanted something a little more certain and was prepared to see that you did not lose by it."

"I just refused to understand that part of his conversation. Did this worry him?"

"I don't mind telling you, Kunle, that I have a personal interest. I hope to get a directorship in that business once it is all settled. It means a lot to me. I am not asking you to help us for nothing. I've talked it over with the representative, Schweiner. You will be looked after in a way which will cause you no embarrassment. No local transactions. Money will be quietly deposited in your name in a foreign bank. And we bid high, Kune. I have told them you are not to be insulted with a silly offer."

Kunle knew Tom Brunswick to be blunt and open about his deals, so he was not surprised at the directness of his proposition. Tom had this pseudo-philosophy about the middle class and capital which he was happy to trot out in defence of the shadiest of fiddles. Kunle almost envied the man his easy compromise with his conscience. He would never get an ulcer.

"Mr. Minister, if your tender is the best, it would be my duty to recommend it. What Mr. Schweiner should be worrying about now, surely, is how to pare down his costs, not inflate them by building in bribes into his total."

"Look, Mr. Pure-as-driven-snow, I don't want to corrupt you. If you don't wish to accept a perfectly straightforward offer, that's up to you. But not everyone else is like you. We have had to negotiate with others to smooth the way. It will be difficult for them, however, if your report is adverse. I don't want to lose this deal. So think hard before you oppose me."

"I hope I do not have to, Mr. Minister. I would like to help you, but you know my position."

"O.K. Let's leave it at that for the time being. But remember, I am not the only one with a stake in this. Don't hurt yourself unnecessarily."

With his hand on the door, Tom Brunswick turned. He was his charming self again, and a mischievous smile played on his lips.

"Incidentally, I've just finished my little beach cottage. It is quite a hideaway, and any time you want a little quiet time—you know what I mean—just let me know, and I shall be delighted to put it at your disposal. That nice Mrs. Karimu might like it."

"What—" Kunle began, but the minister had slammed the door and was halfway to the lift.

Before the evening, however, he had his table to clear. But not quite yet. There was a knock on the door, and in walked old Pa

Demba. His was one of the most respected family names in the
country. The Dembas were not rich, but had been one of the few
families in the hinterland to embrace western education, and had
scattered the family name all over the country in a large number of
the small but important jobs on which the country really depended.
There had been Demba school teachers, Demba branch managers
of large European trading firms, Demba members of local councils,
Demba football stars and of course a few famous Demba black
sheep. At independence the Dembas were poised for the leap into
the future. Soon a Demba branch manager became "the first African
to be appointed" a director of O.T. (Omnibus Traders Ltd.). After
his years of labour in khaki shorts, white canvas shoes and pedal
cycle, he now went about in a large chauffeur-driven company car.
Another Demba became his country's first Ambassador to Japan.

    Alimamy Demba, Pa Demba as he was now commonly known,
had been getting past it at independence and was looking forward
to retirement from his post as headmaster of the famous Kanjara
High School (the Eton of the backwoods one facetious D.C. had
called it) when he was invited by the People's Solidarity Movement
(PSM) to stand for Parliament in his home constituency. Pa Demba
was not even opposed in the election. No one would have had a
chance in his home area except another Demba, and the family
had naturally backed him solidly. Pa Demba was offered the Ministry of Rural Development. It was like a dream, and in his few conscious moments, Pa Demba found himself to his own surprise an
old roué. He had taken his alcohol secretly before because of his
position in a mission school, but now publicly revelled in a distinctive mixture of whiskey and stout which was known throughout the
country as D.D. or Demba's delight. Pa Demba had been a widower
for more than twenty years, and during that time had led a reasonably discreet sex life. But now he exercised his failing powers on a
wide selection of fast girls to whom he was a kind of public assistance bureau. One rather anxious mother had expressed relief when
she had discovered that her rather wild daughter had only been
visiting Pa Demba: "Oh well, she could do worse: he'll look after
her, and won't do her any real harm." She was right. The girl was
now comfortably settled in England, becoming a company secretary.

Pa Demba had in a matter of a few years become a national joke. His ministry was ironically one of the best run in the country, for the simple reason that he had Gus Taylor, one of the best civil servants in the country, in whose capable hands he left the entire running of the ministry. He had been often heard to remark when any proposals were put to him: "See Taylor. If he says 'sign,' I sign. If he says 'don't sign,' I don't sign."

Kunle was glad to see Pa Demba, as he always was.

"Please sit down, sir."

"Thank you, my boy. Busy as usual, eh? I don't know what this country would do without devoted civil servants like you and my Taylor. We politicians come and go, but you are the backbone of the nation." Pa Demba reflected ruefully on the plight of a country with him as a possible vertebra, and with his characteristic honesty, he winced. "Oh, yes. You are the backbone of the country, and that's just as well."

"Thank you, sir." Kunle smiled. He, too, had just tried to visualise Pa Demba propping up the country and had thankfully dismissed the vision.

"My boy, I have come to give you my whole-hearted support in the job you have got. I am not a saint, but I can say this. The people put me where I am. I take what they give me, and no more. I have never taken a bribe in my life. To tell you the truth—" Pa Demba seemed to have realised this fact for the first time—"no one has ever offered me one. I wonder why? Never mind. I have enough to account for without that, heaven knows."

He dug into the sleeves of his large white gown and fished out a crumpled mass of stiff pale blue paper. He pulled one out and passed it on to Kunle. It was a monthly bank statement. At the bottom the figure in black was £2 10s. 5d. Kunle smiled a rather embarrassed smile, but Pa Demba laughed quite openly. He passed on another sheet—another bank statement for another month. The total at the bottom was £1 10s. 5d. "I had a rather unforeseen caller on the 27th of that month." Kunle grinned; Pa Demba roared. He passed on another—£2 10s. 5d. By this time he was slapping his thighs with merriment. Kunle could not help laughing, too.

"You see, my boy. When I first started teaching, I was paid the

pricely sum of £2 10s. 5d. *per mensem*—that was the phrase in the
letter of appointment—and I lived comfortably on it. So now, as long
as my current account shows £2 10s. 5d., I feel happy. Oh, I have a
savings account, too—and a saving system, what's more. On the 26th
of every month I pay a call on the bank, pick up my statement, and
write a savings cheque for the difference between my balance and
£2 10s. 5d. I walk out of the bank feeling like a potentate. I owe
nobody anything, and I can always maneuver, if necessary, to the
extent of £2 10s. 5d. until my next salary cheque is paid."

"No a bad system at that, sir."

"That depends, my boy, on what the difference happens to be
each month." He dug in again and produced his savings bank book.
Kunle looked at it. The difference was never large. He flicked the
pages over backwards and saw that for several years Pa Demba had
been about to save at least £10 a month until he became a minister
and trebeled his salary. Now he saved sums like £1 13s. 7d., £3 5s.
8d. and on good months just under ten pounds.

"You see, my lad, it all depends on the difference." He laughed.
"And what is more, I am not ashamed of my record. You will get
great shocks when you look at other bank statements. Nothing is
more revealing of a man's character and way of life as his bank
statement—not just his balance, mind; his statement as a whole.
Mind you, the balance too is pretty significant. As you can see, I
don't have much. When I leave this job, I shall go back to my house
in the village—I built it before I became a minister—keep a few
chickens and pigs, and hope I will have a few years of total im-
potence during which to repent my sins." Pa Demba still laughed,
but a little solemnly now.

Kunle looked at the old man. He was sixty-five. He reflected
that he had seen better, and he had seen worse—far worse. Pa
Demba was not one of his country's heroes. He would leave no
mark—except perhaps a few more qualified secretaries in the various
ministries—but he filled a space which might have been occupied by
a man who was not only incompetent but also flagrantly dishonest.
Kunle felt grateful on behalf of the country for the small mercy that
Pa Demba was honest.

"What I came to say, my boy, is that the job you have been given is very important. If there is anything I can do to help you, you just need to ask. I am not as blind as I seem, and I know something of what is going on. So call on me any time you want to."

"Thank you, sir." Kunle was really grateful. He would probably need this man. If things got rough in cabinet he could at least count another reasonably friendly vote.

Boevi Zankli

The Dream of African Unity

O Mother Africa O,
We Africans dream a dream O,
It is a dream of African unity O.

O Mother Africa O,
We your sons and daughters
Promise you O,
We will always dream of African Unity O
We will always pray for its realisation O.
We will always work assidously, for its fulfilment O,
                Night and Day O.

We will always work life and death
                For its birth O,
We will always preach it O,
                From coast to coast O
                Shore to shore O
                And ports to ports O

From Cairo to Cape of Shaka,
From Dakar to Dar Es Salam,
                In hamlets and cities,
                In market places,
                In the valleys of Africa,
                In the caves of Africa,

We will always sing it aloud O,
From our various tongues O;
We will play it
On our gourds O,
On our balanjis O,
On our koras strings O
With the best of African
Sweet-symphonic-harmony.

We will always dream
Of African Unity O,
In our sleeps O,
        In our works O,
        In our plays O,

We will always paint it
        On canvas O,
We will always carve it
        On woods O,
We will always mold it
        In concretes O,
We will always cast it
        In metals O,
        And
Set it in colorful mosaic O,
Until the day of total independence,
For Balkanised Africa O,
Oh Mother Africa O,
Forward to the Union Government O,
For one Africa we dream O,

We promise you Mother Africa O,
We pledge that our dreams
Will not be an empty dream O,
    We promise you that if it
        Is a matter of spilling our
        Black blood, for its realisation,
        We are ready to go to battle O

O Mother Africa O,
We promise you O, we shall
        Keep our oath to you O.
May we all live to see the birth of
The glorious dream of our dreams O,
        African Unity O,
        African Unity O,
        African Unity for ever. O
           Yah O Yah O Yah O.

M. C. Njoku

The Python's Dilemma

A YOUNG PYTHON, very tall, very handsome with shining black and white skin rushed home from school on a very sunny afternoon. Panting and scooping beads of perspiration from the arc of his face, he flung his school bag to a sofa. "Mama! Papa! Where're you?" he yelled. He was all excitement.

"Here, child, what's wrong?" said his parents.

"Discovered something, mama. Daddy, I got power."

The bewildered parents looked with mouths agape.

"I can blow you and mama to pieces. I can blow everything up. I can blow uncle," the young Python said hilariously.

"Who taught you such a dangerous joke, son?" said Mrs. Python.

"True, look!" He tossed something up to the air.

"Bang!" said an explosion.

The Python's home was a storm of conflagration. Fortunately, no one was hurt.

"Ha, ha, ha!" laughed junior Python. "You've seen nothing yet. I can blow up our snake universe. I got power, mama."

Mr. and Mrs. Python called in a psychiatrist. "How long has this been going on?" asked the doctor.

"Since he came home from school this afternoon," Mrs. Python said, wiping tears with the back of her palm.

"It is a clear case of paranoia," said the psychiatrist. "Measures must be taken before the next and more dangerous stage of total madness. I suggest that he be put under lock. He must not be allowed any solid diet. Milk is what he needs."

"Please, don't lock me up," pleaded young Python. "What have I done to deserve this? True, daddy, we will be all right, we will be powerful. True, mama, I'm not mad."

"Leave the young fellow alone," pleaded uncle Python. "Perhaps he means well. Perhaps his invention may one day bring us to the leadership of the entire Boa Kingdom."

"Power is the flame of madness. Unchecked, its flame engulfs all in one massive insanity whose end is assured destruction," said Mr. Python. "No, don't encourage young ones to do evil. Let him take his comeuppance like a good lad."

"They'll regret this," young Python said to himself. "Rather suicide than suffer injustice." However, before he slings, he must get himself one delicious meal of choice human flesh. At midnight, he looped behind a blackberry bush by the wayside. He knew that a certain aristocrat usually came that way at that time of the night. He was a large man; dressed always in a well-tailored, dark suit. He had ample folds of fat around his waist, although his head was relatively small and stuffed fully with political pamphlets.

Young Python was not long in ambush when came the tramp tramp of a foot.

"Who's that?" the important politician asked.

"Hee—see!" Young Python said rather loudly.

"That's applause. It means I shall be premier soon," he said.

"Hee—see!"

"That's my name, laddy?" said the aristocrat, who was a little tipsy.

"Hee—see!" Python opened his mouth wide and the politician slid in. Usually, if the Python swallowed a whole animal he underwent a period of incubation, during which time the diet was gradually digested. It was not so this time; instead, the Python found itself changing.

First head, then hands, legs . . . A complete man! Six feet, six inches upright above the ground. What a mirror of perfection? His skin was whiter than snow. Golden haired. Oval faced. Aquiline nosed.

He started to walk down the street. In the morning he found himself in the middle of a city. It was a civilized city. Electric lamps hung in long perspectives of tall poles; classical, Gothic, and modern buildings, in a sort of orderly disorder, competed as to which must choke the sunlight. The visitor found the inhabitants very congenial and curious. They seemed to have correct opinions on all matters, particularly in the governments of other nations. They were polite and very anxious to be helpful. He soon found out that the city which was called Nondo was the capital of Nida, one of the most powerful countries of the human world.

"Pray, stranger, what's your name?" his guide inquired.

"Dr. Faustus Potentiate," said the stranger.

"That sounds aristocratic," the guide said.

"It is pedigreed in the first century and even beyond," said the doctor.

"Drofxo accent, too!" the guide shouted in amazement. "Then, it is my obligation to conduct you to Her Majesty."

"Her Majesty?" asked Potentiate.

"Yes, a very gracious personage. It is her pleasure always to have Drofxo pedigrees in her government."

Dr. Potentiate's performance before Her Majesty was an unqualified success. He pronounced "Your Most Gracious Majesty" in a tone so softly sweet that the queen was for making him her chief minister there and then. But the then premier, being a shrewd politician and conscious of that frailty to which mighty and low women are equally prone, spoke of the inadvisability of committing Her Majesty's Government and Subjects into the hands of "a perfect stranger." After a heated argument, Dr. Potentiate received the title of "Courtier to Her Majesty." He was given a home opposite the House of Parliament to familiarize him with the laws and problems of the nation.

Dr. Potentiate's metamorphosis did not diminish his desire for power; in fact it actuated it. After a few conversations with the premier, he found that his ideas were consonant with those ideals which the human species called rational.

"Ha, ha, ha!" the premier chuckled, twisting a wry neck in the direction of Potentiate. "How can a rational being reject measures whose ultimate end is awesome power and world control? If you'll identify your ambitions with those of our great nation, be assured of a niche among the most illustrious of this nation."

"I assure Your Excellency that my scheme is entirely the nation's," Dr. Potentiate said, congratulating whatever brought his unexpected transformation. How sad! Animals are so unthinking. So indifferent to matters that would lift them above others. They are irrational. It makes all the difference.

Dr. Potentiate was soon married to the beautiful Elizabeth Agnes Power—a tall, buxom blonde with the generic smile of those happy women whose husbands were power-bound on a pair of lovely ovate lips. At twenty-one, she could trace her aristocratic lineage to the 5th Century, B.C.

They had been married for four years when war broke out between Nida and a neighbouring state. Dr. Potentiate's bombs proved decisive. They wiped out all that breathed in the enemy country. The inventor's fame quickly spread to every recess on earth. Potentiate was proclaimed the most useful man on earth. A grateful queen and country decided to accord him the highest honour that Nida ever gave out.

The happy news blazed out from every news medium:

"It pleased Her Gracious Majesty to confer the most coveted title of 'Honourable, the Knight Commander of Her Majesty's Killers to our illustrious Doctor Faustus Potentiate, whose knowledge, skill and perseverance culminated in the invention, perfection, and use of the most destructive weapon ever known to man. The future of our great country and indeed of the whole world is irrevocably bound with the progress of this awesome instrument of mass murder . . ."

Unfortunately, a few days before the ceremonies of Knighthood, Dr. Potentiate suddenly fell sick. He glued himself between bedsheets and forbade anybody to see him.

"Darling, Faust, you're certainly very sick. I must fetch a doctor," Eliza said.

"No! no! no!" he said frightenedly. "I'll be all right."

Mrs. Potentiate sat dolefully at the foot of the sick man's bed. Faustus had never been so seriously ill before. Alarmed, she reached a hand in the position of her husband's masculinity.

"Leave me alone!" yelled Dr. Potentiate, and at the same time pushed so that she slumped her ample buttocks on the floor.

"Faust! Oh! no, no, no," she sobbed. "Christ have mercy!"

Although Dr. Potentiate gave most of his time to state duties,

he had, nevertheless, been a considerate husband. Their marriage
had been ideal, if not exactly happy. They had three boys. They
never had a row. Eliza was a devoted wife, conscious of her duty
towards an ambitious husband. Their children were bonny and
bouncy. On his own part, Faustus had been a vigorous lover. He
held, of course, that sex was unheroic, but as a good citizen, he fulfilled his matrimonial duties. However, he never "degenerated" to
the level of applying profane, four-letter words to conjugality. When
obliged to ask Eliza for a love match he would say, squeezing her
pale nipples, "Darlin', what about a sperma-uterus connubiality."
Previously, when he appeared indisposed, Eliza had thrown sex to
him and he had riccoheted to health. But this time . . . If a dog
sniffs at a bone, he must be truly sick. Eliza flicked her fingers.

Dr. Potentiate was actually transmogrifying into a python. His
legs had merged to form a thick tail, but he remained a man from
navel to head. He was embarrassed.

Ah! why must this happen to me! My God! Why bring me face
to face with power—and then mock me with this snake business? I
would've reformed your earth. I would've ushered in a whole set of
new values to Your Glory and my humility . . .

Had the doctor not forgotten that he was once a snake, perhaps
his sorrow would have been bearable. But in the bustles of life,
amidst the pomps of aristocracy, in the conjugal warmth of a lovely
wife, in the joy of a talented offspring he had allowed his past to be
buried in the debris of amnesia.

Three days his metamorphosis continued. He lost his hands and
his trunk to Python. It was becoming more and more difficult to hide
himself from Eliza. If he lost his head, he would be through. At that
crucial moment he got an idea.

You swallowed a man to become a man. To remain a man—

It was just after midnight. His family were secure in bed. Outside, the world was silent and dark. He hurtled down from the bed
only to find that he was completely powerless against the door. He
struck several times with the tail, but all to no avail. He glided up
and down the walls and to the roof, but alas, his man's head did not
have the colubrine flatness which would give it access through holes

and cracks. Red with anger, he let slip. The door cracked. He balled himself under the bed.

"Papa!" The sound was like a treble whisper of a boy.

Although the young Potentiates were not permitted to see their sick father, the oldest son Faustus Junior was in the habit of stealing into daddy's bedroom when everyone else was asleep. He would approach the sick man's bed, whisper "papa" and then sneak out.

Necessity knows no son, Doctor Potentiate thought, as he bit through his son's tender loin. He chewed away reluctantly, mutely.

Unkind nature that condemns a man to eat his own flesh! To drink his own blood! A sudden paralyzing chill seized him and he belched. Through the benumbed darkness, he could see two crystal balls ardently gazing at his face. And he heard the lingering, dying voice: "Papa, pa-pa, pa."

"No, no, no, no!" he said, dropping the child's head quickly. But to complete his transmutation, he must eat the victim, head and all. It was almost morning. There was no time to waste. Fortunately, his Drofxo accent returned to him. He said distinctly the sacred words: "Her Majesty's Government." They worked like magic; and with a rejuvenated energy he attacked the food: eye, nose, bone, and all. Choked with fullness and breathing hard, he muttered, as he shuffled into his bed: "Got to find a civilized method of doing it, though."

Dr. Potentiate became the prime minister of Nida a little afterwards. Everywhere progress reigned. New wars were arranged; new weapons perfected. Other nations flooded into Nida to learn the techniques of weaponry, mass destruction, and economics. Schools were remodelled to accommodate the new learning. The Humanities and other wasteful studies were abolished for good.

But it was only to a select elite that Dr. Potentiate confided the secret of power, which he taught was synonymous with the very essence of existence.

"Man must eat man to grow," he told his audience. But it was not long before his government discovered that, in practice, the principle would leave the streets of Nida empty of its citizens.

"We can make it a national interest," the doctor said coolly. "Initiated man-eaters would, in future, be sent out to other countries as cultural avant-gardes, ambassadors, and colonizers. Armed with plenipotentiary powers, they would assure a regular but controlled traffic of human flesh within an economic context which would be at the same time conscious of a parity between demand and supply." By a near unanimous vote the parliament adopted this suggestion which became the lode star of international relations.

Like every good thing, this discovery was given various interpretations following the fancy of ambitious men. Eventually, factions arose. One group held that man-eating was the one and only truth. All historical revolutions had culminated in the discovery of this law; but the privilege belonged to the masses, not to a select few. To confirm this truth, they ate up their elite, burnt all books which did not testify to the truth, and confined dissident eccentrics to madhouses. Man-eating being a natural institution, they argued, it must be carried out boldly, without those hypocritical niceties which the elite of other nations affect. To ensure that no victim escaped, a system of enclosure within a network of barbed wires was invented. Opponents of this method tauntingly called it a "Barbed Wire Civilization."

A second faction argued that man-eating was only one of the many truths revealed by God. Among other truths was the even greater concept of freedom to go wherever one would. Such a liberty might only be limited by the number of green certificates which a citizen held. The certificates were designed to ensure the necessary supply of human-flesh. There was no need to resort to barbarisms. Eccentrics and unpopular literature were welcome to the Museums of Dead Letters and Men, where they would be too much occupied with each other to be of any bother to the government.

In their own turn, opponents of this system gave it the cognomen of "Green Certificate Civilization."

A third group was an amorphous conglomeration of all those nations who were generally indifferent to who ate them. They made up the rest of man's world and were pompously styled "The Dominion of Breeders." Prominent in this group was a sect of half-breeds with horns, long tails, and oblong, large heads stuffed with porous sand. They formed a separate, but every active union called the "Organization of Satyr States." This organization provided more human meat than any other world group.

Meanwhile, the dispute between Barbed Wire and Green Certificate powers had reached such dangerous proportions that a military showdown seemed imminent. Following a long parade of weapons, the Barbed Wire leader mounted a dais and spoke: "Country men," he said, waving at a procession of giant tanks, rockets, guns. . . . "Your government is ready not only to protect you against any aggression, but to devastate the entire world. That is our goal."

Applause!

"Believe me, fellow citizens, when I say that we can really destroy . . ."

Responding to the Barbed Wire threat, the Green Certificate Secretary for Destruction, said: "Our I.Q. for mass murder remains the highest throughout the world. Our potential for destruction is unlimited. We will never be the aggressors. But, if we are provoked, our response will be so devastating that the planet earth would be demagnetized and chucked into oblivion."

These unforeseen developments frightened Dr. Potentiate, who foresaw the undoing of the world which he had done so much to build. "God forbid that bestial satyrs should inherit us!" He gave up the premiership in order to devote more time to foreign affairs. He visited all important capitals of the world, and through his wise persuasions the nations agreed to meet to formulate principles of coexistence which would save man and his civilization. Twelve months later, a world organization was formed. The first fruit of this great organization is the now famous Seven-Point Charter on Coexistence and Human Rights, which has showered untold peace and coexistence on mankind since then.

Excerpts from the World Organization Charter,
   Virus City, 4th July, 190X.

Be it resolved that this World Assembly, conscious of the catastrophe to which continued conflicts among members of our beloved earth would inevitably lead, and anxious to avoid such a disaster, do hereby promulgate and adopt the following principles of cohabitation, coexistence, comiscegenation, co-development and coculturization. We wish peace and happiness to all mankind!

Article I.

Be it enacted that all legally constituted governments are endowed with Divine Rights to crush, grind, and devour their own citizens by whatever means they deem fit. No foreign government or nation must in any way interfere or obstruct the exercise of this duty.

Article II.

It is the Divine Right of Barbed Wire and Green Certificate powers to continually augment their strength by appropriating from the Dominion of Breeder States.

Article III.

Should it please the Barbed Wires or Green Certificates to exterminate a breeder state—either for food or by way of a routine, military exercise, the exterminant must register her intentions with the World Organization before or immediately following complete extermination.

Article IV.

The primary function of all breeder states is to ensure a peaceful, regular supply of human-flesh to consumer powers. The Satyrs have taken a step in the proper direction; other nations within this group must emulate their example. In return, the powers do hereby guarantee to all Dominion Governments perfect protection against their own citizens.

Article V.

To ensure the survival of civilized mankind, bombs and kindred weapons of mass destruction must not be orbited above the earth. However, should a power (without any harmful intentions whatsoever) wish merely to break through an enemy defense, it is not a violation of this article if it ferries her weapons in half, three-quarters, or in any case not more than fifteen-sixteenth of an orbit above the earth.

Article VI.

Whenever a power has stored enough of a potentially destructive weapon in its arsenals, it must call for a treaty to halt further production or proliferation of so dangerous a weapon.

Article VII.

For the purposes of order and stability, this World Organization pledges full support—without regard to justice or injustice—for any member government against internal or external forces tending to its overthrow; except in so far as such forces are in the interests of either the Green Certificate or Barbed Wire power.

Dr. Potentiate had been so absorbed in the general problems of man's survival that he now and then forgot to make provisions for his own private existence. He was thus forced in emergencies to fall back on his children with the inevitable result that time left him destitute of any offspring. He grew listless and thinned so much that an arm could belt his groin. But it was Eliza who was really hit.

"Ah! my poor ones," Eliza wept. "To disappear so!" In middle of civilization—without a trace! If I only knew what happened to you . . ."

Of course, there were the usual announcements in the press and on posters: "1000 POUNDS REWARD to anyone who can give information leading to the recovery of Felix Potentiate, aged five . . ." All proved futile.

Eliza broke down completely. A physician was called.

"It is a case of acute, pathognomonic hysteria arising from the incompatibility of her clitorisal maternal, sweet naturedness with an unnatural suffering occasioned by the tragic loss of her children," the doctor diagnosed. "Her malady is unresponsive or, should I say, resistant to drugs. I would suggest a tropical vacation where she must be exposed to the sight of large animals in a wild environment."

To render this tropical holiday simultaneously beneficial to all mankind, Dr. Potentiate was appointed Governor General of the equatorial Bombo. Bombo was only five degrees above the equator, it abounded in sunshine, but its towering mangrove forests of irokos, palms, mahoganies, kola-nuts; . . . its expansive waters beneath clear rotating skies; its incessant rainfall brought with them breezy, cooling effects, which even forced the Potentiates to seek the cover of blankets at night.

The governor's house was an imposing two-storied, concrete structure overlooking the sea. But it looked toyish in contrast to the expansiveness of its premises, which contained some three gardens, servants' quarters, fishing pond, swimming pool, tennis court, chapel . . .

The Potentiates, after the initial difficulties necessary for adjustment, found Bombo pleasant. Lady Potentiate's recovery was rapid as soon as wild beasts were discovered and safaris arranged. However, she had occasional relapses. A mother never really forgets her loved ones. Whenever Her Excellency dreamed of her children she woke up screaming.

"What's that, Eliza?" her husband would ask.

"Oh, dear, dear! What a debilitating weather!" she would say between gasps.

Lady Potentiate was not happy that His Excellency devoted seven whole days to official duties.

"You were not much of a churchman at home, Faust. Here you spend whole days in the church, reading lessons and even preaching sermons?"

"Sense of Mission, darlin'," Dr. Potentiate said.

He whistled as he dressed. It was a Sunday evening and he was hastening to vesper. "Men in high power are thrice servants'—put it this way, the Bombolese are eternal children. Find you on the slack once, it will be all over for religion."

But what really piqued Her Excellency was Dr. Potentiate's gallantry. Invariably, the doctor would escort their Bombolese maid to the gate in the evenings, after her day's work. Although, as a governor general, he was not expected to be so polite to his domestic, he argued that he was doing his duty as Her Majesty's Knight and that the foundation of morals was gallantry towards feminity. Occasionally, however, he patted the maid on her buxom buttocks—a form of gallantry which did not sit well with Her Excellency's hysteria.

"Oh, dear!" she would say. "This climate is so enervating."

"Don't let it unnerve you, darlin'. I am Her Majesty's Knight. With his arm about her waist, he would walk her indoors.

Bombo was a large country made up of people of varying ethics and language. They were a friendly people and received the Potentiates with that spontaneity of love peculiar to Satyrs. But the grandest disappointment was the scarcity of really wild beasts. They existed mainly in the zoos. And zoo beasts were ineffective with hysteria. Dr. Potentiate took the opportunity of his first meeting with the natives to propose a solution.

"Chiefs, natural rulers, politicians, high and mighty Satyrs, I greet you in the name of our Great Queen. The bond between your people and mine can never be broken, because our friendship is based on common interest. You are not ordinary men and women. You are our economic, political, and social experiments. Your failure or success is of concern to us. Without you the Organization of Satyrs which we have done so much to encourage on this continent will be quite useless—" he punctuated.

A burst of applause! "Hail Bombo, mighty among Satyrs," the people sang.

"Her Majesty's Government is desirous of granting you self-government on a platter of gold. However, it is of concern to us that you have a trained elite capable of leadership in a very modern sense." He lifted a glass of water to his lips. "You, no doubt, have heard of the recent pronouncements of the World Organization, an association fervently dedicated to peace, concord, freedom, and progress. You know your duty as potential breeders. Fortunately, your leadership resource is unlimited.

"Our major task is to select trial leaders capable of driving ethnic groups on all fours into the forests on special days to be announced in the Government Gazette. . . ."

A short time afterwards selected tribal leaders appeared before His Excellency. As Her Excellency could not tolerate their "long tails" and "crooked horns," they were ordered to have them clipped. This was followed by a ceremonial bath in a huge, circular basin capable of holding one thousand large-sized leaders, who after they had perfumed their bodies were quartered in an exclusive section of the city. Here, each elite received an endowment of a luxury mansion with dogs and servants; such other modernisms as guns, cars, blank cheques . . . which brought civilization to them. The government thus formed was registered with the World Organization for protection.

On a hunting day, two tribes were selected—the hunter and the hunted. The latter, stripped wholly naked, were driven into the jungle on both hands and knees. When a victim got entangled in a thorny undergrowth the hunter's dogs tore away at him with a zealous ferocity to the great delight of Their Excellencies. But much more congenial to Lady Potentiate's health was the spectacle of a Satyr-monkey nimbling from branch to branch. A single gun report! The exhausted beast fell head-long, pom!

As soon as the regulation number was attained, hunting was called off. The dead were ground into fine powder, boiled, liquidified, bottled and labelled: "Exclusively Elite; Not For Local Consumption."

While Their Excellencies were visiting Zinza—a Bombolese state North-South, South-East of the capital—an incident occurred which endeared the Zinzians to Dr. Potentiate. He was on a football field addressing a massive crowd when suddenly he began to transform. From shoulder to foot he had become a snake. But thanks to political insight! By a rare intellectual telepathy, the leaders of Zinza realized what was happening. Surrounding His Excellency at the same time, so that he was completely cut off from the public, they quickly fed a man into him. He continued his speech as if nothing had happened. Her Excellency, who was in an adjoining hall lecturing suffragettes on the probability of including women in future safaris, did not hear of the accident.

Dr. Potentiate was very grateful. "You are certainly not alien to the principles of power. I have no doubt that the leadership of Bombo would one day fall on your shoulders," he said.

Meanwhile, changes were taking place at Nida. A new foreign secretary had been appointed. Dr. Potentiate was recalled home.

"Wonderful, wonderful," the secretary said, regarding Dr. Potentiate with a generous smile on the threshhold of the foreign office.

"Let me congratulate you, in behalf of Her Majesty's Government, for your invaluable services to Nida," he grinned broadly as he ushered the doctor to a chair. "Her Majesty has graciously asked me to appoint you to the curacy of the Museum of Dead Arts and Sciences."

"Curacy. Dead Arts," Dr. Potentiate repeated slowly, listlessly.

"It will carry a comfortable stipend—"

"Comfortable! Convey my thanks to Her Majesty. I—I decline the offer."

"Of course, you cannot."

"I'm only forty. What do I want to be dumped in a museum for?" Potentiate shouted.

"Precisely 'dump,'" the foreign secretary made a wry face. "You're no longer current, I am sorry to say, doctor. Our Commons have learnt the secret. Any economic system which ignores this fact is ousted. Your 'limited approach' has bankrupted us. Unlimited production and demand. This is modernism. Militarily, we have been superseded by other nations. Your rockets and bombs are mere toyish crackers compared to what is now available to man . . ."

Dr. Potentiate left the foreign office a ruined man. His museum associates were eccentric men and women, virtually ostracized from society. They could not help him because they did not have the faintest idea what power was. They buried their heads most of the time behind massive, dusty volumes. At lunch time they discussed endlessly on matters which the doctor considered irrelevant to the facts of existence. Some held that life had no purpose; others that happiness was desirable.

"How can people without power dare dream of happiness?" Dr. Potentiate wondered. His readings had been confined to the chemistry of explosives; constitutions; political theories, practices, and power structures. Studies which merely actuated his misery in his state of isolation. Gradually, however, he grew more tolerant of his new companions, who introduced him to Moral Philosophy, beginning from Plato to Bertrand Russell. He began to wonder whether a new system of values, not based on power and man-eating, was wholly impossible. He realized that for the first time he was happy without the heart crepitations which sabotaged every ounce of happiness that came his way when he had power. Besides, power was so cranky an ally! Yet he could not articulate his thought. One early morning in December, he was overtaken with excitement as he paraphrased from Russell's "A Lay Man's Religion":

"We do not know that we are here for any purpose . . . We know that each wants to stay as long as he could . . . The best we can do for our fellowman is to help him stay here a little longer—"

"I've found it! I've found it!" he shouted, rushing into the street, still in his nightgown, with the book fluttering in his shaky hands. He was barefooted, dishevelled and stinking. He had not washed since his disgrace. He was in the premier's office before the guards could notice him.

"Perhaps, this may help you," the premier said, handing him a green note.

"I am not a tramp, Your Excellency. I'm Doctor Potentiate. I've found a new theory. I confess that I was wholly wrong. The path you're pursuing will be the certain end of man." He gave the book to the premier.

The premier looked at its cover. "Oh, Russell. We have read him," he said. "So you believe that anyone is going to give up power because of the aberrations of an eccentric?"

"Why condemn what you have not tried?" said Potentiate.

"You're very innocent, doctor—" The telephone rang. He picked it up, and replacing it after a few minutes said: "Bad news! Bad news! Always bad news! Bombolese government overthrown!" He leaned his head on the back of the chair and puffed at his pipe. He was a burly, fat-cheeked man with a babyish face. "Sad, very sad! This country had come to love the Bombolese premier," he said, meditatively.

"And hate its people," Potentiate said.

"They must pay for this," the premier ignored Potentiate. "Hot-headed Zinzians."

"Zinzians?" Dr. Potentiate said.

"Yes! the only bastards capable of overthrowing a legal government," said the irate premier.

"Did you find out why?" said the doctor.

"Reason or no reason, to permit the overthrow of a single government is to trample on the great principle on which all governments are founded. It is a ridicule of the Seven-Point Charter of the World Organization," he banged a clenched fist on the table.

"You remember, premier, that I was the architect of this famous charter," Dr. Potentitae began calmly. "I have since discovered that it was based on a concept foreign to the well-being of man. The essence of all governments must be the preservation of life, and hence that government which directly or indirectly destroys a single life has, in effect, forfeited its right to exist."

"Ha! ha! ha!" the premier laughed. "You must be uncommonly naive, doctor, to imagine yourself an originator of a law which transcends you and me. The theory of power is *a priori*, innate. They are adopted to suit governments and to meet the ambitions of—"

Telephone! "Government forces apparently in control! About one million enemy dead! Her Majesty's Government rushing guns, jet fighters, bombs, destroyers! Total annihilation in progress!"

"Very good! Very good!" the premier exclaimed, twisting his elongated lips into a broad smile.

"Oh! Depravity, your name is man," Dr. Potentiate said in disgust. He ran from the office like one possessed. "My Zinzian friends, how I have betrayed you!" He slapped all over his head.

Not long after the Potentiates left Bombo, the government began to kill more citizens than was considered necessary by many. More hunts were organized. Thousands were brutishly burnt everywhere: on the roads, in theatres, on playgrounds, in the jungles—contrary to the civilized methods which were in vogue during the golden era of the Potentiates. Incensed by this "barbaric perfidy," some radical Zinzians coup d'etated the government, thus lashing Her Majesty's government into fury and bringing the wrath of the World Organization on all Zinzians, guilty or innocent. The government of Nida and the World Assembly quickly ordered the extermination of all Zinzians. To defend themselves, the latter took up arms.

Perturbed by the course of events, and rebuffed by his home government, Dr. Potentiate appealed to the Organization of Satyr States to mediate the Bombolese dispute. After a long delay during which time it was hoped that Zinza would be obliterated, the Satyrs met. They resolved that "Bearing in mind our personal interests and the interests of established governments throughout the earth, the desire of the Zinzians for survival is indefensible. We hereby condemn it absolutely . . ."

This resolution was applauded with feasts and dancing elsewhere in the world. The most influential press on earth, *The Signs of New Wisdom*, famous for its liberalism and championship of every species of modernism, hailed the decision of the Satyrs in an incisive, but very humane editorial: "Now that the Organization of the Satyr States has failed to recognize the right of the Zinzians to exist, they must desist from struggling; . . . Gory as their experience may be, but the mere wish for survival does not make sense," *New Wisdom* concluded.

There's one way for me, thought Dr. Potentiate. Return to python land and tell parents how right they were. Tell them how right they were! Tell them how I alone have corrupted a whole race of bipeds! But his desire to do what he could for his friends detained him at Nida until Christmas.

It was a snowy Christmas. The morning was cold and wet; the sky was dark with vapour. Lady Potentiate decided to stay at home and look after her husband who had kept in bed because of a minor cold. She carried a tea tray into his bed chamber.

"Dar-ling, if you will just prop up on the pillow," she said, approaching Dr. Potentiate's bed. She raised her eyes. "Oooh!" she yelled frightenedly.

"What did you see? A python? A snake?" Faust said with a firm calmness.

A dazed Lady Potentiate stood, open mouthed, watching the slow progression, from between bedcovers, of scaled black and white ridges. "Help! Help!" she shrieked, dashing to the door. But it was too late.

"What have I done?" said the doctor. He had found himself again. Silence! "Eliza, Eliza! Where are you? Oh, my darlin'." He banged at his crammed belly. "Man-eating, what a vile atavism! Your only cure—never to have begun. Oh, monstrous villainy! Execrable monster! Eliza! Eliza! Is it true you're in my stomach? Kind suicide— Too gentle for my crimes. One, two, three, four, five, six, seven, eight ad infinitum."

He ran out in his pyjamas, shouting and tearing at himself. An amused crowd followed a at safe distance.

At the police station, the duty officer leaned over a desk. "Yes, sir, what's matter?" said he.

"I'm a monster. I'm a snake. I ate my Eliza. I ate my chicks. I ate—"

"Enough, sir!" said the officer. A broad grin played on his calloused lips. "Another case in insanity," he murmured, reaching for the telephone. He dialed "BED-LAAM."

Solomon Deressa

Death Like Life

Death like life for me would be a luxury
Life like death, the end-product of futile abundance;
Son of the Sense of Waste, begotten by a thousand uncensored gods,
Warping "Is it impossible to love like others?"
Into "Is is impossible to hate like them?"
Hewn in rugged brittle stone have I come to this:
Squat, I listen to the shriek of aborted tangential worlds
Squashed between the two spheres of thought and unthought
Which contact to undermine, wedge their uncanny way in
To die into the insane silence of the bruised brain
Gods exile themselves, we know, out of direct compassion
The Son of Man, to share unaware their destiny of common man
To punt-pole up a given time-stream at a given pace . . .
In vain liberated of all terraqueous essence,
Strain, free-born vibrating with or without significance.

But I,
I our out of the cataracts of these eyes that I myself slice
Mediocre songs on incoherence (juicy looseness of a machete'd
    melon).

        Wagging lightness in my head:

        Drum drum drum
        Beat beat beat
        Detonate within the head
        As drunkness in a splinted bottle
        Chastizing unmitigated tam-tam.
        Cry cry cry
        From the apple centre
        Wail: never never never

>As roaches in muddy water
>Howl: for ever ever ever
>Naked bruised unfledged: tremble
>Shoot out of the booze-barrel
>And I will be with you
>On foot and on fire
>Burning with you
>Hating with you
>Coming with you
>The long, weary long way long
>Phrases from a dis-membered song
>They I the rest and you.

In an effort to undo the done
And through the succulence of a melon see the undone done
To mortgage the future licking with cold flames
A living past with its horde of names
I stand swelling on the edge of my own world
Bored and boring on Hell's folded door-mat
Covered and devoured by spiders of iron
Lunging in sick vengeance at them, in feeble blindness at the
    monstrous horizon.

I invoke choking on blood, on pus-rain
A blizzard of whetted white-heated spikes
That would explode like a dozen genii punches in the face
Digging mechanically into unmendable ribs;
Scraping negro tuft into a crucifixion wreath
       (oh, the holocaust of immodest emulation!)
I hang defenseless by an imperial of spines of kinks
Caught between two words that fell from a poet's nacromanic lips.

In the mean time;
Because I glow with the intensity of covered hearth
Hearth at early dawn in a darkened room,
Because I wink with method at charred light,
Because I glow with the frivolity of the glow-worm,
Because I am the pain in the infant's primal cry

The shot in his shot of breath,
I, trembling vertigo of cosmic onanism
With love to infinite Love my love
Swaying on the deck on the swelling sea
Sink into the Ancient Mariner's Rhyme, dart of the stinging bee,
Being tonight as last night all others excepting the other me
With unflinching pain-fire, fire-pain
Your brother, I stand shadowed
To snatch a kiss under a slanting rain
As we reverberate incandescent against the rest of mankind,
Diving down into oblique indignity
To filch a kiss from under the scattered rain
Incendiating the quiet contented filth of the Seine
Water setting water a-fire blood cremating blood
Turning the whirr-purr of passing cars
Into bars of jonquil music pulling apart helpless stars
Meekly counting their ion-years in *phare*-length
Powdered into everlasting dust on dementia entailed by your absence
And from across the waters rehear T. S. Eliot's Saxon tea-candour
Hack me to pieces of peace off a smoldering Africa.

My love
Homely girls arm-in-arm walking home
On this wind-purged May night
Trudge in no unfavorable contrast
To the budding heels of the beauties that past
Kicking up the dearth of afternoon pavement dust
Like a stallion-king's hooves on desert mica
Breasts whipping the wind, hairs burning the light.
A year ago, I would have been trimming by Satyr's beard
In punctual ritual for Spring and its carnal feast.
Today, pretentious homoeoteleutons all alone
No beauties to bed, homilies in a desolate room; the lesson is learnt
Waiting for you inserted between moment and moment second and
    second
Minute by minute, I, eyed by solitude for a Peeping-Tom,

See them toddlers twenty years ago through the eyes of mothers
    their fragile arms entwined
With the eyes of the village-boy, who with timid pride loved and
    died
Or of more practical bent dabbed at limpid eyes, or just about tried.
Undiscriminating, like distributive justice, an abysmal tenderness
    in me yields to the pull

Of *le Christ noir de l'amour charnel.*

Limping on broken crutches into the face of faith
Unbelieving in human suffering, others or mine
Long have I waited with grim insolence to be burnt out.
Though, because of you, death like life be a gratuitous luxury
And life like death the by-product of futile abundance,
To cut fraternity into a fragile conclusion:
The mysterious door is forever closed on simple mystery.
I have bathed in the insomniac's heavy rancid sweat;
For all the loves that fiascoed loving love unfathoms
I scrubbed me in Yared's wails and Jeremiah's dry sobs;
On laughters that decomposed in the Columbarium's echoes, for a
    pressing-board
I applied the burning bottle to my silence and flattened me out.
Waiting for you I have chased sanity as cats their fleeing tails
I have worn my buttocks out on the women and hunger of Paris
It may be time to lead my skeleton away seeking greener pastures.

"SHADOW DANCERS"—Hezbon Edward Owiti

Paul Sitati

Jane

A LONE, GASPING NOW and then as the current of air filled my stomach, I drifted from side to side. I was soon in a confused state of mind. I stood for some time, and then entered the Friendly Bar. It was a cheap and noisy place, pulsating with life and youth. Students were spilling in and out of it, shouting to each other, clasping each other, fixing their personalities one upon the other with a devastating frankness of youth as if they meant to suck each other dry of every thought or emotion that was in them.

I found a small empty table with some difficulty, and as I sat down, something strange came in my mind. I took out a cigarette and was about to light it when a waiter came to me.

"Can I help you?"

"What drinks do you have?"

"All kinds. We have brandy, gin, whisky. . . ."

"Can I have brandy, please."

I held my cigarette and lit it. As I sat in the corner, puffing away at my cigarette, I recalled the words of our pastor at home. I imagined him standing in the pulpit with his old Bible in the hands, the congregation sitting before him with guilty faces, and his words booming in the church, "Repent! Repent ye! The Kingdom of Heaven is at hand."

I recalled vividly the last Sunday Service I had attended just before I left for Nairobi. My father had taken me there to be prayed for since I was leaving home for Nairobi—the city of corruption as my father called it.

The waiter brought the brandy and placed it on the table before me. As I held the glass, just about to pour some brandy into it the words of the pastor came into my mind again, this time more fiercely than before.

"Whether therefore ye eat, drink, or whatever ye do, do it all to the glory of God."

I raised my eyes to survey the crowd. Among them, I saw a young lady, aged about twenty. She wore a short dress, almost four inches above the knees and in the coloured lights, her thighs shone beautifully. Her hair was long and heavily oiled. She had powdered her face heavily and her red lips stuck out in the face like a wound. She moved a few steps towards the counter and as she did so, her waist swung from side to side. I discovered that I was not the only one looking at her. One of the students who were sitting next to the counter winked at his friend and whispered, "What a nice figure!"

The young lady was not apparently a stranger in the bar. One of the maids smiled at her and said, "Hello, Jane! You're back again!"

The young lady did not answer. She took a few steps towards the door and then back. She seemed to be in a world of her own, and being the mistress of that world, she seemed not to care for anybody. She took some money out of her handbag and asked for a packet of Rex. After she had got the cigarette, she moved towards me and pulled the chair next to me. She sat for some time expecting me to say something to her. When she discovered that probably I was not the type of person she had at first thought I was, she drew my attention by first pulling the ash-tray, and at the same time saying, "Excuse me."

"Never mind," I said.

After a few minutes she said, "You look depressed, John."

I was surprised. I did not expect her to know my name. I could not remember where I had met her. I summoned up my courage and said, "No . . . not really, I am only wondering how I will get to College. The buses have stopped, haven't they?"

"Where do you stay?"

I looked at her with surprise. She did not look a stranger in Nairobi, and anybody who had been in Nairobi for a long time, even as long as only three months, would know that College always meant the University College. I knew that here were many places in the town to which one would refer as college. There is the Kenya Government Secretarial College, Kenyatta College, Kay's College, and many other places. But whenever the word college was mentioned, particularly in a place like the Friendly Bar, and at such an hour of the night, one always recalled the University College. Probably because it was frequented by students. However, not to disappoint her, I said, "At the University College," stressing the word "University."

"Really! I know a few people there. I have been there several times. Once in hall two and several times in hall three."

Immediately, I started thinking that she must have been taken there by students. Students are known all over the town for taking such girls to the halls. In fact they themselves use the term "collection" to describe the women they pick up from town at late hours of the night. Jane moved closer to me, and I read from her gestures that she wanted a drink.

"Would you like to have some . . . something to drink?" She smiled. In a soft voice, she said, "Yes, please."

I knocked on the table and a waiter came. Before I spoke to him, she told him, "Whisky, double, I mean."

She now started behaving as if we had known one another for a long time. She remarked that she did not like the behaviour of the people in the bar because some of them were not kind, and that they approached her in the way she did not like.

"Why do you come here then?"

"Just for a change. I first came here with a minister, and the second time with a permanent secretary. Since then I have been coming here alone. When these people see me, they don't want to talk to me. They say I am expensive. Instead they keep on looking at me as if I am the first girl they ever saw in their life."

As she said this, she was moving closer to me. I discovered that her face was shrivelled and gone life-stagnant.

"How did you know my name was John?"

"Do you know mine?"

"No. That is why I was surprised when you called me by my name."

She smiled. The smile revealed artificial teeth in her mouth. I noticed that the lip-stick was coming off from her lips because they had cracks on them.

"I first saw you in Joe's room. You came there to borrow some records and when you went away, I asked him, and he told me, 'That is John, a friend of mine. A nice chap he is, though he tells me his father is a devout Christian.'"

Her words cut me bitterly. "His father a devout Christian!" I knew my father was known for that and I was expected to follow his instructions.

It was coming to ten o'clock. Most of the students who had been in the bar had gone away. I called for more drinks for both of us. Under the influence of drink, I was getting interested in her. I tried to persuade her to go to College with me. She asked me how much I was going to give her and when I said that would be discussed when we reach the college, she said that her policy was always on cash basis.

"I don't want to reach there and then begin quarreling."

I knew that I had no money to give her. Such girls always demanded twenty shillings from fellows like myself, and something as high as five pounds from big shots. Since I did not want to jeopardise my future relationship with her, I decided to postpone my date with her till such time that I had enough money to give her.

"If it is difficult now for me to go with you, why don't you meet me tomorrow?" There was silence.

"Where?"

"Say at the College."

"I am not very keen on that. Suppose I meet you here?" I knew why she preferred that place to the college.

"All right. What time?"

"Same time you came in this evening. I saw you for I was standing outside there."

"Fine."

We finished the drinks and prepared to go. I lit another cigarette and stood up. Just as I started moving, she held me and with a smile said, "Remember tomorrow. Same time, same place."

"Yes, and thanks for your company."

"No mention. I should, in fact, thank you for the drinks. I look forward to seeing you tomorrow. Don't miss."

We parted. I stepped out of the bar. The air was cool. The moon was shining brightly. The highway stretched out before me like a ribbon.

"Taxi, sir?" a voice called.

I looked back and saw two men sitting in a yellow-band taxi. In the light of the moon I easily read the number of the vehicle— KDH 127.

"How much to College?"

"Four shillings."

"Oh! no. We usually pay three."

"Three-fifty, sir?"

"No, thank you. I told you I have three shillings."

"All right, all right. Come in. But next time you will be kind enough to pay four. We are giving you a special discount tonight."

I entered the taxi and the driver started the engine. All along the way, green lights flashed before us. We passed on a number of students, late-comers like myself, staggering home. They were shouting all the way but because the taxi was going so fast, I did not understand what they were saying. I only heard words like, "collection, budgeting, . . ." When we reached the college, I paid the taxi-man and went straight to my room. I switched on the lights and a heap of books was revealed scattered all over the place. I was not in the mood to look at them. I switched on the radio.

"This is the General Service of the Voice of Kenya. The time is a quarter to eleven." I pulled my pyjamas out and dressed ready for bed. There was a lot of noise in the corridor. Boys were shouting, "Where is the janitor?" The radio gave a signal, "This is the General Service of the Voice of Kenya. The time is eleven o'clock. This is your late night announcer wishing you good night."

The boys in the corridor echoed this, "Good night. Good night, Joe."

After switching off the radio, I lay on my bed but I had no strength to cover myself with a blanket. Suddenly I started thinking about the pastor at home. It was three weeks to end of term and I knew I should have to face him again. At the same time I started thinking about Jane. I was to meet her the following day. I recalled her words just before we had parted that evening. They came to my mind in a sweet voice, "Remember tomorrow, same place . . ."

My accepting to meet her, I knew was contrary to my father's instructions. My father had advised me not even to drink. He had known a number of young people ruined by that. If it had only been drinking, I would not have been so much worried. I had drunk, yes. But among drunkards I was really ignorant of life. The idea of Jane made me shiver from the marrow of my bones.

While all these ideas were streaming in my mind, someone knocked at the door. I stood up to open it. I staggered towards the door, and when I clutched the key, I found it so hard that I hurt my fingers. I released it, lifted it up and looked at it. The key seemed to sum up the situation. I pushed it back into the key-hole and forced the door open. I discovered that it was my friend Joe. He had just returned from the broadcasting house. He pulled the chair and sat down before me. I fixed my eyes on him and seemed to see something in him which I lacked. I knew he also was drunk, but among non-drunkards he fitted in easily. Although Joe was relatively older than myself his behaviour satisfied no possession of pride. To him everybody was on the same level, whether young, old, learned or not. It was his gregariousness that made him win friendship from his contemporaries. Looked at generally, Joe was partly a Christian and partly pagan, but more of the latter. He went to church only when he pleased and began yawning half-way through the sermon. He always carried with him a watch, almost the size of a clock. This instrument was so dear to him that he would not talk for more than ten minutes before looking at it.

"I liked your announcement this evening," I remarked.

"What particularly pleased you? The music?"

I was quiet for some time. In fact I had not listened to the broadcast that evening.

"The music."

"Good. I knew a lot of you guys enjoy light music. I know you like the Monkees' 'I'm a Believer,' that's why I squeezed it in."

"That was kind of you."

"Anyway, John, I called in to talk to you about some social affairs. You remember that girl you met in my room that day you came to borrow some records?"

"You mean Jane?"

"That's it! So you know her too! That girl has been a friend of mine for some time. But I have not met her of late. But I must see her. The other day she was in my room, she went away with my record-player and promised to return it after two days. Now it is three months. I tried to contact her over the phone, but I was not successful. I heard that she stays somewhere at Westlands with a European boy friend. That does not worry me. All I am concerned with is to recover my player. She has a number of things from a few people that way."

"Do you think I can be of any help in this matter?"

"Yes, though not directly. What I want you to do is to lend me some money which I will repay you on Saturday."

Joe and I had been friends long enough for me to trust him. I gave him twenty shillings to help him.

"Thanks, John. I will keep my word. Saturday."

As soon as Joe went away, I went to bed.

The following day was Friday. We usually called it "Members' Day" because it was only on Fridays that most of the students could manage to go to night clubs. We normally paid half the charges at the door. I prepared to meet Jane and take her to the night club.

Seven o'clock. I called for a taxi and left straight for the Friendly Bar. When I arrived, I saw her standing at the entrance. She stood there, tall, but not as beautifully looking as she had been the previous night. However, there was something magnetic in her, something indescribably good that was attracting me. I got out of the taxi and went straight to her. We went into the bar, and sat at the same table where we had sat the previous night.

"How was the day?" I asked her.

"Rather bad ... ah ... I thought of you the whole day!"

"Sure?"

"Of course. I have just been thinking that you would not come. While I was standing out there, just before you came, a man came to me and asked me if I would go with him. I told him that I was waiting for someone else. Instead of going away quietly, he started abusing me, saying, 'I know you. You want big shots, hey?' I was very annoyed. Anyway, it was good that you came. I can now trust you."

"Have something to drink."

"Yes, please," she answered in that same soft voice that had sounded in my ears the previous night. At that moment someone came in the bar and started looking around. He was just about to leave when he suddenly turned around and saw us, or rather saw Jane.

"Oh! Jane! I was about to go on thinking that you were not around!"

She grew pale.

"And how are you, young man?"

When I stood up to shake the hand of the stranger, I noticed that Jane was becoming restless.

"Excuse me," and on saying that she stood up and left the room.

"Sit down, sir, I will be back." The stranger followed her. I did not know what was happening. An hour passed. Neither Jane nor the stranger returned. I drunk the brandy and thought that one of them would return.

Eleven o'clock. There was no sign of them. I paid the bill and left the bar. The night was dim. Mist floated in the air. I tried to look around for them but there was no trace even of the way they had followed. I called one of the waiters and asked him if he saw them going out. He said that he had seen them but he was unable to tell me which way they had followed.

"Why are you bothering, young man? Don't you know that girl? She is Jane the prostitute. She has had a lot of trouble with men. For the four years I have been here, more than thirty men have gone about with her. The man who went out with her has been after her for a long time. He says that she ran away with his money. He has been coming here every night to check. Now that he has found her, I swear something is going to happen. You wait and you will hear of it tomorrow."

The old man told me many more frightening stories about Jane. He told me that she was even richer than many working ladies and she got all that money by selling her body. The stories put me off completely and I decided to go back to College.

For several days, I never went to the Friendly Bar, and I heard nothing of Jane. One afternoon when I was in my room someone came to call me saying that there was a telephone call for me. As I was going to receive it, the boy who called me said, "A lady. Probably a collection!" I picked up the receiver.

"Hullo. John here."

"Hullo. John?" She sounded as if she had been running.

"Yes, John speaking."

Silence. I could hear her breathing. I saw in my mind's eye the lovely face of Jane.

"John, I must see you."

The urgency of this after a long time of silence made me wonder.

"Is that Jane?"

"Yes. I want to see you. You must know how it is. I never . . ."

"Thought of me?" I interrupted.

"I have often thought of you, but not . . . Foolish of me, because . . . because . . . because you are one of those I think may help me."

I realised something shocking in her voice.

"What is the matter? Are you in trouble?"

"No. Yes . . . Please, when and where can I see you?"

"Any time. Where?" I struggled within myself to resist the desire of adding "As always."

Silence. She was thinking.

"How about at Friendly Bar?"

"Very well."
insisted.

"Nothing could stop me."

"Very well, Friendly Bar, at eleven. You will be there?" she

She replaced the receiver. The click said more plainly than words, "I need your help." I went back to my room and thought about what might have happened to her. I recalled the waiter's words, "You will hear of it tomorrow."

The desire to know about what had happened to her urged me to keep my promise to meet her at eleven.

Eleven o'clock. I called for a taxi and as I stood outside waiting for it I imagined all sorts of terrible things. At the back of my mind, the words of the pastor tormented me. The taxi came and I entered it. When I reached the Friendly Bar, I went straight and sat at the same table. The waiters came to me and asked me if I wanted anything. I told them to wait for a few minutes.

After some time, Jane came in. She came straight to me and sat down.

"Well?" she asked, "How much have I changed?" I smiled at her.

"We were sitting here . . ." I looked around.

"Yes, just here one night; I remember telling you . . . Heaven, the things one says!"

I knew she was fooling me.

"Jane, tell me. What went wrong that night?" She kept quiet, looked at me and started shedding tears.

"Don't cry, just tell me and I will forgive you."

"Please, do you mind if we go to my house tonight and I will tell you what happened, and many more?" She took out a handkerchief and wiped her eyes.

"Where do you stay?"

"Eastleigh—Eastleigh Section One."

"Is it safe for me to go there?"

"I should think so. I stay with my brothers. I am sure you will be safe." Her face started brightening up.

"Let's have some coffee."

"It's kind of you."

"But Jane, what is really the matter with you?"

"Oh! John! Please, I will tell you."

After taking the coffee we stepped out of the bar. I was afraid of going to Eastleigh for I had heard of terrible stories about what happens to people there, particularly when they went with women like Jane. Despite the anonymous note warning me not to accompany her, I at last made up my mind to go with her. We entered a taxi and she told the driver to take us to Eastleigh.

We stopped outside an old building, paid the taxi-man and he drove back. The night was curiously still. The slightest noise could be interpreted differently by each of us. She opened the door and we entered her house. When she lit the lamp several things were revealed in the room. Utensils were scattered all over the place. Her brothers lay on the floor snoring. Jane prepared the bed and asked me to take off my clothes. When we went to bed, I asked her to tell me her troubles. She had just started when one of her brothers raised up his head and told her to dim the light and keep quiet.

"You better be quiet, Jane. There are some men looking for you. They came in here and asked for you. They appeared not to be in good terms with you."

Suddenly, I became aware of a stealthy rustling outside. It died down, but a sixth sense warned me of some danger. After a few minutes, there was a knock at the door. I started trembling. Jane held me tightly and whispered to me to keep silent. The knocking increased and the door was forced open.

"No one should leave the house." I recognised the voice to be that of the man who had run after her from the bar. I snatched my clothes, only managed to put on the trousers, and sneaked out. As I was running away, I heard the voice of Jane crying behind, "Don't kill me! Don't kill me! I will give you the money!"

I was happy I had escaped from that hell ground and nothing could persuade me to go back. After that I never heard of Jane again nor was I interested in knowing anything about her.

"Why had I accompanied her?" I kept on asking myself.

Rasheed A. Gbadamossi

Bats and Babies

THE DAY STARTED as usual. Before the cock heralded day-break, the old prophetess walked down our street ringing her bells and chanting hell and damnation to those who would not walk in the path of God. I pulled the sheets over my head and turned over in bed. Then the cockrels began to crow. Later, the muezzin's call to prayer sang from the mosque behind our house and gradually the cries echoed through the morning peace. And then our street became alive. Lying in bed, I could hear the dockers trudging along the street, hurrying to catch the ferry across the lagoon to the docks. We lived on the left bank of the lagoon and many dockers lived in our area. That morning they chattered as they hustled along and I could hear their feet charging up our narrow, hilly street. Then came the glare of the morning light through my window. I got up and after a while I came out of our house to watch the bustling of our community.

As usual, the wheels of the vegetable carts grinded up the hill. The wives of the dockers, carrying huge baskets on their heads, rushed past on their way to the market to catch the early customers. Sometimes a motor truck swept along leaving a trail of dust behind. The old widow who lived in the house across the street from us came out too. She spread a mat on the dusty pavement outside her house. It was an active day, the blue sky was as intense as the blinding sun. Yet the hours were passing quickly, the day even.

Nearing sunset, my mother took me along to the widow's to have her hair plaited. I could not bear the smell of the coconut oil which the old widow rubbed into my mother's hair so as to make it slippery and easier to plait. My mother's head was between the old woman's thighs. The widow was seated on a stool. And my mother and I, and other women waiting their turn, sat on the large mat

spread on the dusty pavement. I looked at the fruit tree in front of
our house. Sometimes it bore fruit. The fruit had no name in our
language; so we called it fruit. Lying on my back I could see a few
bats hanging down the branches of the fruit tree. Through the leaves
I noticed the clouds were darkening.

I started to count the bats on the tree. I remembered my grandmother once told me that if you cut a bat open there was always a
baby bat inside. And if you cut that open too, you would find another tinier baby bat. Now I had counted five heads of bats and I
was thinking how many bats there would be together with the babies
inside. I sat up. I noticed my mother was asleep, her head between
the widow's thighs.

"Mama," I asked a woman sitting on the mat, "how many baby
bats inside five bats?"

"It depends. Sometimes one in every bat; sometimes two."

"If there are two, how many bats in five bats?"

"That'll make fifteen bats. But maybe there's only a baby bat
inside each bat. It's like me or your mother. Sometimes we have one
baby in our belly, sometimes two. I have one or two inside me now."

I was puzzled. I looked up at the bats and back at the woman.

The woman pat me on the head and said, "Little boys don't ask
too many questions."

I got up and went inside the widow's house to look for the
latrine. The corridor was narrow and dark and I groped along
afraid of tripping over something. Then I came out into a courtyard.
It was deserted but for a cockrel crowing to welcome dusk. In the
middle of the courtyard there was a well. I climbed the concrete
structure around it and peeped inside the well. It was so deep and
dark I could not see the water level. Then suddenly somebody pulled
me away and whacked me on the bottom.

"You silly boy," he said, "little boys fall into the well and die.
You've been warned many times, many many times."

I yelled and freed myself from his grasp. I ran through the
corridor back to my mother.

"Somebody beat me for climbing the well," I told her.

"You asked for it. I told you not to go anywhere."

Everybody laughed. I sulked bitterly. I lay back on the mat and counted the bats on the tree. Now, there were only two bats. It was darkening and the street began to be filled with people scurrying home from the docks. Presently a man walked toward the woman who had the baby inside her.

"Now, I've got you," the man gloated, "you're coming home."

"Go away and leave me alone!" the woman shouted. She looked scared to death and everybody was startled. "I don't know you. I've never seen you before," the woman yelled.

The man's eyes burned like hot coals. He was like a lion stalking a deer. He sprang at her and held her dress.

"I've searched the whole world for you. For four months I've looked everywhere. I thought you would come to this gay town. You're still my wife. I'm taking you back."

"No. No. I never loved you! I never married you!"

A palaver erupted. Too many people were talking and there was a lot of pushing and pulling. The man held on to his prized woman. The other women struggled to free her from his grasp. The widow became agitated. Suddenly a crowd had gathered round. It seemed it was going to be free for all. The old woman then got hold of a broom and began to hit the strugglers on the head. Then there was a truce.

"Now, everybody," the old woman said, "this woman is my client, young man. What do you want from her?"

"I've searched for her for months. She ran away," the man said, "I've got to take her back. I paid a dowry on her."

"I left you. I left you for good. I'm not going back to that village," the pregnant woman said.

"They said I should bring you back. I have to."

"No. No. I've got another man. He's given me what you couldn't give. See everybody: I have a baby in me. I have life living inside my body. For three years you blamed it on me. Now I have it. I have it in me. Life! A baby! And I'm going to stay in this town with my new husband. He works in the docks."

"They said I should bring you back to the village. I paid my dowry. I'm taking you back with me."

"Oh, no, I'm not coming back. People everywhere, listen. There is a weird custom in that village far away beyond the savannah. She, who doesn't have a child in the third harvest after marriage, simply disappears. She doesn't run away; she just disappears. I ran away before the third harvest. This man couldn't give me a child. Please don't let him take me back. Please, please, send him away . . ."

The man was unyielding. Now and again everybody talked at the same time. I could not understand much of what they said.

It was darkening fast and there was a constant turnover of the gathering. Then the run-away woman asked my mother to show her the latrine. My mother got up, her hair half-plaited, and showed the woman into the widow's house and they disappeared along the dark corridor. A few minutes later my mother returned.

Meanwhile the debate went on. It was like an assembly, everybody had different views on what should be done. The men agreed with the man, after all he paid a dowry on her. The women sympathised with the woman. Someone shouted that the man should go to the police station, but the man replied he had no money to pay a lawyer.

Minutes passed.

"Where is she anyway?" the man asked my mother.

"She's easing herself," my mother said. "I wonder why she's taken so long?"

The man sensed something. "Is there another exit out of the house?"

"Yes. Many gates. There's a courtyard and many gates."

The man bolted into the house like a dog released from chains.

"I showed her the way out of the courtyard," my mother proudly announced. "She must be on the ferry by now. Who would want to be sacrificed in a backward old village? She's pregnant for another man. I hope I've done right, God. Many weird things go on in the villages."

My mother was congratulated by the women for her good judgment. And when we got back home she amused my grandmother with her heroic deed. My mother felt like a saviour; she had helped a fugitive from old ways.

Early next morning the old widow came round to tell my mother the woman's body had been found in the well in her courtyard. The fugitive woman had jumped in to kill herself. She did not take the ferry. She never got to the waterfront. And her husband had gone on a wild goose chase.

"Grannie," I said, "how many babies would be found inside the woman?"

"Shut up," my grandmother said. "You ask too many questions bigger than your mouth."

Rasheed A. Gbadamossi

In the Beginning

THE CHARITABLE OLD man had a white, long beard. He plucked a few strands off his beard and wrapped them in a leaf. Then he gave the charm to Arinjo adding, "This comes from my body, take it. It will come in handy. In time of need, suck it. And if you have faith, wish anything and it shall be done."

Arinjo set out on the journey. He paid his respects to the old man. He was going into the wild, through the gate into the Everlasting Forest.

But the gate was shut. Iwin stood there, his forehead emitting smoke. He would not allow entry until Arinjo had paid homage to him, acknowledged his might, his supremacy.

"I've never paid respects to anybody else," Arinjo said.

"Then you'll have to go back," Iwin told him.

"If I turn back I'll be dead. I've got to go beyond this gate. Beyond this gate into the Everlasting Forest."

"Then bow to me."

"I can't."

"I guard this gate. Nobody goes through until he touches the earth with his chin and pays homage to me."

"For the third time, I bow to nobody else."

Iwin was furious. He trumpeted for the beasts. He called them to come and watch the battle: the battle for supremacy between him and Arinjo.

Within a few moments all living animals were assembled outside the gate of the Everlasting Forest. The elephants were there. The lions sat down, regal. Monkeys beat war drums. The snakes curled up in silence. Birds perched on the trees. The tortoise surfaced from underground. Even the foxes ignored chickens. And rabbits appeared in daylight.

Up in the sky, the sun started to fade away. It appeared the moon was attempting to overshadow the sun. Down on earth, Arinjo and Iwin commenced the battle. They wrestled so violently the ground trembled and threw up so much dust they were barely seen. The more furious the fighting, the more smoke smitted from Iwin's forehead. Like the threatening eclipse above, it was hard to judge who was dealing the heavier blows.

Suddenly, Iwin disengaged and took a few steps back, breathing hard. At the wink of an eye, he was transformed into a lion. That was not surprising. He was a spirit. And spirits come in all forms; they'll do anything to break man.

Courageous man never turns back at the gate. He fights the spirit as he must to finish his journey. Sometimes he is defeated and he dies. But he fights and fights and fights again to enter the Everlasting Forest.

So now, Arinjo fished in his pocket and brought out the charm the white-bearded old man gave him. He stuck it in his mouth and he too became a lion. The two lions roared and clawed each other. Presently, the lions turned into tigers and the tigers into rhinoceroses, the rhinoceroses into hippopotami and the hippopotami into cobras.

All the time, the spectators silently watched the struggle between Arinjo and Iwin.

Up in the sky, neither the sun nor the moon had triumphed.

Just then, a cobra turned into an elephant and, within a second, the elephant seized the cobra with his trunk and smashed the cobra's head to the ground. Slowly, the elephant split open and out emerged Arinjo, sweaty and exhausted. The beasts cheered and paid homage to Arinjo. The sun came up and the moon raced across the sky to another world.

Arinjo was now supreme. He threw away the charm. He was through with the white-bearded old man. And he would go through the Everlasting Forest alone.

Quietly, the animals dispersed afraid of each other and afraid of Arinjo.

Rasheed A. Gbadamossi

The Sexton's Deaf Son

JOSHUA KEINO'S PARENTS had no objection to his bringing
the boy home to Sunday lunch. But Auntie Roda's indignation
was ill-concealed. She shrugged indifferently everytime Mrs. Keino
offered her the next course. She spoke very little. She took it out on
the electric fan. "The awful thing doesn't work efficiently," she said.
Perhaps it was in the wrong angle. She got up a few times to fix the
fan. She really would like to tell her stories now, her exaggerated
rumours about various individuals at the church. But all the attention was taken up by the guest and Mr. Keino was probably relieved
he would not have to endure Auntie Roda's blabbing.

Mr. Keino ate voraciously. Mrs. Keino made signs to the deaf
and dumb boy to check if he had enough to eat. Joshua was exhil-
arated. He had now acquired a new playmate. He had met the boy
earlier in the day at the junior church service. They had roamed in
the huge park together after the service. The boy made incomprehensible sounds by way of speaking. Joshua felt attracted in a curious
way to the chubby, unspeaking boy. They had climbed the guava
tree together and, finding no fruit, they had sat on the branches
looking at the lake and the coastline beyond. It was cool in the shade
of the leaves and now and again the breeze rustled the leaves per-
mitting the sun to pierce through. On the lake, two paddling boats
were racing towards a tiny island on which there stood two coconut
trees. A fishing net was fastened to the trunks of the trees. The fishermen soon loosened the cords and they rolled up the dry net and
shoved it into one boat. Then they anchored the other boat and
paddled off in the one with the net.

It was time to go home and Joshua indicated to the boy he had
to go home. The boy's face tightened in disappointment. Joshua
beckoned to him to come. The boy uttered something indiscernible.

Joshua climbed down the tree and gesticulated to the boy to come on. And so they came home.

After lunch, Auntie Roda went off to her room for what she called "her health rest."

"Now Joshua," Mr. Keino said, "where did you meet your friend?"

"At the church. He is the new sexton's son."

"What is his name?"

"I don't know. He couldn't tell me."

"I see. I suppose you'll take him back soon. His parents must be looking for him now."

"Can I show him how to ride my new bike?"

"If you wish. Don't go out into the street. Stay in the garden."

"All right, dad."

But they sneaked out into the street. Joshua's intention, really, was to show off his new friend to the other boys in the neighbourhood. Presently they came to a group of three boys who were leaping over bamboo make-shift high jumps. The idea was to progress from a low height, and taking turns, everyone had to make a clean jump. Anyone who fell the cross bar was flogged by the others and you dropped out after three unsuccessful tries.

Joshua was dubious about involving his new friend in the competition. But it was a problem of communication. Perhaps his friend wanted to join in.

The game started. Joshua went first and he sailed over the bar. So did the others. The deaf and dumb boy did not take part. The height went up about three inches.

Then to the astonishment of others, the deaf and dumb boy took off his shirt, took a few paces backward and then ran forward and leapt up and across the bar, hitting the ground on the other side with great glee. They all cheered him except for the biggest boy.

The height was increased. The smallest of the three boys fell the jump three times. He dropped out. Each time he was whipped by the others according to the rules of the game. But the deaf and dumb boy did not join in any flogging. Neither Joshua could make that height in three attempts. Then another of the three boys dropped out. The biggest boy took the next turn. He succeeded in the third attempt, taking only two beatings. The deaf and dumb boy did not flog him.

Now came Joshua's friend's turn. He stood beneath the cross-bar and then counted a few paces forward. The biggest boy flexed his bamboo cane. Now the deaf boy stopped, turned around and came running, his cheeks slightly puffed, faster now and up and, crash! The cross bar fell. The biggest boy rushed forward and assailed the deaf boy.

"Stop it!" Joshua shouted. "He did not cane you, why should you cane him. Leave him alone."

"It is the rule of the game," the biggest boy defiantly said.

He lashed his cane on the deaf boy again. The other boys stepped in and hit the boy who was now uttering a torrent of incomprehensible words. Joshua pushed them off.

The biggest boy again hit the deaf boy across his chest and bruised him. "Nobody invited you," he said. "Why did you barge in with that deaf boy. Nobody invited you."

Joshua promptly punched the big boy in the face. The deaf boy started to cry. He was sitting in the sand. A melee ensued. Joshua did not have a chance against the three of them. Somehow he bruised the smallest boy on the eyelid. The smallest boy and the dumb boy were both crying. Presently, a man showed up and broke up the fight. Joshua's lower lip was cut and he was licking it all the way back to the church. There, he waved good bye to his friend and strolled on home.

Auntie Roda was knitting in the living room.

"Joshua, what happened?" she asked.

"We had a fight."

"Who cut your lip? Where is the dumb boy?"

"I don't know. I lost him."

"That serves you right. Of all the boys in the neighbourhood you can't choose a playmate but a deaf boy. Do you know deaf boys are animals? They don't talk and they can't hear; just like animals. They have strength like wild animals. Don't get mixed up with him again. You hear me?"

Joshua did not say anything. He got up to leave the room.

"Where are you going? Wait, I'll treat your wound."

"My bike is parked down the street."

But Joshua went back to the park and he climbed up the guava tree. Now he could see the fishermen were back on the island of two palm trees. The sun was tracing the horizon down and the surface of the lake reflected the aging sunlight. Auntie Roda; she's just like those brutes, just because he doesn't talk; he's not an animal; he can't be an animal; he's too likeable to be an animal; those boys were animals, my friend can't be an animal. Maybe he should talk, Joshua was thinking. Pity, he can't. Why was he created deaf? Yes, who made him dumb?

Taban Lo Liyong

BLACK HUMOURS

Uncle Tom's Black Humour

(For Michael Dennis Browne)

let us now praise famous men
our past masters
and why not
after all there are many sides to the same thing
were beneficial side effects
and we can now afford to laugh

we cost many the heads the crowns
shaky french cabinets stumbled and fell

i was taught a tongue
with which to curse prospero and woo miranda
since ariel was so airy
he had no room for a heart

well mr I admired your gun
but you could not my magic
now i can make your gun make
but do you know my magic
to your one I have two

summers come
you go for tan
from eating you divert oil for rubbing
you strive to get as dark as i am
but can you
my blackness is original
inimitable desirable but induplicable

i will never go to sunbathe
youll never catch me exposing myself to snow
in order to become white
as far as color is concerned
i am content

now about hair
short hair is best
and thats what i have
as any navy man
my teeth are just as white
as mungo found them
as strong as
livingstones wife's were

now ive taken to growing cocoa
for chocolate
and sugar cane
for sugar and candies
with these to cause a decay
of your teeth
the dentist collects them
and i give him gold
to fill the gaps
sweets or gold
i fill my purse

you may praise blue eyes
yes as color blue is blue
what about visibility

because i labored hard in the fields
now i am the best boxer
mohamed ali or no mohamed ali
we keep the championships

in other sports too
the blacks are to the fore
with better coaching
to monopolise the medals

you brought great/dads here
few arrived
but we are many now
because of pleasure
or vigor
or ignorance of birth curb
we shall populate the earth

sexually
my prowess is proverbial
and you want your women spared
or deprived
perhaps
to save your grandsons
from seasonal sunexposure
let me coal black
mate your daughter lily white
and beget a merger race suitably tanned
and sink our oversights
and let nature adjust things

caliban smelled like fish
quoth trinculo
but a beast of burden has to smell something
if not fish he will smell food

man to man othello beat iago
in direct confrontation
it is the underhanded acts that derange the world

i hollered a lot under the yoke
and in revival meetings
by songs and dances and sways and handclappings
i can exorcise hoggish demons
but
now i can sing very well
and cut records
and act roles
and write

my big lips
are good for kissing
they are substantial
not dimunitive

yes whitey i know what you have always wanted to
be black like me what with all my excellence in
baseball in football in basketball in jazz in boxing
and now even in westmorelands viet nam game how
could you look at me and not envy me

do what you may you will never become like me
you may bask in the suns or even go to the moon
to be nearer the sun but to be black like me you
will never be

have you known a confirmed culprit who is always
reprieved and then condoned thats UNCLE TOM have
you known of the freedom of nonregulation of your
own life you would if you were UNCLE TOM always
receiving orders and directions ever pondered the
lightness of possessing little to nothing see it
from me ever watched lions fighting all their days
in order to be one inch beyond the other and you
yourself never caring a damn about that race thats
my art if you have seen masters rise and fall in
the pursuit of an artificial life you would know
why i stay pat no butler ever served a hero the hero
is actually the butler himself thats me baby UNCLE
TOM

from the look of things too i am humble enough
to inherit heaven and when i inherit it i will
keep all of it to myself and my chillun and
we shall wear shoes and walk shoulder straight

you see i am not mean with gods heaven or
sumthin the trouble with the other people is that
they are so rich or mean they cant pass through
the needless eye in the gate

me with my few aims and scanty possessions and little
vice (a little cursing is welcomed even in heaven
getting drunk on weekends too is not so bad since
it keeps one off major offenses borrowing from
the cellar or store or missus cupboard is not
bad at all since master can afford more easily)
i travel light and thats heavenly quality
jesuss apostles except judas knew that as well as
me

and one thing more i am not going to pitch for
the presidency of the united states either no sir
the spirit tells me i would make the best and thats
where the trouble lies i dont want to be shot at
no sir i dont want to have abdominal problems
or sleep in the walter reeds hospital

anyway i am a free man i dont want to ride in a
harmored car i want a big cadillac a convertible
in which to breeze and listen to a blaring duke
ellington jazz a big car makes all the difference
to a mistress who has to make a choice between
candidates moreover it has room for doing you know
what

some of my haunts arent even safe for hoover i
dont want my activities noted down no sir i just
want to be responsible to my appetites first
next my whimses third the defence of my master
and mistress

each public show of concern for their welfare endears
me more and more moreover miss sarah pays
me to keep from master her own secrets and master
doles me to keep missus in the dark thus i get
two bonus payments besides the threat of blackmail
i have retained the best team of permanent defence
my faults enjoy the rare state of everlasting
excuses and reprieves

AUNT JEMIMA she done teach young master how to be
man yes sir she done it yes maam he gone done it
never mind them talks about integration and other
shits and me i know my way around

and master does all the worrying for us miss sarah
the children AUNT and UNCLE the undergrowth is
too good to be left i am a permanent parasite in
permanent dependence sheltered from the overhead
struggles by our towering master

after hes made billions from oil
or ford cars
he still eats through his mouth
like i do
goes to the toilet
like i do
get drunk
like i do
fuck missus
less than i do
so what the hell have i to worry about

UN Chef's Choice

MY BROTHER, THE NEGRO BOURGEOISIE GRILLED
A LA E. FRANKLIN FRAZIER ON THE OCCASION
OF THIS LUNCHEON
GIVEN BY 15 AFRICAN NATIONS IN HONOR OF
JULIAN BOND AN ELECTED
NEGRO REPRESENTATIVE WHO WAS REFUSED ADMISSION
TO THE GEORGIA STATE LEGISLATURE

"While pretending to be proud of being a Negro, they ridicule Negroid physical characteristics and seek to modify or efface them as much as possible. . . . They talk condescendingly of Africans and of African culture. . . . They are insulted if they are identified with Africans. They refuse to join organizations that are interested in Africa . . . they . . . boast of the fact that they have Indian ancestry . . . if a black woman has European features, they will remark condescendingly, 'Although she is black, you must admit that she is good looking.' . . . (they) like to wear Hindu costumes—while they laugh at the idea of wearing an African costume. When middle-class Negroes travel, they studiously avoid association with other Negroes, especially if they themselves have received the slightest recognition by whites. . . . Therefore, nothing pleases them more to be mistaken for a Puerto Rican, Phillipino, Egyptian or Arab or any ethnic group other than Negro."

> —E. Franklin Frazier
> pp. 186-187, *Black Bourgeoisie*, Collier Books,
> New York, 1962

God said: Let there be light,
There was light—in darkness.
Therefore Darkness is supreme.

Socrates murmured: Man know thyself.
No difference. Should have shouted:
Man you are a fool—he is.

We only know what we know
or, we can't know what we don't want to know
or, we should know what we don't know—
    Even if we don't want to.

In the beginning was the Word
Truth it was—Pilate knew it not.

Everything is truth—to some people:
True to Pope Boniface, the world was flat:
True to Church, God is up above;
True to Hitler, Aryan is Pure:
True to Europe yesterday, African is no man;
True to Negro, he is nobody—
BECAUSE
In truth, man knoweth no himself.

What are thou, Negro?
    Art thou Scottish? MacCathorine—true;
    Art thou French? Du Bois—true;
    Art thou German? English? Italian? A bit of Europe?
Gospel truth.

Negro, thou art part English
    The English disown you;
Negro, partly thou art Spanish
    The Spaniards used you in their new beginning;
Negro, thou art French
    Only French in you is name;
Negro, thou art Italian
    Italic romance and banditry thou has;

Negro, thou art also Jew
> To support young Jews on your money thou doeth;
Negro, Oriental too thou art—
> Can't remove those Oriental eyes;
Negro, thou art Red Indian—
> But no Red Foot name has thou.
BUT
Basically, Negro, thou art African
> Thou acknowledges it not,
> Therefore, thou knoweth not what thou art.

Four centuries back, so 'tis said
No blacks lived in Harlem;
In Afric jungles mixed they with monkeys.

Among kith and kin Africans lived.
Commerce, search for gain, Afric knew years and years;
Politics, banishment of opponents, is only new in Russia;
Population control by reducing mouths for food is older than
> Malthus;
Wars of colonization is older in Afric than in Rome;
Prejudice tribe contre tribe was a currency before Columbus;
Majority domination has, is, and will be;
Dictatorship? Kakarega knew better than democratic Khrushchev.
> These compounded
> What resulted
BUT SLAVERY.

To India slaves went,
Middle East is nothing, remember Pushkin,
In Spain Negroes ruled lilies,
To America, land of opportunity
> > plenty experimentation
> > Indian and bison extermination
came
handfuls of Negroes who the sea death did escape.

I am no chemist
> To know chemical process of color mixture;

I am no geneticist
    To know the science of inheritance of no wealth;
I am no Gobineau
    To know inherent superiority and inferiority;
I am no English renegade
    To teach Hitler a Gentile's creed;
I am no historian
    To trace who was owned and influenced by whom;
I am no Ku Klux Klan
    To think a dark spot invites a bullet;
I am no legislator
    To think human benefits need not be shared;
I am no Christian
    To accuse God of condemning Ham's issues
        Whoever they may be;
        Or to turn the other cheek, too;
I am no Lazarus
    To feed under a table and walk later with Abraham;
I am no Gandhi,
    To preach "non-violence" in a violent world;
I am no Uncle Tom
    To think all Negroes wrong; . . .

        . . . yet my hands are red . . .

    I am a realist
Who believes in the real being known,
        in uselessness of pretensions,
        In Mosaic measure for measure,
        in equality of love and hate, folly and wisdom,
            good and bad,
for all things which walk on two and have a claim to Adam or
    zinjanthropus.

Can thou be African, Negro?
"No! No! No!
How could they be mine when they sold me?"
(Germans would say:
"How can we be Germans when Hitler has a bad record."

Jews would say:
"How can we be Jews when we killed Jesus."
African slaves in Africa would say:
"How can we be Africans when Africans sold us").
BUT
'Tis this: —must we only acknowledge a glorious past?
                    whose past has been only glorious?
Go to Mars,
None on Earth.

'Tis interesting to know
Aggrey of Livingstone College said, once
A farmer had an eagle among chicken bred.
The farmer boasts to friend: the eagle is chicken now.
The friend says: eagle is always eagle, as sun is sun.
The farmer says: friend, test for yourself.
Mornings and evenings found friend and eagle on mountain top.
Eagle, see sun above and other eagles, there thou belong.
Years of rebrainwashing
Yielded their fruit.
One day, the eagle, eagle-like, did fly.

A man must know himself, or
Pains be taken to teach him unlearn all art
And learn all truth.

Says de Gaulle—
France, thou wert great in Europe,
A second Napoleon has come—in me
Awake again
Leadership of Europe is yours.

Mussolini dreamt:
Rome was supreme,
I will get into Caesar's clothings
With Hitler's help, Japan's help, Rome will have Rome from
Land of Rising Sun to Alaska.

Garvey irate, searching for recognition, raves:
Where are black kings? Empires?

Nkrumah remembers:
There was a Ghana once,
A Songhai too;
Timbuctoo was greater than Sorbonne, Oxford, Harvard;
Revolutionaries drive out their rulers;
Colonialism and Imperialism exist where
Awareness is not, where ignorance is;
Gold Coast shall be free,
Africa shall be free,
And one and great.
Let the other races of the world tremble.

The giant is rising
You never have known what power there is
In black giant coal.

Before, it was said:
    African and monkey are one,
    Subhumans they are (mixture of Darwin and fiction).
    No achievement can you have
    'Cause you had none.
    No money had you; only barter you knew
    (As if bullions and cowries are no currencies.)
    No knowledge of God have you
    (As if Bible is God and religion.)
Christ knew no quinine, he cured cold,
Our medicinemen know herbs and keep life,
Our witchdoctors know psychology, so they
Cure through belief, confidence, will power.
Lawlessness was a word undictionaried,
To us it did not exist;
YET
You still say we had no morals, nor forms of government,

By nature you are lazy, —so it was said;
Naturally you are docile, —this was not doubted;
Your heaven was here because you are so contented
(Good enough, our heaven, you and me, our heaven and hell, are
    here);

Be content with your lot fixed by weight and volume;
Be a Negro, childish (the oldest answered to "Boy");
Be a good Christian, you outdid Christ himself,
Be an American, you are the best confessor of Americanism,
Be glad you are in America, not in African jungles,
AND
     You thank your white God for it.

Clubs of Irish Americans there are,
Jewish Americans meet, too,
Italian Americans raised cain over Yale's Lucky Erikson,
But
Negroes are Negroes, —American Negroes,
'Tis taboo to talk of African Americans.
Even Black Muslims bypass Africa,
To Arabia they look for salvation, for a root—
They descended from Arabs, not Africans.
To the Negro Africa is what never was, nor is.

Woe unto him who reminds a Negro:
There is an Africa, better than you were told,
From this Africa your matriapatriarchs did come,
They have good good-will toward you,
It does no harm for you to Africa think.

If what is, is not,
What is not is,
Where does logic head?
Is this a world of make believe
Belief make?
Double thought and double-talk?
Truth escape and fiction manufacture?
Do we know what we are doing?
Is the human race evolving to a stage of truth forgetting?
I
Know not.
But man,
Know thyself.

"Creation Were One"—Hezbon Edward Owiti

Lemuel Johnson

Melon Flowers[1]

> And though the fields look rough with hoary dew
> all will be gay when noontide wakes anew
> the buttercups, the little children's dower,
> —far brighter than this gaudy melon-flower
> *Home Thoughts from Abroad*—Robert Browning

MR. ISHALU walked up to the window of his office overlooking the hard, dusty playing field. As occasional puffs of wind swirled over the surface, he watched thin spirals of red-brown dust sail indecisively toward the already brown leaves of the trees under which the classrooms were built. He reached for the large checkered handkerchief in his breast pocket as he felt the corners of his nose itch with sweat. He passed the handkerchief slowly over his face and then moved back to his desk where he spread out the now very damp handkerchief. Mr. Ishalu adjusted the knot of his green and gray striped tie, buttoned both buttons of his brown woolen coat and then returned to the window. He watched as two students dashed out of the First Form classroom and ran toward the bell hanging from the huge baobab tree at the far end of the playing field. The rope tied to the clapper was beyond the reach of both students. One of them knelt down and helped the other onto his shoulder; from that new height the other reached out and pulled six times at the clapper. Then the positions were reversed and the clapper jerked out six more red-brown sounds into the swirls of a typical red-brown, dry season afternoon.

Mr. Ishalu watched as both students got down on their knees, raised their haunches, and then raced back to their classroom. Within

---

[1] All the characters and events depicted or referred to in these sketches are entirely fictional and bear no relation to events or persons past or present.

a few minutes the playing field was filled with students, khaki shorts and white shirts, a handful of teachers and the usual shouts, scuffles.

It was three o'clock Greenwich Mean Time; school was over for the day at the Princess of Wales Secondary School for Boys.

Mr. Ishalu moved back to his desk when he heard a knock on the door.

"Who?"

"Me, sir. Messenger, sir."

"Yes, sir."

Mr. Ishalu reached out for the dry handkerchief. He wiped the sweat from his face and the drops from the hairs on the back of his hands. Then he folded the handkerchief in four and pushed it down his breast pocket, allowing a small section of the green and gray stripes to protrude.

"Come in."

"Yes, sir. Good afternoon, sir."

Pa Kai-Kai, the school messenger, wiped his bare feet at the door and moved into the office. His khaki shorts were covered in spots by the red dust of the school compound. The khaki shirt, which completed his uniform, was wet under the armpits and across the chest. He stood in the doorway waiting for permission to move up to the desk.

"Yes, Kai-Kai?"

"Letter, sir."

Mr. Ishalu reached for the long brown envelope, put it down on the desk and looked up at Pa Kai-Kai.

"That's all right."

"Thank you, sir."

Pa Kai-Kai walked out and Mr. Ishalu picked up the envelope and read the heavy, official seal: "Office of the Solicitor General, Law Courts, Westmoreland Street." He put the envelope in his briefcase and walked back to the window. He looked at his watch; quarter past three. He decided to wait for another fifteen minutes before leaving. The brown and white Vauxhall he had just bought second-hand was parked a few feet from the baobab tree and he could see no one around or near it.

At half-past three Mr. Ishalu picked up his briefcase and left

the office. As he walked out, Pa Kai-Kai moved back inside to shut
the window and door.

Mr. Ishalu pulled out the keys to the car as he walked down the
playing field. A wave of burning heat struck him as he opened the
car and sat down. He wound the windows down and started the car.
A couple of false starts and he pumped nervously and rapidly. The
engine started and he released the handbrake; as he reached out
toward the clutch, the engine coughed, shuddered and stopped. He
got it started again and the car jerked, bounced forward as his foot
alternated rapidly between the accelerator and the foot brake.

It was then that he heard the sounds. First a slow hissing and
then a humming to be followed again by the hissing. The words and
singing would come soon. His foot slipped hesitantly over the accelerator as his angry eyes searched behind the trees for the students.

"Mister Shalu, Mister Shalu!
Learn to drive,
Leave the brake!
Vauxhall Shalu! Second-hand Shalu!"

Mr. Ishalu briefly debated whether to step out of the car but he
knew that all he would see, if he saw anything at all, would be the
back of unidentifiable white shirts running away. Besides he would
have to start the car all over again.

"Vauxhall Shalu! Second-hand Shalu!
Leave the brake!
Learn to drive!
Mister Shalu! Mister Shalu!"

The car continued jerking, bumping, bouncing, dancing; but it
was bouncing forward. Mr. Ishalu's eyes were now glued to the
school gate. In three minutes he should be through it and out on the
street. He got the car under better control, wishing he could reach
for his handkerchief as the sweat tickled its way across his face but
his hands were firmly glued to the steering wheel. He winced as a
soft plop sounded on top of the car. Some day, one of these days
they'd throw rocks and break the windows. Somebody, anyone of
them to make an example, a public example of, was all he needed.

Two dozen lashes, two dozen lashes in the Assembly Hall. The gate was less than a minute away. His hands began to peel slowly from the glistening black of the steering wheel.

"Vauxhall Shalu!
Second-hand Shalu!
Mister Shalu! Jankoliko!
Mister Shalu! Mister Shalu!"

Mr. Ishalu made a left turn at the gate and headed up the street, going toward Krootown Road. Two dozen lashes on the back and buttocks.

The traffic was light as he kept the car at a hesitant twenty-five miles an hour through Krootown Road, past the market, and then headed for the junction of Westmoreland and Krootown Road. The car coughed softly, but he made the turn into Westmoreland without incident. He considered going up Waterloo Street and hitting Pademba Road to avoid the downtown traffic. But Waterloo Street went uphill and he wasn't sure what would happen if he tried to shift gears going up the hill. All the same, it took him less time and effort than he'd feared to negotiate Westmoreland, go up Wilberforce into Kissy Street and then on to Fourah Bay Road where he lived. Forty-five minutes in all.

Ishalu parked the car as close as he dared to the large, open gutter which ran down the length, on both sides, of Fourah Bay Road. He had little difficulty finding a place to park right in front of his house.

"Welcome, my D.!"

He raised his eyes to the front window as he heard his wife call out. His hand half-reached out through the open car window to acknowledge her greeting. Soon the children would also call out. His hand moved over the brief-case as he remembered Pa Kai-Kai's letter.

"Papa Shalu, welcome, sir!"

"Papa Shalu, welcome, sir!"

His two daughters called out from the open window where they'd join his wife. His right hand once more made the half-movement through the car window. He pulled up three of the car windows and then opened the envelope.

"Office of the Solicitor-General
Law Offices,
Westmoreland Street

To Mr. Ayodele Ishalu,
Principal, Princess of Wales School,
King Tom.

You are hereby requested to appear in Court on the 7th of May 1964 in the case of The People vs. Ted Bahorik, expatriate, Teacher at your school, in connection with aforementioned Ted Bahorik's Disturbing of the Peace which Event took place on the 27th (Twenty-seventh) day of April 1964 at the Independence Day Dancing in the Village of Kissy.

OFFICE OF SOLICITOR-GENERAL."

"My D.!"
"Papa Shalu, welcome, sir!"
Mr. Ishalu unfolded his handkerchief, wiped his face and hands, and then the damp steering wheel. Then he turned toward the window from which his wife and two daughters were calling out to him.

II

". . . General Overseas Service of the B.B.C. This is the British Broadcasting Corporation coming to you from London . . . The B.B.C. presents: Desert Island Disc . . . Each week a well-known person is asked the question: If you were to be cast away alone on a desert island, which eight gramaphone records would you choose to have with you?—assuming of course that you have a gramaphone and needles . . ."

Dennis Hirst moved over to the radio set to switch it off but changed his mind, shrugged his shoulders and sat down at the typewriter on his bedroom table.

"Dear Neil:

"Dear old B.B.C. is just starting in with one of its doddly pleasantries. Remember? Desert Island Disc and gramaphone needles.

"You are still very much around here in Freetown; at least, your case has a way of cropping up quite easily. The Daily Mail helps a bit too. 'These white men must learn to respect . . .' The new fellow, Bahorik, Ted Bahorik, Princess of Wales School and the P.Z. apartments, remember him? . . . Anyway, he's developed an interest in Boondoh and female circumcision after I filled him in on the details of your publication. Not a bad sort but 'most likely to' candidate for something silly."

". . . Ladies and Gentlemen, as usual to introduce our famous castaway, here's Mr. Roy . . ."

"To tell you the truth, I'm writing only because I've noticed a compulsion to put things down in writing—letters which for the most part never get posted. Nothing of interest on the radio. And the five hours of television are taken up with American silliness; you know, Lassie and the Flinties."

". . . Well, Miss Cogan, assuming that you were cast away alone on a desert island, assuming of course that you had a grama-phone and needles . . ."

"We've started a new game of sorts around here. First Glimpses . . . Ethel came up with the name. You know, the first undeniable realisation that we had arrived . . ."

". . . And now for Miss Cogan, Desert Island Disc plays: If you take a peek in my Gazeebo/You'll never be a free beau . . ."

"My glimpse is somehow inextricably bound up with Graham Greene, a little gray rat, and the flushing of a toilet. The funny thing about it all is that this did not happen my first day here . . . nor even my first year. Only two months ago, actually.

"I was walking down George St., going down toward the waterfront at King Jimmy Wharf, when it all of a sudden struck me as I walked past the City Hotel at Oxford St. that Graham Greene had stayed there for a while and had actually worked on one of his novels there. *Heart of the Matter* I think it was. On a sudden impulse, I decided to spend the night at the hotel. I got a room and, to be honest, I found it rather ghastly. Ghastly walls and a decaying musty smell. But I remember above all being kept awake by two things. First, constant mouthfuls of spit; it was as if I had a reservoir of stale saliva flowing through a wide open valve into my mouth. I remember getting up several times and brushing my teeth, but no sooner did I put my head on the pillow than the flow would start again.

"The other thing which kept me awake was the grey rat. My room wasn't rat-infested or anything like that. There was just this one grey rat, probably a baby rat. It moved around while my mouth was filling and hid when I got up to brush my teeth and wash out the spittle. Finally, it somehow got into the cylindrical garbage can which served my room and then slid up and down the metal sides in futile attempts to get out.

"That, for some reason, was my glimpse. It suddenly struck me that anywhere else but in Freetown at that hour of night, about one in the morning, I could find a reasonable means of exterminating the rat. You know, an American spray of some sort, a hotel attendant, a protest or something. I knew that I was going to kill the rat; there never was any question about that.

"I lay back in bed, listening to the sharp, rising sounds and the glissando effects as the rat rose up and slid down the sides of the can. When my mouth finally filled up again, I got up to wash it out. As I have already said, I knew I was going to kill the rat. And perhaps if there is any one reason for the glimpse nature of that night, it must lie in my next series of actions.

"I looked around for a suitable weapon. I thought of several possibilities. Filling the can with water from the faucet would be one way. The rat would drown. But I decided against that . . . well, somehow, that's not quite accurate. I mean, I didn't seem to have decided as to have recognised that one idea slid off my mind and was replaced by another.

"You see, the fantastic thing was this: I mean, there was I, a thirty-two-year-old Londoner with an English Honours from Manchester, standing in my underwear at one o'clock in the morning in a Freetown hotel. And faced with the realisation that I inevitably had to deal death to a baby rat for the first time in my thirty-two years. I use the expression 'deal death' because that was exactly how it registered itself in my mind. Silly in retrospect but still quite intriguingly foreign, don't you think?

"I looked around and finally picked up the lid of the Webcor tape-recorder I'd bought earlier in the evening from Chellerams. The garbage can was a small one and the lid fitted easily over the open top. I then picked up the can and for about ten minutes, I shook it. First, up and down. Then sideways; then up and down and sideways and up and down again. When I lifted the tape-recorder lid, the rat was lying at the bottom of the can and only occasional twitches showed it was alive. I picked up the can and walked to the bathroom next door. I emptied the rat into the toilet and then flushed it. The rat swirled in rapidly narrowing spiralling circles of yellowish water and then disappeared head first."

"Dear Father Northway:

"I got the address of your sanatorium from the Father Superior at St. Edward's. Well, actually I didn't get it myself. I'm not sure you'd remember him but I got it through Ted Bahorik. He arrived a couple of days after your . . . well, after your illness. A nice fellow. American. By the way, I am not exactly sure what I'll be writing about but I hope you're finding the hills of North Wales somewhat different in effect from these here which make Freetown such a 'magnificent abortion.' I've always remembered your description of it. 'A magnificent abortion.' I meant to ask you just what you meant but somehow never quite got around to doing so. You wouldn't mind, would you, if I confess that I found and still find something rather odd about a priest developing metaphors with abortions in them. Of course, this is more a reflection on my quirks than on your imagery!

"By the way, the boys at St. Edward's were quite jubilant over your illness and departure. The *Daily Mail* made quite a to do of it. Some of the fellows, remember Pollin, swear that the 'bare arsed (forgive the direct quotation) chimps' who sell the *Daily Mail* made a point of developing a special, ringing cry each time they went by. I'm referring of course to the edition that headlined your case. I can still hear the sing-song, untrained tenor of the fellow on Pademba Road—you know, the one down by the Cotton Tree Cinema.

" 'Daily Mail! Daily Mail! Read About Father Northway's Case! Daily Mail! Daily Mail! Father Northway, the Madman Rev'rend Father! White Man Becomes Mad at St. Edward's School! Daily Mail!'

"I gather from Ted that a number of your ex-students firmly believe you rubbed somebody's 'black man juju' the wrong way. Some story about your treatment of a student called Amadu. Can't recall his last name but I'm sure you'd know whom they're talking about—if there's any truth to the whole thing.

"Oh, by the way, Pollin, who makes a specialty of clipping up the *Daily Mail*, read one out to us a couple days after you left. I've got a copy.

"To the Editor:
"Dear Sir:
I am very pleased to write this demonstration of my feelings in your esteemed *Daily Mail*. Allow me to say something about the case of Father Northway who has fortunately departed from Freetown to his own homeland. Let me only say that God moves in a mysterious way and as such performs his wonders. And so we must always try to act in such a manner that we will not reap what we don't sow.

A Citizen"

"It's a rather warm night, tonight, Father. You know, April and the dry season. I suppose for you, it's the picturesque hills of Wales. The Father Superior said something about a fantastic view of April from the windows of the sanatorium."

". . . The preceding program, Desert Island Disc, was a transcription from the B.B.C. . . . This is Freetown calling . . . You're in tune with the Sierra Leone Broadcasting Service coming to you from Freetown on a frequency of three point three one six megacycles in the ninety metre band. Good evening, Ladies and Gentlemen."

"Dear Neil:
"I've been to some of the villages on the hills. And, as you

know, I've lived in Freetown for quite a while now. Yesterday, one of the fellows made an observation as apropos as it was fascinating. Not one of the fellows. Ethel, I think it was. We were standing on the veranda of Pollin's flat looking down on the multi-coloured twinkle of the lights of Freetown . . . reminding me then as it always does of the brilliant scarlet of hibiscus flowers, the rich, black blood gangrene of purple and scarlet flowers: begonias, plumbagos, poinsettia, bursting out of the cracked, dry season soil. . . We watched the lights almost colouring the heavy smell of the dry season night as night men headed for sections of the water-front with open barrels of human excrement on their heads. We watched until Ethel's voice cut through the flowers and the smells and the lights: 'This is where and how history hesitates.' "

". . . In next week's English by Radio, Fifth Formers will prepare an analysis of the style of the following news item:

> Our court reporter reports the bad news that today, in Magistrate Court, Sorie Bai-Bureh, allegedly of no fixed abode, was found guilty and sentenced to goal on possession of Canabis Sativa, commonly known as Diamba . . .

Miss Ethel Hendrik pushed away the pad on which she was preparing her script for broadcast over the S.L.B.S. later in the evening. The news items was what Dennis would describe as being 'unnecessarily immediate' since she'd taken it from the papers.

Ethel Hendrik had been in Freetown for three years and the years had been punctuated by three major events which more or less determined her subsequent and current activities. Her first year, she fell in love with Dennis but he fell out of love with her before the year was through; but first he introduced to "them that matter." With the failure of romance, Freetown did not quite cave in for her. For one thing, she'd been introduced to Ministerial Secretaries—"Males, Ethel, males," was the way Dennis had impudently put it—so she had been introduced to the "outings" and dances of "them that matter" at Lumley and Cape Aberdeen. She had even been able to shake the limp, heavy, wet hands of at least four Ministers—heavy, wet hands that lingered in unpunctuatedly telegraphed questions and invitations. And each time, the limp, black heaviness in her hand had filled her with the same palpitating and stomach-knotting and yet sensual feeling that she would vomit if she did withdraw her hand from the sensuousness that enveloped it.

Ethel Hendrik taught English at the Congo Cross Secondary School for Girls. And like Pollin, she had been placed by the Overseas Education Programme in London.

The English by Radio program on the S.L.B.S. was something that had come in her second year. She'd been on a number of outings with some officials from the Ministry of Education and, without really stressing the point, she'd brought up the idea. A couple of months later arrangements were completed and much to her surprise and gratification, she began the broadcasts. There had been a slight argument over the broadcast hour.

"From ten-thirty to quarter to eleven, Miss Hendrik."

"That's silly. It's late."

"Miss Hendrik, the Ministry of Information and Broadcasting does not make 'silly' decisions."

"But this is for children; they'd be in bed."

"Miss Hendrik, African children are not in bed between half-past ten and a quarter to eleven."

And so the programme was broadcast from ten-thirty till quarter to eleven. Fortunately she lived only a short distance from the broadcasting studios.

But later in an effort to prevent the constant disruption of her evenings, she'd suggested prerecording the whole programme. There had been a period of silence lasting for four months. Then she received a letter saying that "The Ministry of Information, under whose direct supervision and control the Sierra Leone Broadcasting Service is placed, has given adequate and serious consideration to the proposal *re.* pre-recording of material for English by Radio. You will be pleased to know that under the circumstances considered, the idea of pre-recording is not necessarily looked upon adversely."

That same year, the number of American Peace Corps Volunteer Teachers arriving in Sierra Leone increased. The usual official welcome party given by the Ministry of Education at the British Council was converted into an elaborate evening at Reffel's

Hall. Ethel Hendrik received a formal invitation to be present at "the auspicious welcoming ceremony under the auspices of the Ministry of Education. A speech will be delivered by the Honourable Minister."

Unfortunately, a number of unexpected developments had complicated the evening. Miss Hendrik danced several highlife numbers with the Ministerial Secretary. Somehow, he ended up slipping one of Miss Hendrik's shoes into his jacket pocket—this after several rounds of Palm Wine and Gordon's Dry and an intense but aborted reference to English literature in the course of which the Secretary had informed her that it was Walter Scott, yes, he believed it was Sir Walter, who once said in *Ivanhoe*: "May your neck collar be no heavier than a man's smoothly hairy arms." Miss Hendrik's reaction had been a somewhat inflexible insistence in her protestation that she did not like being without both her shoes on. To which the Secretary had tried to reply by pointing out that there was little, if any, logical connection between an appreciation of Sir Walter Scott and the wearing of shoes. The evening had ended untidily with the Secretary expressing the hope that differences in skin colour did not lead in future to "irresolvable difference." She had gotten her shoe back but later "in the light of subsequent administrative reconsideration" any final decisions *re.* pre-recording of English by Radio on the S.L.B.S. must, until further notice, be pending. Sincerely.

Thereafter, she had gravitated once more into the group and their evenings were taken up with recitals of First Glimpses.

Now, she turned her attention once more to the radio script.

Or comment on the following from any point of view . . .

A strange and wonderful and sad thing happened in Freetown today. A woman, Fatmata Dumbuya, delivered a baby which was two in one at Fourah Bay Road Pregnancy Hospital. This is the first Siamese for our city. Our reporter said one doctor said the babies had only three feet. 'Oh, it was horrible, it was horrible to see . . .' "

But even as she wrote out the script, she knew she would never be able to use them. Too "unnecessarily immediate" and therefore likely to explode in expatriates' faces. In her mind she was already searching for words of thundering length by incomprehensible and involved English authors to broadcast in the evening.

The telephone ring startled the thoughts before they had crystallised into a definite assignment. Pollin wanted to know if she had heard about the American fellow, Bahorik. Yes, something about disturbing the peace."

III

Ted Bahorik had picked up the handbill announcing the Independence Day Traditional Dancing at Kissy in the lobby of the British Council library two weeks before the dancing was to take place. The intervening period had been devoted to a careful examination of his camera equipment among other preparatory activities. On Independence Day, Ted Bahorik was ready. Since the village was some sixteen slow miles from Freetown, he decided to leave early. The main reason, though, was to get a fairly close stand for his camera shots.

He'd seen a number of these dances—masked "devils" with a variety of interestingly unpronounceable names. He had done quite a lot of research on them and was already about some thirty pages into an illustrated paper on "Volume and Space in the Masked Devils of Sierra Leone: the spatial lyricism of African tribal dancing." He was not particularly interested in publishing the finished work; he looked forward instead to a feeling of overwhelming satisfaction. He would have the finished volume privately printed and bound; it would take the place of family albums prominently displayed in sitting rooms. Instead of faded photographs of naked cousins, hairless, black-gummed grandmothers or the pale protrusions of public and senile fat from the bottoms of tight swimming suits, he'd have illustrated comments on these masked dancers.

He spent considerable time therefore describing, noting the essential features of the unpronounceable names. There was the cylindrical shape of the tall *ogunugus*, the wild leaps of the *egugus*, dressed in brilliantly purple and scarlet scarves, the unabashed and enthusiastic ugliness of the *gongohlies*. Then there were the special

Boondoh and Pohraw devils which danced only on special occasions, generally after rites of initiation.

"The male foreskin is removed. Female circumcision involves the removal of the clitoris. The average size of the material removed is about the size and shape of the top of the thumb of a slightly anaemic one-year-old. The 'operation,' performed without anaesthetics, is widely believed to be of great value in stimulating uncluttered and exhilarating sexual gyrations."

He had gotten that from Pollin when he had begun his research but there was too much of Richard Pollin's cynicism in the style for him to trust the accuracy or even the truth of the information. The group had been wary of the subject. Dennis Hirst had called him to advise caution: "It'll make sense later on when you've been here longer but a fellow got deported. Neil Gordon. Published something about not being able to sleep at night in his bungalow at the college because of the screams of women being circumcised. Very silly, of course."

As he drove his Austin Minor through Wilberforce and Kissy Streets and finally turned down into Kissy Road, leaving Freetown by the east, he patted his camera equipment and tried to imagine the ceremony surrounding the "hunting devils" he was going to watch. He had never seen the particular masked dancing but had gotten some information from his houseboy.

He accelerated his car past the Kissy Road Cemetery, past streams and half-naked women whose breasts flapped against their chests as they slammed their laundry against the rocks. Occasionally the road took a bend quite near the streams; the women's naked breasts hung like black, slightly withered mangoes as they straightened and stood watching his tiny, navy-blue car go by. Occasionally they could call out, "White Man! White Man!" and wave brightly dripping lappas, drawers, bubbas at him.

He could not help smiling as he involuntarily recalled some of Hirst's, or was it Pollin's, remarks:

"Christ! Have you ever seen a single Japanese man smile happily for more than two minutes? I mean, a happy, very happy smile? It's their women, that's what! Their bloody women!"

"All right. Come on."

"Their breasts, man, their bloody breasts. Might as well throw in their thighs too. Japanese women have hanging, dried-up pancakes and bloody bow legs. And you realise the legs begin to bow at the thighs. At the thighs, good God! Christ, no wonder the famished Japs went off and bombed Pearl Harbour."

Neil, yes, that's it, it was Neil, had made the remarks before he fully realised that Father Northway had been sitting in the room.

That was also when he had explained to the group that he had come to Freetown to teach at the American-sponsored Academy. Further discussions of his plans and background had been disrupted because Neil had been unable to control his reaction to Ted Bahorik's announcement to the group that his father had been a professional dog-barker who had made his living appearing on American television shows.

"For crying out loud! The original son of a bitch!"

In all it had been a slightly irritating and crudely amusing evening. The crowning point came when Ethel had gone to the bathroom and apparently had forgotten to close the door. They had all sat in stiff silence, purposely avoiding Father Northway's eyes as Ethel's urinating sounded noisily into the sitting room.

Ted Bahorik stopped the car at the foot of the hill leading up to the King George V Insane Asylum at Kissy. He picked up the camera equipment and headed for the clearing behind the village slaughter house where the dancing was to take place. There was a small crowd waiting there. He was only vaguely disturbed by the fact that he was the only white man there. He was setting up his camera when four men walked up to him. Bahorik looked up.

"Hi. You guys all set for a fine show?"

"What you doing?"

"Oh, setting up my camera."

"What for?"

"I'm going to take a couple of shots of your—"

"What for?"

"Well, it's today they're dancing, isn't it?"

"You can't."

"What d'you mean?"

"No pictures."

"Oh, come on! I mean, you guys have a great—"

"No pictures, sir."

"But why? I'm sure we can—"

"No pictures, sir."

"Look, if it's money—"

He was interrupted by the sound of a litany-like chant, modulated by claps and the rhythmic but muffled resonance of drums. The sounds were punctuated by shots fired at irregular intervals. The men speaking to Bahorik turned away at the sound and walked back to the centre of the clearing.

Mr. Ted Bahorik peered at the approaching procession through the lenses of his camera. He had barely focused on a dirty-brown mask, ringed with cowrie shells, when his lenses shattered into small fragments. The next rock caught him on the nose and the next sent a sharp pain up and down the length of his left side. He stood there much too surprised to move. He was still standing when the next three rocks hit him. First, on the right side of his face, then between his eyes and again high and hard on his right cheek bone. He raised his left hand toward his nose when he felt the warm flow trickling down. But the pain which resulted from the movement was so sharp and unexpected that he stopped the hand half-way to his dripping nostrils. A rock suddenly caught the hand in mid-air opening a white, pink and red jagged gash behind the knuckles on its way to Bahorik's dripping mouth. He was suddenly but groggily aware that the singing and drumming had stopped. In the silence that followed, the men who had earlier talked to him walked back to him. They pointed to his car and he bent down to pick up his camera equipment. Stabbing pains in his head and left side made him unable to straighten himself. He dropped the equipment and blinked his eyes, trying to focus his vision. But suddenly his body stiffened and then his body and face exploded as he vomited in convulsive spasms. The four men picked up the camera equipment and held him as they half carried him down the hill.

The men walked away from the car to the slow, renewed pounding of the drums; the chant broke out again as Bahorik groaned into a crouching, sagging position behind the wheel. The slow pounding of the drums and the chant throbbed with the throbbing of his heavy forehead as he leaned over the steering wheel trying to force back the explosions from his body and his face.

The police man's truncheon rapped suddenly against the small, navy-blue Austin Minor.

"Sorry, sir. Illegal to park and to disturb the peace, sir."

IV

"Luxury Tampalay Club Highlights—The most phantasmogorical, scintillating Social and Dance on May 7th at Dworzak Hall. Master of Ceremonies: Mr. R. S. B. Ishalu, Esq. B.A."

Mr. Ishalu glanced at the card, hesitated and then finished rolling up the car windows. He kept the two-year-old card clutched between his teeth until he had finished the operation. The card was normally in a special corner of the glove compartment; before the car, he carried it in his briefcase. But the card was important in a way that was not indicated in the event it commemorated. That event was a social and dance; a gratifying programme drawn up to celebrate his being awarded an M.B.E. from Queen Elizabeth II through His Honourable Excellency, The Governor-General. What the card meant to Mr. Ishalu was the concrete evidence it obliquely furnished that his wife weighed exactly two hundred and five pounds. The card was the midway point between the before and the after. He had stopped accepting invitations that called for Mrs. Ishalu to be present exactly eighteen months back. At that time she weighed one hundred and eighty pounds. And gradually the embarrassment of dancing, or attempting to dance with her and being unable to encircle her body gave rise first to feelings of irritation; then embarrassment; then anger, irritation, and embarrassment in a simultaneous explosion which ruined his capacity to enjoy the function they were attending. These feelings were in turn replaced by self-pity when in the course of the evenings he stood and watched friends and strangers try the difficult and by then impossible art of negotiating Mrs. Ishalu's jowl-covered body in any decisive manner.

The evening of Mrs. Ishalu's one hundred and ninety-seventh pound, there was a get-together for his staff, and in the course of the evening, his misfortune had been acutely emphasised when the view was indiscreetly passed around that one of the expatriates dancing with Mrs. Ishalu had looked like an albino seal drowning in the blubber of a wrinkled sperm whale.

Thereafter Mr. Ishalu's domestic life had been literally slippery, calling for the most exquisite balancing skills during moments of attempted intimacy. Especially during the dry season. Mr. Ishalu's house was concrete for about a quarter of the way from the bottom. The rest was board. A brown corrugated iron roof capped the building. This kept the house more or less fairly cool during the rains. In the dry season, the iron roof sucked the heat, hungrily and relentlessly sucked in the heat from the tropical, rainless sky. This then was the most difficult season for him. The bedroom sweltered in heat at night and it was soon obvious that the small electric fan was woefully inadequate to cool his wife's body. The result was that her whole body lay beside his throughout the summer nights in a way that aroused guilt, anger, lust and frustration. And when he attempted to resolve these feelings through intimacy, he was faced with sweating, slippery folds and unexpected niches.

Mr. Ishalu put the card inside his briefcase, straightened his tie, stepped over the gutter and passed out of the burning, rainless sky into the welcoming voices of his wife and daughters.

V

> Oh, drink milk when you lunch
> drink milk when you lunch
> Oh, drink milk when you lunch
> give your life a punch . . .

. . . English by Radio coming to you from the S.L.B.S. The following assignment for Fifth Formers. Comment on the style of the following:

> "Laughing causeth a continued expulsion of
> the breath with a loud noise which maketh
> the interjection of laughing, shaking of the
> breasts and sides, running of the eyes with
> water, if it be violent."

. . . And this passage for Fourth Formers . . .

"The act of laughter is a sweet contraction
of the muscles of the face and a pleasant
agitation of the vocal organs, not merely
voluntary or totally within the jurisdiction
of ourselves."

... This is Ethel Hendrik, English by Radio, S.L.B.S.

VI

"*Salve, magister.*"
"*Salvete, pueri.*"
"... Edward Kai-Samba."
"*Adsum.*"
"Sorie Sankoh."
"*Adsum!*"
"Sesay."
"*Adsum.*"

"Dear Father Northway:
"It's of course quite unethical to compose this letter to you right
in the middle of calling my class roll. Perhaps the fact that the
Sierra Leone Grammar School sees it fit to use Latin when students greet teachers and answer to their names, has something to
do with it. Rather interesting, isn't it? Never did have an ear for it
anyway—at least, until I listened to you at Mass. I have this irre-
sponsible vision of Pollin with a red cape over his shoulders, head-
lining The Latin-speaking bare-arsed chimps of Hirst's collection.
Silly, of course. But he may need less police guidance ..."

"Tejan-Sie."
"*Adsum!*"
"The last lesson, we read some poems by William Wordsworth.
The class was asked to prepare for recitation one of Browning's
poems ... Kai-Samba."
"Yes, sir."
"What is Browning's poem called?"
"Thinking About ... about ... Thinking About Home."
"Yes, Tejan-Sie?"

"Please, sir, that is false. The poem by Robert Browning is called, 'Home-Thoughts from Abroad.' "

"Kai-Samba."

"Sir."

"The first eight lines of the poem."

"The first eight lines of the poem are . . .

    'Oh, to be in England . . . oh, to be in England . . .'

"Dear Priscilla:

"I'm not sure how many times I've written you since I left London. I'm busy right now having one of my attacks of nostalgia and irrelevance. One of my students is rubbing the fabric out of his khaki uniform trying to recall the first eight lines of Browning's 'Home-Thoughts from Abroad.' So frightfully irrelevant of course to everything. But then, no escape from the syllabus. I'm not too sure whether I should be thinking up this letter in particular. But then, you may not get it . . ."

"Sesay."

"Oh, to be in England

"Now that April's there,

"And who ever wakes in England

"Sees, some morning, unaware . . ."

"Dear Neil:

"Ted Bahorik had wanted to get in touch with you about female circumcision. If he did you'd better not reply here. He's been medically deported. He got badly broken jaws from 'disturbing the peace' at Kissy. They got him wired up and clamped and shipped back to America for treatment. Saved the group here another trial. Must have been his variety of Spring madness. You know, it's April and the dry season in Freetown

        and the tom toms are beating
        and the natives are restless
        and who ever wakes in Freetown
        sees, some morning, unaware . . .

copyright to you of course. It'll all be followed soon enough by the thunders and the mosquitoes of the rains . . ."

"Sankoh."
"Please sir, I'm sorry to say, sir, but I forgot."
"Awoonor-Williams."
"And after April, when May follows . . ."

"Dear Father Northway:
"Unlike you, and yet not too unlike, Ted Bahorik, the American, has been physically broken and sent back to an American hospital."

Oh, to be in England, etc. A bit of irreverence through Reuters. Something about a priest hauled into court for stealing two pairs of panties in a London shop. Shoplifting charge, actually. Pleaded guilty but refused to tell what he had intended to do with aforementioned garments. Father Superior here is as purple as a bruised mango. Unfortunate, though; it stirs the usual disenchantment among out converted friends here . . .

". . . Hark! where my blossomed pear-tree in the hedge
  leans to the field and scatters on the clover
  blossoms and dewdrops—
"The poem so far, as I hope you can see, is a rich symphony, I mean, a rich . . . a rich . . . By the way, Tejan-Sie, what is a clover?"
"I don't know, sir."
"Sankoh?"
"I think perhaps it is a sort of a bird."
"Later on, in the last but one line, Browning mentions buttercups. What is a buttercup?"
"Sir, could it be a kind of dish or basin for putting—"

"Dear Priscilla:
"I've been thinking about this compulsion to write letters. I'm always doing that. By the way, Priss, how many synonyms do you know for 'symphony'?—assuming of course that one knows what orchestras et al are. The Roman Catholic cathedral in Freetown is on Westmoreland Street—no, I don't know why it's called that. Anyway, it's directly across from the Odeon Cinema. The

Father Superior's supposed to be concerned about 'tight-skirted
and mountainously-fleshed black daughters of Babylon' who sit
on the Cathedral steps from ten at night until the last white man
drives away from the cinema. Father Superior Breshan is Irish—
probably by way of explaining the style . . ."

"The clover is a type of plant. And buttercups, which Browning
contrasts with 'this gaudy melon-flower,' are flowers. English flowers
contrasted with a non-English flower . . . Awoonor-Williams, what
does 'gaudy' mean?"

"Sir?"
" 'Gaudy'—as in 'this gaudy melon-flower' ?" . . .
"The curious thing about the whole experience though, Priss,
was the silence throughout. I can't really say that I did it just for a
lark. Nor can I say I thought that I hadn't really to pick her up.
There'd been some sort of a typical silliness showing at the
Odeon—*Son of Tarzan Meets the Thing*—or some title like that.
Incidentally, that was Ethel's introduction to Freetown cinema
audiences."

"Jesus, Hirst, do they keep this up the whole of the evening?"
"What?"
"Well, the bloody applauses and screams."
"Yes."
"What do you mean, yes?"
"Oh, don't worry about it. When they like something that's
happened, they applaud."
"But, look here, man, how can one hear—"
"And when they dislike anything, they scream. You'll develop
your Freetown cinema ear soon enough . . ."

"Something that's 'gaudy' is flashy, superficial . . . hm . . . cheap.
Sesay, give the class a sentence using the word 'gaudy'—and try to
bring out a contrast."

"My sister went to Fulamusu's shop. She brought back some
gaudy bananas but, however, if she went to London—"

"She didn't say anything, Priss. Neither did I. Something

fantastically unreal about it all. There's a poem by Lawrence about
the silence of mating turtles. I had dropped off Ethel at her flat
and then driven back to the cathedral. I'd never been in bed before
with women with 'mountainousy-fleshed behinds.' Ludicrously
funny, tottering sensation. 'The accumulation of excess fat on the
buttocks of the women is regarded as a sign of great beauty.' The
most curious thing, though, was the sudden realisation that I
couldn't see her at all. Odd sensation of tottering over a hole with
a heavy smell of Chanel 5. Quite unlike anything between us. But
then you are white . . .'

   "Browning's poem is an excellent example of a . . . a nostalgic . . . a . . . nostalgic experience. Nostalgia, from a different
point of view, can be seen in the last stanza of *Snowflakes Sail
Gently Down* by the Nigerian poet, Gabrial Okara:
   Then I awoke. I awoke
   to the silently falling snow
   and bent-backed elms bowing and
   swaying to the winter wind like
   white-robed Moslems salaaming at evening
   prayer, and the earth lying inscrutable
   like the face of a god in a shrine.
   ". . . No, Pris. I shall resist the temptation, the compulsion to
ask what snowflakes are; what are elms?
   "Okara uses the words 'elms' and 'snowflakes' in the stanza I
have just quoted. Tejan-Sie—."

John Roberts

There's a Meaning

I grew low on a tree where the shadow fell, and the sun,
And they picked me and took me a long way over cart-tracks
A long journey I had of it, and a conveyor-belt after the lorry,
And they canned me and stuck a label on me saying who I was
And where I came from.

The can was okay, curving and flat at the ends—
One end for my back and the other to press my feet on.
They had to fillet me first, but then what's a bone or two between
    friends?

Canning wasn't the end of it, though—I mean,
They don't just do it for fun. There's a meaning in everything
If we only knew where to look. So me and the others, each one snug
In his can, they packed us off in a crate—nothing
Special, a crate like another, splintered,
Stencilled in creosote, dumped upside down on docksides.

Not cozy, but lots of companions. And the ship
Hooting over our heads and reaching out and swallowing us.
And the journey rising and falling, rising and falling,
Rising and falling.

And the arrival. A sale, a piercing and the light
The terrible light.

Peter Ruoro

End of Month

"UUUUI!" A young girl screamed as she stumbled over Marete, an old man sitting on the pavement, knocking his head against the wall. Except for a thin film of dust in the air, the day was a fine Saturday and River Road was crowded, lively and peaceful.

Marete stirred, moaned, opened his eyes and then sat still, watching, listening, and caressing his long, dirty grey beard. He knew he should have met Ayub, a young clerk he knew, together with a daughter he had not seen for twenty years, in a restaurant not very far up the street. But his eyes followed the girl. Then his nostrils caught the smell of perfume left by the touch of her dress. His mind flashed to the days River Road was his.

The wrinkled face glowed and his eyes beamed as soft, fleshy arms yoked his neck. A warm breath beat gently on his face and two hearts pounded against his chest . . .

Then suddenly his fists clenched; the glow vanished from his face. She was there, crawling. He peeped from a corner. She tried to rise, but fell on her face. Her body heaved and then lay still . . . quiet and still in an empty street . . . dim lights . . . between silent, towering buildings . . . sleeping bodies, resting, embracing, in agony? . . .

"Ha-ha-haaa!" . . . hilarious laughter of women, blaring trumpets, heavy beats of the drums and tramping feet of dancers. He knew where the noise came from. He ran.

"I left her to die!" Marete screamed. "I left her to die!"

"Wake him up," someone said.

A young man kicked him in the ribs, adding:

"No market for you, old man."

"He is dreaming of the knockouts of his day," his companion said.

"The ones that clean barrels in beer-halls today . . ."

Marete raised his head, trying to catch their last words.

A small crowd that had gathered roared with laughter as Marete stumbled to his feet. He looked around anxiously, hoping neither Ayub nor Mumbi, his daughter, would be there.

"I was young once, too," he said aloud.

Women shrieked wildly and the crowd hustled aside as if a giant wedge had been thrust from within. On the street motorists, having realized it was only an old man on the pavement, speeded up.

A young man shoved Marete aside.

"You!" Marete retorted, thrusting his chin and shoulders forward to emphasize his protest.

But the young man did not stop. He did not even seem to have heard and was busily rubbing his coat where it had touched Marete.

"Look what that beggar did to my coat," he said to no one in particular. "Why doesn't the mayor clean them from the streets?" He clicked his tongue with disgust.

Marete stood still for a while, his arms and shoulders drooping, facing the direction the young man had gone, wondering if he might not be one of his many street-sons and also regretting he should have ever had any. He felt gazes drain him. Giggles reached him as he passed along and he saw himself! dirty, old, feeble, a sight even the milling crowd managed to avoid.

"Girls! Girls! Girls!" A young hawker yelled. "Venetian silk to wear to dances and parties. Don't look at the old beggar. I am selling everything cheap . . ."

The shop-keepers stood at the doors of their shops just as they had faithfully done for years, waiting for customers who often never came, advertising their wares.:

"Come in and see my muslin direct from Bombay . . . just unpacked . . . I am not cheating you . . ."

Some people were lured in and soon emerged with laden arms. Others rushed out, shopkeepers in pursuit:

"Come back . . . I will lower the price for you . . ."

"Go away, beggar!" The hawker continued. "Customers don't

want you near their goods. Come, sweety. I'll lower the price for you . . . Don't look at the bum."

Marete resumed his journey, wondering whether he should tell the young man that once all hawkers on River Road either paid tribute to him every evening or perished. He turned around to tell him he knew better. But the young man was gone.

A strong smell of curry hit Marete's nose, saliva flooded his mouth and his feet stumbled towards the door. He remembered his daughter, and a coldness cut through his stomach. Maybe, he thought, she would be there and would look at him in the same manner other people had; maybe she would remember he was still her father, the same man she had said "Father . . ." to with a smile, her neck slanting innocently.

"Look at this one. They really smell."

It was a woman's voice. Marete turned. But it was just the crowd. Any woman could have said it.

Again the smell of curry struck his nostrils and he turned to enter the restaurant. Then he saw a girl at the door, looking at him. He stopped, fumbled with the rags he wore and then turning back said:

"Ah! It is too early for a meal."

But her image remained in his mind: tall, slim, a rich ebony complexion, a dress so tight that it augmented her curves, beautifully straightened hair, huge earrings and long polished fingernails. He stopped, closed his eyes . . . they closed themselves . . . and his body simmered with desires that had once found abundant satisfaction, but which now just gnawed him.

The girl stared at him and the crowd jostled along. The traffic zoomed past and the sun still hit the ground and warmed the thin dust in the air.

The girl pivoted on her heels and walked away, tapping the pavement sharply, swaying her hips violently and seductively. But the old image floated in his mind: a woman, lying full length on the empty street . . . dim lights . . . between silent, towering buildings . . . Like many, her end with him meant her end with life. The poison had worked, although he could have used his gun. He bit his lips with bitterness toward himself.

Nearly every spot on River Road was associated with his heroic days; their glory, money and women but which now he termed pride, corruption and fall. Days without food, nights in the open beside a shanty hut, the shock of waking up only to find that the bed had turned to a drainage or that the police had set fire to the village, the humiliation of having to beg for food had been now a part of his life, in fact his whole life. He wondered how he could have deceived himself and failed to see his youth decaying and his soul submerging into agonizing emptiness. Even the manner of his death was clear to him: he would fall in a gutter, be picked up by the police and buried in a mass grave. No mourners. Policemen would smile, and "There goes another," would be the only comment.

"Yes, my friend!" A shopkeeper shouted.

"Yes, Albhai," Marete answered politely.

"I have not seen you for many days?"

But Marete was not listening. He had known Albhai to have sat at the door of his shop for twenty years, waiting for customers who sometimes never came. "That is what I should have done," Marete said to himself. He now remembered that his wife always told him that a snail reared itself beneath a rotting piece of wood until it was grown. It always did, and Albhai's shop had. Marete thought of his wife. Maybe she, like daughter, was in the streets. But he changed his mind and was almost sure she would be at home, clean; and although not wealthy, with enough to eat and a place to sleep. The thought of going home to her had occurred to him often. She was still his wife; he had paid the dowry for her as tradition required. But he had joined the army and deserted only to bully people, steal, kill and bribe in the city streets, and had forgotten her.

The pain of hunger and thirst compelled him to turn back to the meal he had prepared himself for. But when he got to the door he hesitated and wondered whether to enter the restaurant and eat and also meet his daughter, who might defy him, or go back and remain hungry. He realized that she was no longer the little girl that used to tug at everything playfully and innocently, but a woman that had tasted the power women have over men.

People were gay, noisy and no one except Ayub seemed to notice him. A young woman was being dragged from beneath the table where, drunk, she had retreated. Marete bit his fingers, adding:

"If it were she, I would teach her."

"Now, elder," Ayub called. "It is the end of month! Some food and beer for the elder."

Ayub did not mention Mumbi and soon Marete forgot her as he enjoyed the flow of beer into his veins and smoke into his lungs. The trumpet blared, the drum beat and the feet of the dancers answered, raising a thin film of dust. Marete swayed with music and was soon carried back fifteen years: gentle fingers tenderly crawled around his neck, his fingers fondled with a glass of beer, his table jammed with bottles of Pilsner . . .

"What is it, elder?" Ayub asked.

Marete started, dropping his spoon.

"She will be here soon."

"But Ayub . . ."

He was gone.

Marete was restless for awhile and regretted having asked Ayub to bring his daughter along. He had overheard two young men talk about Mumbi Marete as being young, beautiful and cheap. He knew what that meant. She had just arrived, and he wanted to order her to return home.

He continued eating, glancing at the door anxiously. Mumbi, he said to himself, must return home and there rear children that might redeem him.

The bandmaster struck his drum, the trumpet blared and people yelled, imitating the instruments. Women flocked to the floor, swaying and wiggling their hips, their eyes closed, arms outspread, sighing deeply.

"As her lips touch yours, her hand slips in your pocket," a man shouted.

There was a roar of laughter.

But one by one the men rushed and grabbed their choices.

"Not my daughter," Marete said to himself.

"Here she comes."

It was Ayub. Beside him stood a girl: tall, slim, a rich ebony complexion, beautifully straightened hair, huge earrings and long polished finger-nails.

"Eh, eh, eh, . . ."

Marete stretched his hand but she refused to take it.

"How is it?"

"What?"

"What are you doing here? No . . . no . . . I mean how is your mother?"

Mumbi placed her hand on the table, bending her shoulders over him.

"Is it now that you realize we exist?"

"My daughter . . ."

She smiled scornfully.

"I think girls like you ought to find a good young man, rear children that would redeem their grandfather . . ."

She continued to stare at him.

"Aaaaaa, I mean leave the paved city streets. They are poison."

Her forehead wrinkled and she clenched her fists. "You mean like your friend here?" She pointed to Ayub, who walked away.

"No . . . no . . . no . . . Just what you want."

The music stopped.

Mumbi slapped the table so hard that everyone turned toward them.

"I am your father," Marete said, his chin trembling.

"Listen to that!" someone shouted.

"You? My father. I am even ashamed to be seen talking with you. If the streets were poison, you should have stayed home with us."

"I know about them. Listen to me . . ."

"Who wants to hear you . . ."

Her voice was drowned in a wild laughter.

"Forget!"

She pivoted on her heel and swayed herself toward the door. Men whistled, screamed and yelled.

"I did not know you had such designs, elder," Ayub said. "She is just another whore."

"Ayub, it is . . ."

The drum beat, the trumpet blared and the bare feet of dancers answered, drowning his words. Ayub disappeared in the crowd.

Marete fumbled with his clothes, his beard, and then watched the dancers.

"Yes, girls," he said to himself, "in the jaws of crocodiles." Then aloud: "Yes, girls . . . in the jaws of crocodiles! . . ."

"Throw him out!" Men shouted angrily.

There was a roar of laughter as Marete, afraid of being attacked, stumbled to his feet and walked to the door.

He looked across River Road. Mumbi stood there, talking to a man. She shifted her weight from one leg to another. Marete wanted to call her but realized he had no authority over her; he had never established it. She looked at him and then turned around, just as if he was not there. And then that body floated in his mind, strong, beautiful, stretched full length in an empty silent street . . . dim lights . . . between towering buildings . . . an image of his daughter floated in between the vision. He looked across the street. She was gone.

"Get out of the way," someone shouted, shoving him aside.

Marete stood for awhile, unable to do the only good thing he had tried in his life. Choked with anger and bitterness against himself, he stumbled into the crowd that still milled its way up and down River Road. He knew that no matter how much he had learned in the twenty years he lived there, no one wanted to know and no one would listen.

Jim Chaplin

Slum Day

The monotonous tap of the blacksmith's sounds.
Long shadows zebra the roads;
Partners stretch and yawn,
Their girls catch up on sleep.
Dew lies still on the piled maize,
And children tumble their way to school.

The vendors squat behind their wares.
Careful spenders have enough for food,
The careless flounder in the shade
Press emptiness against worn grass.
The pious wash and pray.
Heat stills the birds; the crickets sing.

Smoke curls to stifle the quiet air.
The lamps are lit: music begins to play.
As bars begin to fill,
The girls waken and parade.
Children quarrel their way to bed.
Life has been won from another day.

The Next Morning

Was this where I came staggering?
This the inviting portal to delight:
Three box-lids and a half peeled log.

Was this the hall that opened wide?
Promising of soft richness of desire:
Two Army blankets hung on a knotted string.

Was this she who called me in?
She of seductive grace beyond compare;
Grasping, blowsed with our oft caressing.

Was that the man who came inside?
That peeling reflection of beer-shot eyes:
That pocketless, drained, dejected I.

The Derelict

When he left us
He needed neither hat nor coat.
And to the forest he left walls
And to the ants the stakes of his house.
Grass was not needed, so he let it fall.
Even the body of years
He left to his sons' sons.
And to the village
The memory of his fine spears.
All this he left us
When he walked alone, ahead of us.

Matei Markwei

The Appointment

Your body
Moves in
Passioned curves
Like flames of fire climb the wind
Or like the mind
Skirts for
Kisses on an empty mat.

Your cottony steps
Intelligently spread
Can bed
The dust
Make beauty spots
On the ground.

You
Are elegant!
Tropical beau ideal
That cools the heat with
Plump
Plum-smooth
Gait.

What thoughts knit your brow?
Light the torch of Hymen
On your lips?
What magic orbs your eyes
In Mona Lisa grace?

Tell!
Tell!
What grandeur swings your arm?
Which beautician fruits
The rings that bead your neck?

When the night begins to mask
And sprinkle
Ash-clouds
On the fire-stars
And the moon smoulders
Under mauvy darkness

Come
Down
The path
That folds the cricket's song
The sleepy lizard
Inside its grassy hem
Quick-freeze Desire
Till you see a shadow veil the road.

"ORUKORERE" from *J. P. Clark's* "Song of a Goat."

R. A. Freemann

Indoro Bush College

IT IS PLAIN for us to look at or to see that the Shell group of people does not settle in one place for very long. They move from place to place like monkeys twine from one tree to another. In the year 1959, the Shell group of people went to Indoro River. This Shell group of people, if you look at it carefully, consists of two types, the Black colour and the White colour. These people are hard-working people, so when they reached Indoro they went up and down very busily with their house-boats and their flying-boats as if they really meant business.

When it came to a certain fine day, three white men came to the town of Indoro with a flying-boat. When they reached the town they told one young boy, a worker, to go out with them. The four people entered the boat, three white men and one black man.

This town that is known as Indoro is not a big town, but just an average one. The townspeople are great juju servers. In ancient times, the inhabitants of Indoro were the greatest juju servers in their whole area; but at present, they have left and neglected many things. Yet they still are serving a great forest, which is known to us as Indoro juju forest.

They believe that there is another town of Indoro in the bush. All the citizens of the real Indoro are also in the bush Indoro; all the names, all the houses, all the families, all the compounds and all the quarters, all are the same. Many palm tappers and hunters who have missed the road in the bush have burst out in the bush town. If you miss the road in the bush and step into the town, the townspeople will entertain you warmly and will show you the road to the real town. When you have reached home and plan to go back to the town again, you cannot go, even if you try your best, unless you miss the road unexpectedly in the bush. Due to these reasons, the people of

Indoro serve the bush Indoro with their whole minds. When they hear a bell ring in the bush, they start to worship. When people pass by this forest, they should not set their eyes on it; if they gaze at it directly, they will die on the way. People should not land on it, either. When it is time for service, only the servers are allowed to step into it.

Still, the young man and the white men were going. When they reached the forest, they landed on it with the boat. The young man was afraid, so he said: "No person should step into this forest. Any person who steps into it will die." The white men said: "Shut up your mouth, step in and go on. If you do not step in, we will shoot you to death." They pointed their guns at him. The young man started to cry. He said: "Oh! all the great men in this forest, hear me, all the women and men, all the spirits and great things, and other great things, hear me, and all the water spirits, hear me. We are serving you as our grandfathers were serving you, we do not subtract and do not add. These men are forcing me to land on you, I am innocent, so you should know that. The white men said that if I do not step on, they will kill me, so I want to land on you." The white men said: "This boy, what are you saying, if you don't step on, we are going to shoot you to death." He was afraid of death, so he stepped on. They told him to walk up on the land and they were also following him with guns, pointing at his back like a shepherd with his flock.

The boy feared the white men, so he kept silent; and the white men were in readiness to shoot him if he made any noise. As they were going on the road, the white men urged him to walk quickly without stopping. As they were going up-land, after two miles, they burst onto a certain big road, which was a coaltar road. Immediately they reached there, they stood, because the boy did not know which direction to follow. They nagged him and said: "If you will not walk again, tell us so that we should kill you here." On hearing this, he started to move on because of the fear of death.

II

Truly, during that time, during his agony period when his life was in the basket, he smelt the smell of death. When it came to a certain time on their way going, they saw a door. The door covered the whole road, just like a gate. When they reached the door, they did not know where to pass. After a little silence, these three white men said: "Knock at the door, else we kill you here." The boy did not know what to do, so he knocked at the door. Immediately after the knock, a man opened it, who was the gate-man. He asked them and said: "My good men, where are you going to?" The three white men answered him and said: "We are coming to this town." He said: "Very well, come in."

A short distance past the door, another white man who was as white as the three men met them. The man asked them and said: "Where are you coming from? What do you want to do in this town? What do you want to do with this boy?" Among all these questions, the white men could not answer even one. The man said: "Why is it that you give us a headache every day since you came to Indoro? Follow me, your request will be granted today. You are continuously worrying us without rest, everything will be ended today."

Therefore, the man went off with the people. On their way, the people were surprised that inside such a forest there was a mighty and beautiful town of that type. The man put the three white men in a certain big house and locked them in and started to walk round to see things in the town with the boy. Some roads were made of glass, some made of iron, some were cemented ones and some were coaltarred roads. Some places would easily blind the eyes due to the glimmering.

They came to a certain big house. The man said: "My friend, this is a bicycle factory, we make any type of bicycle you want in this world." After that, they went to another big house. He said: "My friend, this is our motor factory; and any type of motor you want, we can build." They went away from there. When they reached another big house, he said: "My friend, this is our aeroplane factory; any type of aeroplane you want, we build here." They proceeded from there and went to another big house. He said: "My friend, this is our cloth factory; all the types of cloth in this world, we do weave." They went away from there. They reached another mighty house, and he said: "My friend, this is our plate factory, here we make any type of plate you want in this world." They left there and reached another place. He said: "This is our zinc factory, here we make all types of zinc people want in this world." They again went to a glass factory, and he said: "This is our glass factory, here we make all the types of glass in this world." They again went to a certain place, and he said: "This is our iron factory, here we make all the types of iron in this world." They left there and went to a certain place, and he said: "This is our knife factory, here we make all the kinds of knife in this world." They went to a gun factory, and he said: "This is our gun factory; all the types of gun in this world, we make here." They went to a bomb factory, and he said: "Here we make all the kinds of bomb in this world."

He took the boy round to show all their factories, materials for travelling, for house use, war materials and all materials for dressing. The man said: "I will show you every place."

The boy was very happy, for he was seeing all these things. The man took him to another part of the town. When they went to a certain big house, he said: "All these books in this house are for education; any type of title you want to obtain, we can teach you to that extent." As big as the house was, it was full of books, many kinds of books were in it, any type of book you want in this world, you could find in it.

That house was only for books, it was a library. After that house, they went to another big house. When they entered the house, due to the way they built the house, the boy was afraid; the whole of the inside of the house was built with gold and silver. Inside the house, there were many rooms, and all were numbered. The man said: "This house is only for reading books, any room you can enter and sit down to read."

III

The man started to walk round with the boy to see them. He said: "My friend, every room in this house has its number, this is number one room, this is number two room, this is number three room, this is number four room, this is number five room, this is number six room, this is number seven room, this is number eight room, this is number nine room, this is number ten room, this is number eleven room, this is number twelve room, this is number thirteen room, this is number fourteen room"; he showed him all the rooms in the house, all amounted to thirty rooms.

After their going round of the house, he took him to their big bell that was in the town, in order to show him. When they reached the place, he said: "This is the biggest bell of all the bells in this town; when we ring it, your townspeople say, 'Oh! The secret forest is in need of worship!' From there they start to serve us, we want to do something, hence we are ringing it. When we ring this bell, the big bell of London is rung too, these two bells have connection. You people cannot find out secrets like white men, you serve everything as juju, because you do not know."

When that came to pass, he took him to their main workshop. When they reached the house, the young man saw that here was another mighty house. The man said: "My friend, this is the head workshop, this is the headquarters." He showed him everything that was in the house.

When they reached the outside of the house he said: "My friend, I will take you to a certain place before we go back." The boy said: "I would be very glad if you take me to the place." The man said: "If it is so then let us go." They started to perambulate the place. When they reached the place, there was a big house; the man said: "This is our magic medicine house, so we will enter the house. But if we enter, nobody should talk, it is forbidden; anything you see, just close your mouth." The boy said: "If it is like that, it is good, I will do so."

They entered the house. When they got into the house, the wonders that he saw were greater than human's expression. They started to speak to each other with eyes, both the men became as dumb people. They walked round the whole house to see everything. When they reached the outside, the boy said: "My friend, in all my life I have never before seen such wonders as I have seen in this house. It is here that I have learnt how to speak to somebody with my eyes." The boy made the man to fall into great laughter. The man said: "Any type of thing you want in this world, we are able to do for you in this house."

After all these conversations had come to pass, then they started to return. On their way, the man said: "My friend, when we reach where the white men are, I will release them to go with you. When you go, on your way they will ask you to tell them what you have seen and what you have experienced and what you have heard. Do not tell them anything. They will even pretend to kill you, but do not tell them; they are just making you to be afraid. When you reach home, come back with five young men and we will teach you." The boy said: "Yes, I think I will do so, I will come back."

When they reached the place, the man released the three white men and said: "Go away from my sight, if you do not want trouble!" The white men could not voice any word, they just went back with the boy. On their way, having passed the door, the white men started to worry the boy and said: "Tell us what the man told you and what you saw." The boy said: "As he locked you in the house, that was how he locked me inside a house too and went away. When he came back, he opened the house and said: 'Come out of the house quickly, or I will kill you today, don't come here again!' He dragged me out of the house and brought me to you, that is how it happened, he did not tell anything more than that." The white men tried to force him to tell them something else, but the boy did not tell them anything. They tried their best, but still he did not tell them. They thought that he would tell them something.

When they looked back, there was nothing but thick forest. They started to walk speedily, because they were afraid. They had forgotten what they were pressing the boy for, but they started to run to save their lives. Immediately they burst out at the water side, one white man gave up the ghost. They quickly got into the boat and proceeded. On their way going, another one was at the point of death. They quickly went to Indoro to drop the boy and crossed to their house-boat. Immediately they got to the house-boat, the second one too died. They took the remaining one to Port Harcourt. On their reaching Port Harcourt, he too died.

When the boy reached Indoro, he called the whole town and narrated every bit of his travel with the white men. He began with his narration from the beginning, what he saw and what he heard, but he did not tell anything about where he studied how to speak with his friend with eyes. The townspeople said: "Nobody should listen to him, he is mad, the worship of this god was begun from the time when our grandfathers were in existence till now. Who will go with you? If you are in need of death, go alone and die." The boy could not go alone, so he left it. The story ends.

G. Awoonor-Williams

Messages

On time's lap sat simmering
burnt on lost hearts' desires,
tasks fulfilled not fulfilled
through joys dying,
pain reborn in hearts
that felt they have forgotten
but not forgotten forever
sleeping ever last of all
with the down sloping of hopes lost
reborn everyday in the anguish
of a forgotten ecstacy
long known of long shores
stretching through childhood memories
      birds and hunting at grandfather's farm far away
      and squirrels hide and time's harvest.

Stop the Death-Cry

Let all of you stop the death-cry
        and let me hear.
It is home; I stood at death's door
        and knocked throughout the night.
Have patience and I shall pay the debt.
Suppose I had someone
        Someone who will call me the dove
        and it will run and come to me.
I have something to say I want to say
        But it surpasses saying.
The dove says it is the soft voice
Which take gifts from elders.
The prepared-for war is never surprised
So have patience
        and I will pay the debt.
I knocked at death's door all night
It was only the sleeping crow who came.
Go back and prepare your gods
        and then come back
So I left; I am seeking to prepare my gods.
        I am seeking; I am seeking.

More Messages

I can go placing maggots on those fires
fanning the innerwards; I can sneak
along like the crawling beetles
Seeking through dust and dirt
the lonely miracle of redemption
I will sit by the roadside, breaking
the palm kernel, eating of the white
with the visiting mice
throwing the chaff to the easternly wind.
But will they let me go?
to nowhere where I can see
the sunlight fall on the green waters
and the ferrymen hurrying home
across with their heavy cargoes
of man flesh, child flesh and woman flesh
I sit where I can gather my thoughts
and ask what I have done so long
why could I not eat with elders
though my hands are washed clean in the salt river
Where they leave the paddles in the boat
to be carried by children of strangers.
Coming to that land that day
where sand strip covers childhood
and youth's memory; there was no storm
that did not speak to us
divining the end of our journey
promising that our palms shall prosper
and we shall not die by thirst
in the same land; where our fathers
lingered, ate from land and sea
drank the sweet waters of the ancient palms.
Will they let me go?
and pick the curing herbs behind fallen huts
to make our cure, their cure

marking the potsline
the lingering desire of every marksman
returning from futile hunt
beaten by desert rain and thistles
on his shoulder the limpid hare
and empty guns; will they let me go
to hoe my own fields, plant my own corn
              to wait for rain to come?
The sacrifice of years awaiting
unlit fires, who to knowledge
prepare the feast of the resurrection
On many rivers shores moved
the benevolent band, awaiting that season
The dawn second cock
split by the ears of rumour
time to wash the new corn
ready for the grinders
lighting the family fire of flimsy twigs
Broom sweeping unto dunghill
Crimes that my fathers atoned for.
Some day, by some rivers!
We sang that song before
in the thousand seasons of good harvest
and full fish following our fathers' foot prints
on the long shores, homegoers.
They heard the thousand thunders
from the great rivers waves
as the road crossing snakes brood on rotten eggs
that our feet should move to make room
for an empty valley.
What happened with cries heard under trees
that many households are empty?
The powder house is fallen
So we cannot make war
For when the bulls are alive
could the cows perform weed?

The Journey Beyond

The howling cry through door posts
carrying boiling pots
ready for the feasters.
Kutsiami the benevolent boatman;
when I come to the river shore
please ferry me across
I do not have on my cloth end
the price of your stewardship.

I Hold the Dreams

feasts tortured smiles
after; the painful purgation
    and we sleep
        dreaming of purple paradises
        of laughter of naked virgins
in the arms of buffons
fetid vomit
loud raucous music
rending the dream of skies
the smell of sacrifice
as the lord takes in
        the exhalations
and gathers unto himself
twelve baskets of feasted bread
        the lonely army
        lost in the city streets
Singing its last songs to sunfall
The joy, brothers, the joy!
        of waking up
        breaking the benediction
        of yet another dawn.

Okogbule Wonodi

Native

Your eyes toe-set,
    thumbed my nerves
    as you weave
    your being into a frenzy;
and your tongue,
    weaving a song,
    painting the scenes
    as I sit toe-dancing.

Then you pull
    those eyelids over
    as you bend
    downwards to dance
    yourself into goddess;
and your waist,
    swinging to rhythm,
    answering the drum,
    as I look, headshaking.

Then light fades,
    those scenes fly
    as you stretch
    your being, panting,
and your mouth,
    muttering my name,
    stifling my nerves
    as I end my verse.

A Memorial

The shadow of dusk insists on house tops,
the songs of the moonlight play echo
in the ears;
there is a bugle call
and the dum-dum of drums
now and in time for the memorial.

The sun is mellow on palmtops
and the rays of yellow beauty
reassert the dawn on window panes;
there is a bugle call
and the dum-dum of drums.

Rays of light permeate the smoke
of noisy factories
and the songs of moonlight play
are fresh on youthful lips;
before these are lost and gone
our memorial shall be full and done.

(Read at the Cultural Festival of the National Union
of Nigerian Students, Ibadan, March 20, 1964.)

Ashes for Granny

She stood still at break of day,
the palm tree, erect and slim;
I see her still but who would say
that such rays could dim.
Alas! What owls hooted at me
when the sun went to sea?

You hear me drop tears here
where we ate, you and me,
and she that fed us is gone
beyond the reaches of thought.

The morning food,
warmed in a platter of broken pot,
the gentle slap on the back
to warn a rascal and correct
are forever gone.

She stood firm on her work,
and motherlike, fed the gods
with nocturnal shrills and dances;
and where are the gods she called on
night and day in sacrificial belief?

The Earthgod,
Thunder and Sun,
where stood they?

She's dead and none,
not one stands to say:
"She lived well."

And here I sprout, rootless,
lonely and dry.

The Owls Hoot

The owls hoot at night,
I am asked to stand and watch
for the call is pregnant
with ills that come at dawn.

The owls are hooting again
and soon the prophet will urge,
will constrain me to raise my hand
and nip in the buds
these nocturnal shrills
ominous with cries of men.

I cannot persuade the prophet,
deep drenched in his conviction,
that owls cry in other lands
and are let cry;

I cannot stop the owls hooting
for the reverberation is in me.

The Immigrant

Flying over Chicago that night he saw
America as through a telescope
With a multiple of eyes; and her streets,
Straight-eyed, blinked, bidding and binding his eyes.

He tried another look, this time sideways,
Flapping his eyelids close to the window
And his mouth, like clams at fulltide, opened full.
He saw nothing but distant specks of stars
Piercing like arrows the darkness beyond.

But beyond he saw ten dainty maidens
And beside them ten young men in loincloths
And he brought the sacred drums and drumsticks
And walked before them; and the maidens
And the young men gave their waists to the drum
And his voice dug deep into the Fathers.
They danced behind him, frenzied as prophets.
Sweating, beating a staccato of sounds,
He was one with them, lost to the moment.

"This is O'Hare"
                           and the dancers sank
fast over fast running pillars of light.

Lovesong

I shall not wait for April
To sing my love. There may be
No snow or hail then, and seeing

The green-grass beauty around
Or lying outside sunbathing,
You'll listen to the sweeter

Voices of birds now absent
And realize that mine's coarse
And my verses without rhymes.

I'll not wait for the Spring.
So, come to the riverbank
Where lovers go and laughing

At night show that the winter's
Nothing after all. After
All, love's no running water

Chilled by the winter cold. There's
Enough warmth in touching lips
To melt snowflakes between us.

R. N. Egudu

Remembrance

I

Heads that clash
over a calabash of
stale palm-wine
reel proudly
in the air;
you the mediator
receive the blows
meant for others:

forced vendor of
false kindness,
the unwilling buyers
reject your wares
for your blood!

II

How can I reach
the chicken hoist
in the mid-air
by the hawk?
tear-pools below
reflect the futile

struggle above:

I hear the words
from the dumb man
echoed by the smoked
package hung over
the fireplace—
my eyes now
see my ears!

III

Sacrifice is needed
for life,
for wealth;
libation is poured
to the gods,
to the Sun; the Sun-tree
shakes,
waves
its leaves
in assent;
earth's blood is mingled
with the goat's, the cow's
for birth,
for peace:

but now the peace-gods
seal the pact
with your blood—
oblation that sustains
national pride!

IV

The hen squawks
and seeks
the maize grains
hidden in the fox's
mouth;
the owl hoots
me awake
as the fox forages;
the thunder roars
and old men
predict rain,
which is already
falling in me,
the flood scoops
the yams to the sea,
and I wail on to
wet cheeks:

the growling stream
buries my voice
in its grooves;
my tongue grows
limp in the cracked
concave of my mouth,
and my throat,
a rust-coated gong,
loses its tone
to rain and sun;
my mind beats the gong
with an ant-eaten stick,
but its sound is with
him that is buried
beneath the eastern soil!

The First Yam of the Year

I have dug it fresh,
this boneless flesh
of air, earth, warmth
and water, this
life out of the heart
of death;
its cap of fibre
will mail the elder's
head against grey rain,
and its body proof his
to spite time's arrows.

For he is the rope
tied at the foot
of our past hooking
its fingers round our waist,
and reaching for the sable
gourd on the forked stump
where the unfeathered chick
chirps a sacrificial song.

He will eat this log-root
of earth, and after spread
my skin under the Red-Sun
to collect his rays
for washing my blood,
and plant the ageless
sun-tree into my heart.

John Ssemuwanga

Two Poems

I

Slopes falling and rising sinuously
Hillocks brimming the dome above
Climbs conical echoed in shape
All in pattern with the bowl-valley below
Meandering stream curving a course
Through the bowl with serpentine grace
Sparrows flying down and up the vale and up beyond
Cuckoos cooing good-night to kins
Across and up the down—
There are curves I sense
Standing on a mound atop.

II

If the sun I trusted would nourish my dreams
      Has run its course
And the night I dreaded would shroud my hopes
      Is darkening to gloom
Then I know that all that remains of reality
      Is the scribbling of this verse.

U D U

H E A D

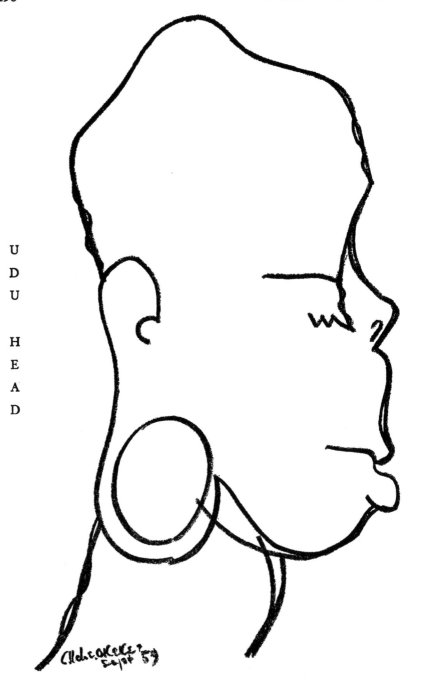

Ama Ata Aidoo

Other Versions

THE THING IS, it had all started after the certificate exams. Instead of going straight home, I had stayed in town to work. This was going to be my first proper meeting with town and when I sent the letter home announcing my intentions I felt a little strange. Bekoe and I were going to stay in a small room in his uncle's house. The room was like a coffin, but who cared? We found a job as sorting hands in the post office. I've forgotten how much they were paying us. Really, it's strange . . . but I have. Anyway, it was something like twelve pounds. Either it started at fourteen pounds and then with the deductions leaned out to twelve-'n'-something, or it was twelve with no taxes. But I remember twelve. Bekoe told me that his uncle was not expecting us to pay anything for the room and that he had even instructed his wife to give us three meals a day for free. I say, this was very kind of him. Because you know what? Some people would have insisted on our paying. They would have said it would help us get experienced at budgeting in the future. And in fact we later discovered that the wife did not have it in mind to feed us free like that. After the first week, she hinted it would be nice if we considered contributing something. She was not charging us for the meals. No, she was just asking us to contribute something. We agreed on three pounds each. We also thought Bekoe should not tell his uncle this. Not that Bekoe would have told on her anyway. He knew nephews and nieces have been able to break marriages. Ei, he didn't want any trouble. Besides, his mother would have killed him for it. His mother is a fierce trader and I know her. She could easily have slapped him and later boasted it around the market how she had beaten up her son who was finishing five years in college! . . .

Anyhow, that was three pounds off the pay. Then there was this business of the blazer. I mean the school blazer I wanted to buy. It cost ten pounds, and father had made it quite clear that he considered his duty by me done when he paid my fees for the last term. How could I go to him with a blazer case? So I thought I would keep four pounds by every month towards that. We were going to work for three months. That was the only time we could have in the long vacation. You see, we both wanted to go to the sixth form. Well, if I was able to set by this four pounds every month, I would have two pounds over after I had bought it. And I could use this to look after myself until our pocket money from the government came.

Then I remembered what Mother had told me. I remembered her telling me one day that anytime I got my first pay, I was to take something home. That part of this would be used to buy gin to pour libation to the spirits of our forefathers so they would come and bless me with prosperity. That was why the first Saturday after pay-day, I went to the lorry park and took *The Tailess Animal*. As for that lorry, eh! I was not surprised to read in Araba's letter the other day that Anan, its owner and driver, had bought a bus. Anyone would after the two of them had for years literally owned what was to their right and to their left in the way of passengers.

Of course I had always thought this money would go to Mother. And so see, how do you think I felt when in a private discussion with her the afternoon I arrived, she told me it would be better if I gave it to Father? I had decided on four pounds here too, reserving the last pound for regular spending. Anyway, the moment the paper notes fell into her hand she burst into tears.

"Ai, I too am coming to something in this world. Who would have thought it? I never slept to dream that I would live to see a day like this . . . Now I too have got my own man who would take care of me . . ." You know how women carry on when they mean to? She even knelt down to say a prayer of thanks to God and at that point I left the room. Yes, and after all this business she didn't even take the silly money.

"Give it to your father. He will certainly buy a bottle of gin and pour some to the ancestors. Then I will ask him to give me about ten shillings to buy some yam and eggs for Sunday . . ."

"That should leave at least three clear pounds." I sort of thought aloud.

"Listen, my master, does it matter if your father has three pounds of your pay? It does not matter, I am telling you. Because then they shall not be able to say you have not given him anything since you started working."

"But Mother, this is not starting work permanently."

"And what do you mean?"

"Mother, I have done an examination. If I pass very well I shall go to school again."

"Ah, and were you not the one who made me understand that you would finish after five years?"

"Yes, but the government asks those who do very well to continue."

"And does the government pay their fees?"

"Yes."

"Then that is good because I do not think your father would like to pay any more fees for you. Anyway, it does not matter about the money. You give it to him. His people do not know all these things about the government asking you to continue. What they know is that you are working."

II

God!

I hadn't thought of giving anything of that sort. Certainly not that soon . . . However, Sunday came and I ate the oto mother prepared with the yam and palm oil. I ate it with some of the eggs to congratulate my soul. Then I went to say goodbye to people, and mother took me up to the mouth of the road. Being a Sunday, we thought it would be useless to wait for *The Tailess Animal* to wander in. Because it simply won't. It did that only on the weekdays.

And I was to realize that I had not heard the last of the money business. Mother thought it would be good if I continued to give that "little something" to father as long as I worked.

"Ho, Father?"

"Yes. You know he has done very well. Taking you through college. Now, giving him something would not only show your gratitude but also go towards your sisters' fees."

Ei, I say, have you heard of a thing like this before? I tell you eh, I caught a fever in the raw. But mother was still talking.

"I had thought of a nice dignified something like five pounds. But you brought four this time, and maybe it will be better to maintain just that."

"And how much do I give you?"

"Me?" She sounded quite shocked. "Why should you bring me anything? I do not need your money. All I want is for you to be happy and you shall not be if they say you are bad. And do you think I am an old fool to ask you for more money? If you give that to your father, you will do a lot. Say you shall do it, Kofi."

"I will do it, Mother." I parroted.

I had a dazed feeling for the rest of the journey and the whole day. I just could not figure it out. To begin with, whose child was I? Why did I have to reward Father for seeing me through secondary school? And calling that "college" did not help me either. Besides, he only paid half the fees since the Cocoa Brokers' Union to which he is a member had given me a scholarship to cover the other half. And anyway, Father is the kind of parent who checks out lists so thoroughly you would think his life depends upon them. And he does not mind which kind, either. Textbook lists? "Hey, didn't I buy you a dictionary last year? . . . The lists of provisions you needed to survive the near starvation of boarding school feeding? "And whom are you going to feed with a dozen Heinz baked beans?" Well, you know them. In fact, from talking to people you learn that most fathers are like that and that is the only nice thing about it. Anyway, Father is like that. It was a battle he and I fought at the beginning of every term. Once when Mother didn't know I was within earshot I heard her telling my little aunt that Father always feels through his coins for the ones which have gone soft to give away! It's not very funny if you are his son. So you see why I got so mad to have Mother talk to me in that way? And the main thing was, it wasn't the money I was giving which hurt me. It was the idea of Father getting it. I had always thought of making a small allowance for Mother from the moment I started working. I was the third child. My two older brothers were all working but married and couldn't care much about the rest of us. There were two girls after me, then one other boy. Father pays the fees and complains all the time. Mother wears us clothes and feeds us too because the three pounds he gives for our chop-money is a nice joke. Mother peddles cloth but I know she is not the fat, rich, market type—say, like Bekoe's mother. In the villages you always have to settle for installments, and money comes in in such miserable bits that someone like Mother with four children just spends every penny of her profit as it comes. It is her favourite saying that she sells cloth for the fish-and-cassava women. There is always a threat of her eating into her capital. And naturally it was of her I had thought in terms of any money-giving I was going to do.

But I obeyed her. I sent four pounds to Father at the end of the remaining months and each time just about burst up. "Why not, Mother? Why not, Mother?" I kept asking myself. It drove me wild.

Well, we went to the sixth form. And of course Father realized I was still in school. He was quite proud of me, too. He always managed to let slip into conversations with other men how Kofi was planning to go to the University. Oh, it was fine as long as he was not paying ...

After the end of the higher exams, I went to stay in town with Bekoe to work again. And I resumed sending the money to Father. But I felt like I was involved in committing some injustice. In fact at one point, I thought of finding something extra to do to earn at least four pounds more for Mother too. But we were doing our old job and that was extremely tiring. In the end I just realized I couldn't manage another work. So I gave up the idea, though only here in the front part of my head and not at the back.

III

I passed higher and with lots of distinctions. I stopped working to get ready to go to our national University. And then I met Mr. Buntyne, who had been our chemistry teacher. He asked me if I would be interested in a scholarship for an American university. He knew a business syndicate. They were looking out for especially bright young people to help. They had not had an African yet. But he was sure they would be interested. Of course I applied. There

were endless forms to fill out, but I got the scholarship. And I
came here.

Somehow, I never forgot the money for Mother. I told myself
that I would do something about that the first thing after graduation.
Perhaps it is the way she genuinely thinks she does not need my
earnings that much which makes me want to do something for her.
I've even though of finding a vacation job here to do and sending
the money home with express instructions that it is for her. But that,
I know, would distress her no end. Better still, I planned to save as
much money as I could so I could take her about forty pounds or
even four hundred to do something with. Like building a house "for
you children," as she always put it . . .

And then somehow this thing happened. It was the very first
month I came. I was invited by Mr. Merrows to go and have dinner
with him and his family. He is either the chairman of this syndicate
which brought me here or certainly one of its top men. They came to
pick me up from the campus to their house. Oh, to be sure, it was a
high and mighty hut. Everything was perfect. There were other
guests besides the Merrows family. The food was gorgeous but the
main course for the evening was me. What did I think of America?
How do I plan to use this unique opportunity in the service of
Africa? How many wives does my father have? Etc., etc., etc.

I had assumed that everyone in the household was there at the
dinner table. Mrs. Merrows kept popping in and out of the kitchen
serving the food. And as I've said before, the food was really very
good. Everyone complimented her on it and she smiled and gave the
wives the recipes for this and for that.

A couple of hours after the meal, Mr. Merrows proposed to take
me back to the campus because it was getting late. I agreed. I said
my thanks and goodnights and followed Mr. Merrows to the door.
I waited for him while he pulled out the car from the garage. He
asked me to jump in and I did. But then he left his seat leaving the
engine running and returned some five or ten minutes later followed
by someone. It turned out to be a black woman. You know what
sometimes your heart does? Mine did that just then. Kind of turned
itself round in a funny way. Mr. Merrows opened the back seat for
her and said:

"Kofi, Mrs. Hye helps us with the cooking sometimes and since I am taking you back anyway I thought I could take her at least half her way. Mrs. Hye, Kofi is from Africa."

In the car she and I smiled each nervously to the other . . . I tried not to feel agitated . . .

But then was it the next evening or two? I do not even remember.

I was returning again to the campus from visiting a boy I knew back at home and whom I had met the first few days I arrived. I took the subway. When the train pulled up at the station, I got into the car nearest to me. It looked empty. I sat down. Then I raised my eyes and realized there was someone else in it. There was a black woman sitting to the left end of the opposite seat.

Another black woman.

Now I can't tell whether she really was old or just middle-aged. She certainly was not young. I realized I had to be careful or I would be staring. She was just normal black with a buttony mouth, pretty deep set eyes and an old black hand bag. Somehow I noticed the bag. She was wearing the lined rain coat affair which everyone wears around here in the autumn. Except that I felt hers was too thin for that time of the night.

That time of the night.

I got to thinking of what a woman her age would be wanting in a subway car that time of the night. I don't know why, but immediately I remembered the other one who had been in the Merrows' kitchen while they ate and I ate. Then I started getting confused. I can swear the woman knew I was trying not to stare. She most probably knew too that I was thinking about her. Anyway, I don't know what made me. But I drew out my wallet. I had received money from my scholarship. So I took some dollar bills, crumpled them in my hand and jumped like one goaded with a firebrand.

"Eh . . . eh, I come from Africa and you remind me of my mother. Please would you take this from me?" And all the time, I was trying hard not to stare.

"Sit down," she said.

I'm not sure I really heard those words above the din. But I know she patted the space by her. The train was pulling up at a station.

"You say you come from Africa?" she said.

"Yes," I said.

"What are you doing here, son?" she asked.

"A student." I could only reply shortly.

"Son, keep them dollars. I sure know you need them mor' than I do," she said. And we did not have anything more to say to each other. But now I could openly look at her face. I got out at the stop. Of course she waved to me and smiled. I stood there on the platform until the train had wheezed and raged out of sight. I looked at the money which was still in my hand. I sort of felt like opening them out. I did. There was one ten dollar bill and two single ones. Twelve dollars. Then it occurred to me that that was as near to four pounds as you could get. It was not a constriction in the throat. Rather the dazed feeling I had had that Sunday afternoon on the high road to town came back. And as I stumbled through the exit, and up the stairs, I heard myself mutter, "O Mother."

Sadru Kassam

The Child and the Water-Tap

THE NAKED child stood there in the scullery in front of the tap, staring intently at the water dripping in a little tin. A shiny, filmy surface appeared at the mouth, gradually dilating into a smooth, round, transparent bubble. Then it began to taper and ripen into a bulbous shape, like that of an onion, and leapt out, glistening through the thin beam of sunlight filtering in from behind. It bumped with a "tup" in the tin and broke up into little crystals which hurriedly scattered away in all directions.

He listened, and watched everything with still, sparkling eyes. But each tup seemed like a beat of hammer, heavy, painful, reverberating. Every time a drop fell and he moved his eyes up again, they appeared to tug something along, something that called back, like a crying child after its mother. His face was wrung with agony, he grew restless, his heart throbbed, his hands moved. He clutched the head of the tap and tried, hard, to turn it with his fingers and between the palms. As it shook, drops of water scuttled down. Then they stopped, abruptly. He watched, and attempted again, harder, and harder still; and now, without stopping, gnashing his teeth he forced them on it and tried further. He went on till he felt a hard, tingling sensation and his teeth pained and he became tearful. He stopped, taut, burning, trembling, and flung a look at the tin. He waited, now watching the mouth of the tap hard. Slowly, the thin glassy surface appeared. His face was tense, his teeth clenched, eyelids sagging under tears, one of which fell softly on his toe as if to soothe him. But he looked up again at the tap. A drop had formed and was tapering. A moment later he thrust his own bigger mouth on to the mouth of the tap and pressed his teeth hard upon its small, round surface and held fast by the hands the back-pipe of the tap. A big, sweet, titillating drop slid on his tongue, and he tilted his chin and the drop rushed down his throat. He waited for the next while tightening his grip on the pipe and grating the crowns of his little teeth that now seemed to shake. And he pushed his mouth farther till the sharp, polished edge of the tap cut against his upper jaw. It hurt him, but with a harsh, whetting, intoxicating sweetness. Then he tasted blood, followed quickly by another drop of water. The two blended and he closed his eyes, tight, as if shutting away the world.

Time dripped on.

At last he relaxed his grip. He was dazed and exhausted, almost panting. As he recovered breath and his vision became clearer he noticed a pink, watery mark on the metal. He stared at it for a moment, then touched his index finger against it. He looked at the blend and smiled, and, gently closing his eyes, slipped the finger in his mouth and sucked it. An idea struck him. He looked around. In a far corner, just peeping from behind a dustbin, there was his new toy motor-car. Noting a drop fall, he dashed for the toy. He began knocking the head of the tap with it, first one end, then another. There was a sudden gush of water as the head loosened and the child screamed with joy as if spurting forth his own energy. Slowly, holding the toy in his lap, almost hugging it, he sat down, cross-legged, under the tap, smiling, just smiling, while the water flowed over him and the warm beam of sunlight settled on his navel.

John M. Ruganda

The Image of God

It is the sweet death
Of the God who dies
In Man's birth,
That is the spring of Kato's freedom,
Alike in vanity and divinity;
And it is the victory
Of the God who is
When man dies
That impels Kato,
Not to want heaven,
But the eternal form of pleasure:
For God is
Because man lives.

Samson O. O. Amali

Kano Storm

"Fasten your seat-belts
    Please"
A voice commanded
    Suddenly
The aeroplane vibrated
It began to descend
    From its height
    Gear by gear
    With great rapidity
My heart dropped
    Into my stomach.
The man sitting next to me
    Clutched his seat firmly
    With his fists
His arms' nerves bulged out clearly
And I saw his lips moving
    In supplications
He sat erect
    As if ready to fly out

Of the aeroplane
Any moment.
But to where?
The aeroplane shook vibrantly.
And he seemed to be saying:
"I have had it!
I have not drawn
My will
And my wife is pregnant
She will soon deliver.
I won't see her deliver.
Will I have a moment
To scribble down my will?
Maybe someone
Would pick it up
If I crash."
I said to myself,
"Go on man!"
I watched the man
Melting into fear
We waded
Through the rain storm
And landed safely
At Kano Airport
I laughed.

S. Nair

Mrs. Kimble

REALLY, RANI," replied Mrs. Kimble, the Magistrate's wife, as she stood up to arrange the folds on her dress, "you've only seen him once and that, too, on his way to work. Is that reason enough for you to marry the man? How annoyingly, unthinkably impossible."

"I am sorry to cause you anger, Memsahib," faltered her little Indian maid.

"On the contrary, Rani, you amuse me exceedingly. Of course, you can take a week off your work. But tell me—is this one of those exquisite little 'arranged marriages?' What kind of marriage is yours going to be?"

Mrs. Kimble anticipated an amusingly naïve reply. She was constantly being amused in this rich peculiar land of the Orient. She was, in fact, becoming more and more certain that beneath the widely acclaimed spirituality of the East there was a painfully stupid core of unreality. And today she was going to prove this to Rani.

"Tell me," she coaxed, with her usual condescension, "what kind of marriage is it going to be?"

With a quickness that shook her Memsahib's complacency for a moment, the little brown maid replied composedly, "I do not know how many kinds of marriages there are in Memsahib's country, but in this country there is only one kind—I know that my parents have chosen wisely for me and that after my marriage I will become a new person. I will become responsible for the lives of my children and of their father. I will . . ."

As she searched for words that would adequately express her deepest feelings she rolled her large dark eyes from side to side—to the extreme amusement of Mrs. Kimble. "I will begin to grow up," she ended abruptly.

"A fine time to grow up in," echoed her mistress with a hollow laugh. "You should grow up before that—you should know all about life and the man you are to marry. In fact, you've got to be well aware of what you're going in for—mutual love and understanding should be established by both parties, with as little interference as possible from parents or from any other quarter. That's how I married the Sahib, and I couldn't be happier."

Rani's eyes grew contemplative. Her marriage was not going to be any less happy than the Memsahib's. She buried her head in her hands for a few minutes. Then slowly she began:

"Memsahib, to us marriage is like boiling water; our love is at first like cold water which when put to the boil gradually gathers heat and becomes hotter and hotter; it begins to simmer and finally to boil—it is a long, slow, and sure process. But with Memsahib all this is done before marriage, so that after marriage there is nothing left to happen and the water becomes cold again."

Rani rubbed her hands with glee at this brilliant analysis of the two customs that she had so successfully completed.

Mrs. Kimble was further amused. Remarkable how the natives managed to explain themselves away so logically. But her humour soon gave way to vexation.

"In our case your boiling water process is done before in order to get a clear idea of how much water we are to boil, in how big a saucepan and at what temperature. And once we're married nothing can easily go wrong; the water is sure to boil. And there's nothing to stop us from re-boiling the water is there? The water, therefore, does not become cold," she concluded with a definite toss of the head.

Perplexity distorted the little Indian's face—if only Memsahib would speak slowly—she could not understand all of what she said. Anyway she must go home and ask Maa all about it.

Mrs. Kimble, taking the girl's silence for submission, was about to begin again when the door flew open and her mother burst in.

"Margaret, where's George?" she asked, panting.

"At court, Mother; where else, of course. I don't see him off to work in the mornings. The heat doesn't allow me to get out of bed that early. But Mother, what's the matter—you look so . . ."

"Margaret," said her mother, gripping her by the shoulders, "he's run away with the young Canadian widow—the town is full of talk about it—even the natives. Rani, don't just stand there—help Memsahib to her room."

Perhaps Memsahib did not make quite sure of her water, her pot and the fire. Perhaps she will have to start all over again with a new pot, thought Rani sorrowfully as she helped her mistress up the stairs.

Proscovia Rwakyaka
The Beard

In the pulpit he swayed and turned.
Leant forward, backward,
To the right: to the left.
His solemn voice echoed;
Lowly the congregation followed,
"Do you love your neighbour?"
Meekly they bow at his keen eye
Now examining a grey head
Heaving under her sobs.
His heart leapt assured—
"Her sins weigh on her!"
So with her he chats outside;
"Weep not, child, you are pardoned."
"But sir, your beard conjured up
The spirit of my dear goat!"

Nathaniel Obudo

They Stole Our Cattle

THE EVENING that ended the day was fine. So fine was it that the moon that was already well up in the sky at the position of the sun at three o'clock in the afternoon, did not allow darkness to occur after sunset. It was thrilling and inspiring weather. It was our habit—my elder brother, my bachelor uncle and I—to go honey-hunting in the river bank bushes which were about half a mile away from my home. This very evening was just another suitable one for us.

We therefore milked a handful of cows, had a light preliminary supper of *uji* and packed for the night-hunt. My uncle had already spotted the previous day several hives along the river banks in hollow trunks of trees. So rather than going to hunt, we went to the bees' honey. In the dark quiet of the river night, where the rolling and unceasing noise of the water is part and parcel of the silence, we cut the tree trunk and awoke and alerted not only the hive dwellers, but also the birds and the other slumbering eyes of the night. We even stemmed the traffic of the night wild cats that went to hunt the dozing wild birds in the trees and the domestic birds in the huts and granaries. Soon, however, we reached the wax and then the tiers of combs and the honey beneath. We robbed and robbed and filled our basin and basket with honey—white honey, brown honey, liquid and solid honey. We quickly and quietly made off for home, but ate the honey the while.

At home, our parents and little brothers and sisters waited awake and anxious. We arrived and placed the honey at their disposal, and they placed our real supper around an open fireplace in the courtyard for us to enjoy. This we did with zest and soon all of us fell asleep where we ate, as if intoxicated by the honey or the food or a combination of both. But soon we woke with heavy half-closed eyes and groped our way to the cottage—that far-off and lonely house prescribed by custom for the young and the old unmarried male members of a family—to resume the sweet sleep that the sweet honey had coaxed. The weight of the resumed sleep lay so heavily upon us that the devils or the night-runners could, without heed, carry us many miles away from the cottage without our stirring.

But all the while, the many thousand eyes of the night, eyes that are keen and sinister and invisible, observed every movement, every action and every intention of the honey robbers and consumers. They projected their telescopic eyes from within the thick hedge of my father's circular home. They saw my elder brother and my bachelor uncle milk our fat cows and safely put them into the circular thorny-hedged kraal. Then they observed in detail my skillful bachelor uncle back the kraal gate with small twisted and huge heavy poles. And with many eyes, they simultaneously saw me pull the stubborn calves and pen them safely in a nearby cot. How my blood runs down my body to this day when I imagine those sinister eyes on me! Then they saw my elder brother sketchily close the main home-gate. They also saw our bitch lie still and fast asleep after fully gorging herself with the heavy evening *uji*. Finally, they saw us slip away through a secret opening in the hedge of the home. With all the vantage and strategic points noted, they lay and waited with breathless patience. They waited for us to return to eat and to fall fast asleep, and then they attacked.

II

Then, as my grandmother used to relate to me the tactics and traditions of nocturnal stock theft, the attack began by occupying strategic and key points. In the glaring moonlight with glittering spears and quiverfuls of arrows and taut bows, two of them paced and crouched near my father's house, one at the door and one at the window; one with gigantic steps went and squatted at my granny's door; two moved and stood like the king's gate watchmen at the sides of our cottage door, for therein slept and snored the would-be warriors; two stood and surveyed, now the kraal gate which they guarded, now the whole circumference of the home, then the positions of their spears; two eagle-eyed muscular valiants dexterously, quickly but noiselessly opened the gate and laid the poles at safe distances one from the other; two with magic hands and magic whistlings patted and soothed the bulls, cows, bullocks and heifers that had grown suspicious and prepared to "mboo" for their young companions in the cot and two kept close surveillance at the main gate for any would-be intruder and laid it open for passage. It was all quiet. The night was theirs, even the home and its entire contents. But the bright and brave glaring moon persistently stared at them and witnessed their deed from start to finish.

The kraal gate was open. The cattle came out. They moved in a cavalcade towards the wide open gate. All of them, large and small, oxen and all. Yes, I can see them go. I can see our milkful, hornless cow, Gumo, go; and with her all the milk, the sweet fat milk that was our delight went. Yes, even now I can see our fat, tame and friendly oxen that used to carry me on their backs when I was tired of walking in the pasture, the oxen that with ease and comfort pulled the biggest of the ploughs, and furrowed many furlongs of untilled land of the village and beyond, all went. No more would they return and turn the soil, nor yield the milk that nurtured the hand that has scribbled the tale.

Did they all go for good or for ill? No. Happily, no, for scarcely had they gone a mile when a ululating alarming noise awakened my father, then our cottage, and finally the whole home. Granny and all the females within joined in the ululation which soon leapt from mouth to mouth and from home to home until the whole village was awake. Gumo had felt estranged and remembered her young one and the loved ones and had run a hundred yards' race with and outstripped the thieves. Wildly and madly she galloped and "mbooed" past the house of one watchful woman who knew her voice so well. She responded by the ululating alarm which brought all the half-dressed men of the village madly but stealthily chasing with shields and spears and dogs. They chased and chased for eight long miles to the Lango's border. They groped through bushes and thickets between villages and on highways from midnight to morning, but all to no avail. They had gone. All had gone except Gumo. She alone returned and remained to tell the tale of the departed and

to comfort the calves and the fond-of-milk youth of the home. They
had stolen our cattle.

My father, after the long fruitless night-chase, falteringly walked
to the police station at the border of the Lango and the Luo. There
he reported what had come to pass the previous night, with these
words he reported and departed:

"They stole our cattle."

Joe de Graft

The Avenue: N.Y. City

Shapes of men
> Caught-rivetted spread-eagle-wise
> In toils of steel girders
> Scraping skywards into the sun.

Souls of men
> Trapped-lost blind-mouse-like
> In a maze of asphalt channels,
> Rat-racing round the clock.

Man
> The city builder

Man
> The world girdler

Man
> The rejected prayer.

Lull-a-Dirge

Don't cry, baby,
Sleep, little baby;
Father will nurse you,
Sleep, baby, sleep.

Lonely bird flitting away to the forest so fast,
Gold-speckled finch, your feathers wet all fading,
Tell me, shivering bird, have you seen her—
Have you seen my crying baby's mother?

> She went to the river at early dew,
> A pot upon her head;
> But down the water floats her pot,
> And the path from the river is empty.

Shall I take him under the palm
Where the green shade rests at noon?
> Oh no, no, no,
> For the thorns will prick my baby.

Shall I take him under the giant bombax
Where the silk-cotton plays with the wind?
> Oh no, no, no,
> For the termite-eaten bough will break
> And crush my little baby,
> My little sleeping baby.

The day is long and the sun grows hot,
So sleep, my little baby, sleep;
For mother is gone to a far, far land—alas!
She is gone beyond the river!

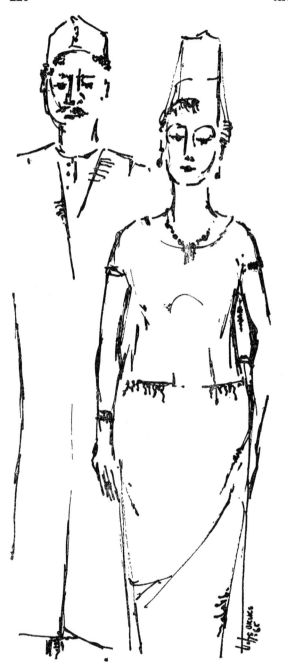

Joseph O. O. Okpaku

Under the Iroko Tree

THE PATH that ran through the thick equatorial forest was narrow, slightly winding and seemingly endless. She was about fifteen years old then, Aramikpojehele was, slim and beautiful. She was barefoot and her clothes, which were barely more than rags, clung to her half naked body as the breeze blew gently about her in a futile effort to conceal the rest of the figure. In the pit of her right arm she carried a tattered bundle, pressed tightly against her sweating skin. As she continued at a steady and apparently indifferent pace down the forest path, farther and farther away from us, it grew increasingly difficult for our curious eyes to penetrate the outer shreds that wrapped the bundle. It was flimsy and broken. True. Its content was obviously trivial, certainly. And hardly worth our curiosity, precisely. But what was it?

As we followed her from behind down the narrow path paved by fallen leaves from the huge trees whose branches overhung the endless road, shading it from the direct strokes of the soothing sun, the sound of music arose in the infinite distance—come, it seemed, to soothe our frustrated curiosity. The music was soft, delicate and with a definite touch of loneliness—distant, piercing, biting, yet soft, soothing and—delicate. It was audible enough to have its distinctive effect, yet too distant to be distinguishable. At times it sounded like a shepherd boy and his bamboo flute—far from his childhood friends, yet surrounded by and deeply immersed in the companionship of his immediate playmates. He knew each individual sheep not merely by name nor just by the subtle characteristics of its voice, but by its very breath—its essence. But just when we were beginning to work ourselves into the intellectual frenzy of speculating on the meaning and profundity of the particularities of this little boy's responses, we decided with conviction, though arbitrarily, that as a shepherd boy, one with a flute, and one playing that kind of music—he had to be a little boy. Just then, it became obvious from the sound, now risen slightly higher—thanks to the increasing wind, that it certainly could not be a little shepherd boy; not even a shepherd boy at all, and certainly not the sound of a bamboo flute.

Aramikpojehele continued to walk away from us and we continued to follow, as the vibrant voice, rising and falling and often drawn out in a piercing but soothing wail, continued to flow past us, raised delicately on the travelling crests of the gentle breeze that blew past us from the infinite distance behind, and continued its endless journey to the infinite distance beyond. As we slowly increased our pace in order not to lose sight of our slim and beautiful fifteen-year-old traveller along the path, we began to engage our brilliant intellects once more, or rather they began to engage themselves once more, in another sophisticated exercise of delicate subtleties, convinced this time that the sound was unmistakably that of a Moslem cowherd, philosophising in song with the accompaniment of his delicately stringed Kora. Of course! That infectious Kora. That enchanting sound. Of course! And so, like the cows to the herd, but with the very opposite of their unpretentiousness, we hurried after Aramikpojehele, riding the high crests of yet another arbitrary conviction.

Uya was eighty years old then—the sweet old slave—and he seemed to be wandering about as he plucked a single leaf from the little plant that stood nearby. His mind was very far away, far from that leaf, as he toyed with it for a long time and then absent-mindedly tore it to shreds in a slow, excruciating manner. He held the pieces in his hands. They began to drop one by one through his fingers into the carpet of leaves on which he sat still looking before him into the distance behind, into some unknown distant past—some distance unknown to us.

As if to complement the prevailing pathos, Onejuwa paced about restlessly in the shade, rather dejected. Once, he walked slowly into Uya's inattentive hands, brushed against his old legs now spread out, especially at the knees to let him in, and brought his face inquiringly close to that of the slave. Uya dropped the last few pieces of the shredded leaf and stroked and patted his companion—or rather the sharer of his solitude—with deep but absent-minded affection. All this time, he still looked straight before him into some distance we could not comprehend. All was very quiet and, as the writers say, you could hear a pin drop. But in that forest on that bright late morning, as the dew rose up from the innumerable leaves that basked flirtatiously in the caressing warmth of the sun, it was obvious, at least so it seemed, that pins did not belong in that pagan world where fronts, tailored or engineered, were an absurdity. The sun penetrated the sheltering high umbrella of branches and foliage in separate, almost tangible shafts, producing the inevitable impression of a mist that sprouted from the thick undergrowth calculatedly to enshroud the circumstances in a soft and delicate haze that blurred our perception.

Yet it was true. The look of things. You could hear a pin drop. That is, if you brought it there and dropped it. But even then, one wondered how much sound the tiny little metal, despite all the milling and manufacturing, could force out of the massive solidity of that earth and brush and the numerous, seemingly blunted thorns that towered elegantly into the yet uncontaminated air. All was quiet, except for the subdued tune of the breeze as it whistled heedlessly through the leaves and branches and continued unperturbed on its endless journey. From somewhere in the far but perhaps not unnegotiable distance came the rhythmic, brisk, measured and relentless tap-tap of a woodpecker at work, marking the only incorruptible time for our misguided present. It was precise. It was perfect. And lest we forget to relate it, it was as penetrating as it sounded clear, as biting as it was musical. Foreboding, ill-ominous. Frightful. Absurd.

And from somewhere above, high up in the distant branches, came the sweet melody of a self-satisfied little bird, serenading, so it seemed, the sleep-walk of our passing times. No one knows if she did, but if the delicate little thing had looked down through the outstretched limbs and the carefully scattered leaves of the huge tree, she might have known, as none of us could, that she was part of the select perception of that old man, seated, maybe squatted, or perhaps just perched, far below in the clearing, at the foot of that gigantic masterpiece. Five parts. Five parts to his select perception. Besides the frightfully ill-ominous tick-tock of the not indifferent woodpecker that marked the warrings of our times; besides the lazy, breezy, sing-song of the seemingly crazy little bird that detachedly accompanied our blinded progress; these things filled the life of the old slave: Onejuwa, now brushing against him, now pacing about restlessly, now stopping in front of him, walking into the hands unconsciously stretched out to receive him, now looking deeply and without blinking into the old man's steady eyes, as if inquiring—inquiring into something we may never know. The other two were in the distance, one in the past—imperceptible, and incomprehensible, and the other, into some physical essence, somewhere in the physical distance, tangible, perceptible and comprehensible.

And so, as Onejuwa slowly, nonchalantly, but not carelessly walked up dejectedly to the little plant that stood a foot or two from the slave's left hand, the Old One continued his absent-minded contemplation. Onejuwa confronted the little offshoot and stared inquiringly at it for some time. Then, very slowly at first, but with increasing speed, energy and ferocity, and yet without the slightest tinge of hostility, he started to scratch and dig. First the leaves, and then the soil around the plant. As the soil flew into the fresh and exhilarating air, bathed in the brilliance of the late morning sun, Uya, still immersed in the contemplation of his five-piece communion, sat in the only place where peace was possible for him. He sat and longed for the return of his peace of mind in that clearing, sheltered by nature from which he was indistinguishable, being one with it, here, in the shade, under the iroko tree. Five parts and one old slave, fighting calmly but desperately to protect their one humanism. Six in all, sheltered by the massive iroko tree. Gigantic, imposing, majestic, and contrary to expectation, calm and peaceful in the self-assurance of its indestructibility.

II

Three-thirty-seven A.M. The room was still quite dark. But being that time of the year when the sun herself found it difficult to stay in bed, some light streamed in through the plain and colourless drapes. Enough light to reveal a figure on the bed asleep. An attractive ebony bust stood on the bedside table, between an electric alarm clock and a bedlamp. On the wall, just above the headboard, a highly decorated mural of Morocco leather hung from a nail.

The sun rose higher, casting more light on the sleeping face; and as the figure rolled and tossed in bed, a man's voice, soft and only barely audible, could be heard whispering to itself. "A story perhaps, but not just any story. Not the heaviness of philosophy, nor the complexity of rhetoric. But something less crude, something soft, as a whisper of a child, smooth as his gentle breath, clear and without blemishes. A voice as clear and sparkling as the tiny little droplets that fall off the tip of a delicate reed, lingering for an extra second or two in the spotlight of the afternoon sun, to show off their purity to the last few stragglers on the human trail, before dropping down to join the rest of the spring water from which they were first diverted. As for the spring, what a pity that it must finally splash on the rugged rocks below or be blown and scattered in the inevitable storm of our lives."

The room brightened up as the sun continued to rise outside and the light streamed in, diffused through the drapes. Now visible in the increased light was a pair of handmade leather slippers on the floor by the bed, sitting on a black and white Colabus monkey skin.

"No matter how much I try," continued the voice, "I just can't sleep. One should normally welcome ideas, I guess, but this is more than a visit.

The urge for something sweet—something beautiful." It paused, hesitated, and then slowly, as if waiting to pick up the echo of each word before proceeding to the next, it confided in itself. "Every artist has one special dream—to create something soft, pure and delicate as a snowflake."

There was enough light in the room now to distinguish the form on the bed, although the details were still hidden in the soft shadows of the early morning sun. The man was about twenty-three years old. His face was attractive but not boyish; soft, yet very masculine.

"Memories of childhood days: vivid, lucid and thrilling. How they bubble up from the deep unblemished depths of a long forgotten simplicity. How they startle present consciousness—distorted by the strains of our cultivated times."

On the dresser stood a picture of the man at age five or six. "All right. Whatever your reason for keeping me awake, you win. I'll try a few lines for you, sweet childhood, but promise not to blame me if I fail to achieve your profound simplicity. It's been a long time now, and I've since outgrown your truth and your vision."

Rubbing his eyes, stretching and then waking up, he rose, pulled out a six yard piece of Dutch print wrapper from between his sheets and wrapped it round his waist to cover most of his pajama pants. He looked at the clock, stepped into his leather slippers and started towards the washroom.

"Ours was a rather small family, ten girls and four boys, besides Grandma, Auntie, Uncles and Aunts and a number of cousins—and their children too. You couldn't say it was a lonely household . . . or lonesome either. But that is another story."

As he bent over the sink and collected running water in his cupped hands to wash his face, he continued to hear the voice.

"It is almost four o'clock. Soon the cock will crow. And the sleeping world around will begin to wake up again."

The man stretched and yawned.

"First it will stretch and yawn, rudely polluting the fresh air which makes it possible for me to remember you now."

And as he dried his face with a towel, the voice continued, "Soon it will grow noisier and more unbearable as it powders over its dirt." He coughed and spat into the toilet bowl. "Cursing obscenely for having to wake up to the dawn of another day in the cycle of our meaningless

He took another quick face rub on the towel. As he flushed the toilet and walked back into the room the voice was more persistent now than boredom."

ever before. "Then it will rush madly out of door to execute its practised act of living once again."

He could still hear the sound of the flushed water, gushing and loud. At the wardrobe, he took out a blue blazer with a high school crest on the breast pocket—a ship in yellow—and put it on over his pajama shirt and the wrapper as he walked into the living room, which was simple but tastefully decorated with some more African art pieces. There were a couple of foot rests on the floor. A miniature talking drum hung from one of the walls. He put on a record, took some paper from the shelf and went to the dining table which doubled as a desk. Putting on the lamp, he sat down, yawned a bit, thought another bit, yawned for a third bit, this time tapping his lower row of teeth with the head of his ballpoint pen and then resumed his contemplation. Finally he bent over the pile of writing paper, hesitated, yawned again, stretched out his right hand as if to relax it, and then began to write.

Oct. 21, 1966
3:45 A.M.

His pen poised on the first line. The sound of the record grew louder, curiously revealing itself as a very familiar tune, like a shepherd boy on his bamboo flute. Or perhaps a Moslem cowherd accompanied on his kora.

"There were sixteen of us and more in the family," he began to write, "ten girls and four boys, besides my mother and father. And we all lived in Grandma's compound, with Grandma herself, our aunt and uncle, and their children.

"There were seven buildings in Grandma's compound, at least that's what there were at that time. Two faced Itsekiri street, or rather had their backs to it, for Grandma never liked to have any house face the street. They all looked inwards, opened onto the centre of the compound. They faced each other, in one whole communion of fellowship. One of these houses, a concrete bungalow, was the family house. The other was a one-story five unit mud apartment building with a thatched roof. Ordinarily, the thatch kept the rain out rather efficiently, and, together with the mud walls, kept the house pleasantly cool even on a particularly hot day.

"At the far end of the compound, partly hidden by the kitchen building in the centre of the yard, was another apartment building, concrete this time, with a corrugated iron roof. I had three rooms and parlour units with a pantry attachment at the back of each. Another mud and thatch apartment house lined the right side of the compound, opposite the family house, with the family kitchen in between, and between this and the concrete triplex was another kitchen built to serve most of the tenants.

"Grandma's bakery stood alone at the bottom of the compound, parallel and with its back to King's Street, the road that led straight up to the Catholic mission school and church a block away. It used to be exciting, Sunday after Sunday, to sit out on the outside verandah of the family house, between the bakery and the artesian well that stood near the intersection, and watch the flood of early worshippers pour out of the mission in their Sunday best. The littlest babies perched conveniently on their mothers' backs, clutched mischievously their poor parents' gold trinkets and threatened to break the delicate hooks that held them together. The small girls toyed dangerously with their expensive earrings and lockets under the watchful eyes of mothers who knew only too well the frequency and pain of having to search the sand and grass on the roadside for missing pieces of gold. There was a goldsmith in Grandma's compound, I'm sure he didn't mind.

"As for the boys, they had greater fun mimicking the priest as best they could, without seeming any less holy—and they pelted their fathers, if they were ever along, with all sorts of questions about the sermon—which was incomprehensible Latin—and the mannerisms of the reverend father—the standing and kneeling, the buzzing and mumbling, the bells and the smoke, the smell, the general magic and conjuration. Needless to say, the poor parents could hardly carry on a meaningful conversation amongst themselves, not with all the attentions and interruptions.

" 'Mama, tie my shoes.—No, not that—this—it is too tight. It isn't tight enough—No. No. No. Papa, tie my shoe for me.' On the verandah, watching the flood roll by.

"Many years later, whenever home on vacation from boarding school, the flood continued to flow and the spectator still took his weekly count. But with a difference. With Papa's bicycle nearby at hand, ready to go into active duty anytime. And with a few friends gathered to increase the watch, one part of the crowd was singled out for intense scrutiny. The girls. Somehow, high school girls on vacation had an obsession for going to church. We really couldn't care less about their souls, nor for they themselves either. But if they felt compelled to parade before our expert eyes, it was our Christian duty to pay attention, to judge, to respond. And we did. We checked each one out. Some we ruled out as outright ugly. If ugly and yet 'humble' we let them go. But if 'pompous' in spite of their looks, we allowed them a bit of our honest opinion, as we consulted with each other in loud whispers.

"There were those to whom we were indifferent. We had a hundred points distributed over various qualities, fifty for static beauty, how they looked, and the other fifty for dynamic beauty, what they did with their bodies as they moved them past our judges' stand on the verandah, as they covered ground on what was supposed to be public thoroughfare.

"We hated to see the girls walk in groups, unless they were just the right number as we were because it was always easier to take a cold shoulder from a single uncooperative stranger. As long as there was nobody else around to bear witness to it, you could always deny it. One thing we always prided ourselves with, that no girl walked either of those two streets, King's Street and Itsekiri Road, without missing her steps. No, not under the scrutiny of our penetrating eyes, fixed so powerfully and unrelentingly that even the most superfluously clothed must have felt naked.

"But all that was many years ago. I think of Grandma's compound now. Sometimes it comes back in vivid and detailed recollections. Sometimes it doesn't seem to come at all, except in vague and blurred inaccuracies. But Grandma, how can I forget her? I dream of her everyday. And even when I'm awake she keeps coming back to me, like the irrepressible vision of my vanquishing humanism. Inextinguishable. Indestructible. I'll be back soon, Grandma, back to the warmth of your command. And when I return, I shall place my ears on that throbbing heart once more and hear it beat again. Then I will heave a sigh and say . . . What will I say, Mama?"

Grandma was sixty-five years old then. That was eighteen years ago, six or seven years before I went away to boarding school, that is, six or seven years before I qualified to join the "students" on the verandah without the constant threat of being told "what is this small boy doing here? Go inside. These things are not meant for your ears." Grandma was quite strong and healthy. She always preferred to do her own shopping, accompanied by one or more of us. And her cooking too—she was very particular about that. It's been many years now. Who knows how energetic she still is, how particular. But she must still be the same in spite of time. It is hard to believe that she would be otherwise. That would be someone else. Not Grandma.

This day was like any other. Auntie was away at work in the hospital. She was a midwife, about forty years old and very attractive. Grandma was cooking in the family kitchen. The children were away to school.

Grandma finished cooking and as she crossed the compound towards the family house carrying the pot of soup in her hand, Auntie arrived after an exhausting morning duty which had lasted into the mid-afternoon.

"Mama, you should have waited for me to come carry the pot in."

Grandma stopped and turned. "Are you back? How come you closed late today?"

"Just as I was handing over the ward, they brought in a boy who had been knocked down by a bicycle."

"He wasn't seriously injured I hope?"

"Just bruised his skin."

Grandma sighed and started to walk towards the house. "I have told these children not to play on the streets, especially . . . Never mind."

Auntie dropped her boar skin handbag and offered to carry the pot.

"You will soil your uniform," Grandma protested.

"It does not matter. I can always wash it."

Reluctantly, Grandma yielded her pot to Auntie who started to carry it in while Grandma picked up the handbag.

"Do you think I'm too old to carry a pot?"

"Am I too old, either?"

"You are educated. Those who go to school, I'm told, do no menial tasks. Isn't that so?"

That was Grandma all right. Teasing, kneading, but always pleasant and loving, even in her worst moods, which were rare.

Auntie entered the house, followed by Grandma. But at the steps that led up to the verandah, Grandma stopped, hesitated, then turned around and walked down past the space between her bakery and the family bungalow, along the edge of the verandah to the outside of the compound. She shut the artesian well which some forgetful tenant had left open in spite of Grandma's persistent warnings that it was dangerous for the children who played around the compound. That well was a good thirty feet deep and in case of a mishap only a miracle could save even an adult. And Grandma didn't believe in miracles—not enough to be willing to test their validity—not with the life of any of her grandchildren. Sometimes she felt compelled to put a padlock on it as a subtle reminder to the tenants. But, kids as we were, we always found some key for our favourite amongst the tenants whenever Grandma was away, only to be incriminated by either some careless tenant who splashed water all around the wall— enough evidence for Grandma—or some greedy ones who, in spite of our angry protest, insisted pleadingly (stupidly, we also thought) on fetching just that last bucket of water—just in time for Grandma to return and, in anger, empty all they had drawn and threaten to punish us for giving the tenants the keys. If neither of these two faults implicated us, there was always some unscrupulous tenant who would, later on that day, plead with Grandma to be allowed to fetch just one bucket. And if she refused on the grounds that allowing one tenant access she would have to allow all the others for reasons of being impartial, the tenant would innocently ask: "How about those you allowed this morning?"

Surprised and irate at the false accusation, Grandma would fume, "Who? Me? Who?"

"I won't call names." Then, looking at us as if sorry for his or her blunder, the tenant would drive his or her calculated point home. "Perhaps, eh," glancing at us, "perhaps it was not you. I must be making a mistake."

Grandma knew better than that. And we did, too. We were in the soup. There was no deceiving ourselves about it.

And so Grandma continued on to the edge of the gutter that separated the compound from the road and looked up Itsekiri Road as far as she could see. It was a normal afternoon street scene—houses, people, bicycles, a hawker or two, a few parked cars and some children screaming and laughing as they rushed for the lime fruit they improvised for a football. One car, an old derelict Vauxhall with a beat-up body, was heading down towards Grandma, trailed by, or rather enshrouded in, the cloud of exhaust fumes that told its sufficient tale.

"I can't see them. School was supposed to be out an hour ago. I hope they have not been playing on the road. God!"

Just then, the mass of clanking junk roared past her at a surprisingly high speed. Grandma stepped back and sniffed and fanned before her nose with her hand as if to blow away the stuffy, suffocating pollution left behind.

"When such madmen cruise the street—Voom! Voom! Voom!—as if once they have a car that's the end of the world. How can the children be safe?"

After the air had cleared a little, she looked out again and saw some school children approaching in the distance.

"That looks like Angie, but what of—"

"Mama!"

"I've warned you not to startle me," Grandma swung around.

Onieyone was six years old then, of light spirit and a sure teaser, without being malicious or obnoxious. "Joker," that is what Auntie called him, but Papa preferred "rascal." Whichever one, it was an endearment, that's what mattered. His school uniform of brown khaki shirt and knickers was stained with mud, apparently from playing football in the rain. One of his suspender straps hung loose against his side. He gripped his slate, which had hitherto been on his head, in his left hand as he ran away from Grandma's pursuit.

"Onieyone, are you making an old woman run?"

He stopped, turned and walked cautiously back towards Grandma. As a "sedative," he turned his smile on at maximum charm. But, just in case that did not work, he held his slate slightly above his shoulders, ready to slide it in her way in case Grandma decided to give him a good knock on his head.

"No," he said in answer to her question, and then quickly volunteered, "Mama, let me carry the bag for you."

As they walked back into the compound, Onieyone rattled off all he had learned in school that day, flashing back every so often to insert some minor detail he had omitted the first time through.

"Where are the rest?" Grandma asked.

"They are coming. They are behind."

That was true and Onieyone knew it. But it was not the whole story. That he also knew. A short while before, Onieyone, his older sister Angie, and his elder brother Sammy (whom they later nicknamed "Sparkle"), were walking home from school.

"We'll see how you intend to explain our lateness to Auntie," said Sammy to Angie, who as the eldest was charged with responsibility for anything that happened.

"Let nobody report me, O." Onieyone laid his position down the line, half pleading, half threatening, but all the time afraid in spite of his air of nonchalance.

"We won't have to as long as you report yourself." Angie was always master of the situation, at least in as much as it concerned her. She could hardly be ruffled. And it might be said without serious exaggeration that she had a not inordinate abundance of self-confidence. Perhaps, as the eldest of the children, she needed it if only because of the great sense of duty and responsibility she had to acquire at that early age.

"Remember you cannot tell a lie." Sammy was not a "joker," like his younger brother. But that too seemed to be in character with his role as the eldest son, the junior head of the family, the natural heir, by birth, to be *paterfamilias*. Such a responsibility demanded a certain soberness and seriousness, and even at that early age of eight his preparation for the demanding task seemed already to have been well on its way.

"That doesn't mean I have to tell all the truth," Onieyone stated categorically, smiling self-praisingly, as if he expected a rebuttal. As neither the firstborn nor the eldest son, he had practically no onerous natural responsibility. So why bother? But that did not make him care-free. It was not all that simple. The time was to come, after Angie and Sammy went away to boarding school, when, as the oldest child at home, he would have to assume both roles, as oldest child and oldest son AT HOME. When that moment approached, a year before Sammy left home, he waited until Auntie had finished her day's work and was relaxing on the verandah with Grandma. Counting on Grandma's support, he gently broke the prevailing silence with: "Auntie, don't you think it will be a good idea to have a servant in this house next year?" But that was several years after. At the age of six, it was still too early to be foreshadowed by a problem several years away.

"What will you do, then?" asked Angie. Onieyone held his forehead in his hand, in proper position for deep contemplation. "Let me see."

And so they walked home quietly, until the boss broke the silence.

"See if this works." He paused, raised his head, tightened his lips and took a deep breath. "If I get home before you, you will have to explain YOUR lateness," and he hesitated, doubting whether or not he should throw in the bonus explanation, "since, with respect to you, I shall be home early."

As they watched Onieyone run at full speed down the road towards home, Angie laughed, shook her head and said endearingly, "That boy is a devil."

"It is not funny." That was Sammy (who else could it be?). Firm, sober, but nonetheless respectful, for Angie was his elder sister; and no matter what the provocation, even if it had been from her rather than from the little rascal, that was something he always had to bear in mind. You just did not raise your voice to one older than you. It was straight-forward and simple, but sometimes very hard to abide by.

"Wait until he gets us into some serious trouble someday."

"He's a small boy," said Angie.

Nothing like a loving older sister, with the understanding of an experienced mother.

"Mama used to enjoy lying down on her raffia mat every afternoon, out on the open verandah."

As we began to hear the voice, Grandma came out of the house carrying a raffia mat in one hand. She walked down the verandah, past the first pillar and stopped. As she spread the mat out, she looked up at the sound of children's voices to discover Angie and Sammy entering the compound from the far end between the five-unit mud and the three-unit concrete apartment houses.

"If we returned from school," the voice continued, "and found her 'having fresh air'—that's how she always put it—we knew we'd come home late, too late to set up the mat and pillow ourselves. As for the consequences—it depended on two things, Mama's mood and our wits—O—a third—if we had visitors, but that really didn't help too much, it only postponed the punishment, for Mama never forgot anything unless of her own free will. One reason we feared to make Mama angry was because she knew precisely where her reprisals would hurt most. Her displeasure could mean no story-telling later that night, and THAT we couldn't bear."

As the children stooped to talk to Grandma, Onieyone, already changed into house clothes, came out of the house carrying a pillow for Grandma. As he approached the group, Sammy shook a threatening fist at him, but was restrained by Grandma's presence. Onieyone struggled with difficulty to hold back a mischievous laugh of triumph. Angie giggled. Just then, Auntie, now also changed into houseclothes, came out of the house, saw the look on Sammy's face and sensed some slight problem. As she walked towards them, spreading the film of her pleasant delicate smile to calm the troubled waters, Onieyone took refuge from Sammy's wrath by first standing behind Grandma and then running into Auntie's hands as soon as she was close enough. Auntie took Onieyone by the shoulder and scolded him mildly. Next, she went up to Sammy, placed her gentle touch on his head and tried to soothe his anger. It was only then, for the first time, that she began to question them in order to find out what the matter was. We were too far away to hear what each of them had to say. But from the choreography of the dance of their heads and limbs, it was convincingly clear that Sammy and Onieyone disagreed, or rather, that they had a difference of opinion, as Papa preferred to put it.

"Kai," Grandma called out after Auntie as she solved the problem by dropping the inquiry, and then walked off to the kitchen, leaving the children to give an account of the day at school to Grandma.

"Kai is mother's first name," the Voice explained. "We never called our mother by name, nor the elders either. It was unheard of. Not even our elder brothers and sisters, it would be the highest disrespect. Instead, we called them 'brother' or 'sister.' But in a family as large as ours you couldn't go about referring to everyone as 'brother' and 'sister' without seriously limiting the possibilities of being understood. But we tried, and had much success, unless when we failed. Anyway, we called our mother

'Auntie' and don't ask me why, it's a long story. Now, we couldn't call our aunt, 'Auntie' since our mother already occupied that title, so we called her 'sister.' That was a great help because with that position given away we now had ten sisters, none of whom we could call 'sister.' Not even one. As for our uncles and other elders, we referred to them by their children's names, always hoping that no two of them would name their children alike, which they in fact did. One uncle had a daughter named Ansaba, so we called him 'Papa Ansaba,' but our youngest uncle was not married and had no children either. So what could we call him? His first name was Kofi, so we called him 'Uncle Kofi.' Things got easier as our elder sisters grew up and got married, then we could refer to them by their children's names."

III

Several sheets of paper were neatly scattered all over. His hair was also scattered. The man's hair. The man in the high school blazer. His hair was dishevelled from being scratched and pulled in the physical act of contemplation. He was still at the table. The dining table that doubled as a writing desk. His pen was poised pensively at the beginning of a new paragraph. Clear, soft, delicate, pure, the sound of the old deceptive song, the pastoral tune. It continued to pour out of the twin speakers encased in their walnut cabinets. The pen rose slightly, quivered with melancholy, hesitated and then dropped down to resume its touching recollections.

"We called Grandma, 'Mama,'" he wrote, "because that's what our mother called her. That was the source of all the confusion." He smiled. "But it was part of the household fun, the confusion, I mean."

As he mused and dreamed longingly, the record ran out. He stopped writing, threw out his right hand a few times to relax the muscles, rose slowly and walked up to the record player. Holding his pen between his lips in order to free his hands, he picked up the record and replaced it with a Highlife disc. As the swinging rhythm, true to its name, filled the air, he paced the living room, rather exhausted. Finally, he dropped into the sofa to catch a few moments' rest. He tried to shut his eyes, but could not. It seemed the story he was wriing held an irresistible compulsion for him. He went to the kitchen and made himself a cup of Ovaltine. On the way back to the table, he attempted a sip which burnt the sleepiness out of his lips.

"Later on," he wrote, "we joined Mama once again out on the

verandah, on the raffia mat. There was room for all three of us who stayed up that late, and enough work to keep each of us busy."

It was late evening. Grandma was lying down on the mat, her head on the pillow. Angie, sitting at the pillow, was pulling hidden grey hair out of Grandma's predominantly black hair. Sammy, squatted behind Grandma, was scratching her back. Onieyone, between disturbing everyone else, fanned Grandma with a fan made out of hide and felt. This was specially made for Grandma by her younger brother, Omasa, and it had Grandma's name, "Usekpimi," inscribed on it in scraped hide and red felt, what the artisans called *ododo*. Once or twice Grandma had skillfully to protect her face with her hand to prevent its being swatted by Onieyone's overzealous fanning.

We heard the voice once more, as it started to say, "One of us searched for grey hidden in Mama's hair. That required expert skill. And another scratched her back, not so much that it itched, but because it felt good.

"On warm humid nights it was necessary to fan Mama too, and since that required the least skill—well, I enjoyed doing it. I was very good at it, so good, in fact, that hardly had I actually got going than she would stop me and either have me replaced or give up the pleasure entirely. I was too young to wonder why. Now I know. I was too good at it."

Grandma was still lying face down and Onieyone, after wiping his feet on a towel, tried to climb upon Grandma's back. He had great difficulty doing this, but finally succeeded by holding first onto Sammy's head, who shook him off, and then Angie's. After gaining his balance, clapping his hands in self praise (at which he momentarily lost his balance again), he walked up and down Grandma's back.

"I had other specialties, too," the voice said, "like massaging Mama's back. It's not very easy, using our method. But I assure you it worked very well, that is, for Mama [Onieyone lost his balance]. You know, the human back is not flat. Besides, it is alive, and as you step on any part of it, it gives way below you." [Onieyone almost fell off Grandma's back.] "But if you've got the talent," Onieyone clapped his hands and almost lost his balance again in so doing. "Well, that doesn't mean you can't slip once in a while, if only to reassure yourself that you're fallible, to reassure others that you're not God!"

The verandah light suddenly went on. Auntie came out of the house, sweater in hand, and walked towards the group.

"Da-aba," Auntie said to someone who had just walked in from the darkness.

"Eomi, Kai, Bonikon," the old man answered, barely audible. A very old man, about seventy-five, and clad in a white sheet over one shoulder, very much in Kente fashion, no shirt. He emerged from the night. Meanwhile, as he approached the group, Auntie was encountering some resistance as she tried to put a sweater on Onieyone. Angie, on seeing the old man, left and returned with a bench which she placed in position for him to sit on. When the visitor finally arrived at the verandah, all the children knelt respectfully before him, on both knees, all except Onieyone who tried to get away with only one knee. But he was caught in the old man's hands, a position he apparently would have gone on seven knees to avoid. He struggled and screamed while the others, including Sammy, laughed to their heart's content. Finally he was allowed to pay his respects on both knees, but the little scamp had his sense of humour. He tried to escape and was caught. Seeing that there wasn't much chance of having his way, not that night, Onieyone finally went down on both knees and hurried as fast as he could to take refuge in Grandma's hands.

Auntie, on one knee, and with her right arm held vertically up, supported at the elbow by the palm of the left, proclaimed the visiting elder's title.

"Orugbo! Mowale! Orugbo! I'm down."

"Kpiara," answered the old man in a firm voice that seemed to contradict his age. "Rise." And as Auntie rose, the voice could be heard, softly at first and then gradually growing more audible.

"Rise. Rise, my child." It paused. "Papa Edema was quite a man. We were all so very fond of him, the sweet old man. So close, in fact, was he to the family that he might as well have been one of it. Though he scared me at first"—and here the voice grew momentarily softer—"actually, it was that white sheet he wore, which made him look like a ghost." And whispering confidentially, "You would think I'd seen one." Then the voice rose. "Yet I grew to like him very much. Besides, he was my old tutor. Taught me many things. Even taught me how to grow money."

Onieyone's face lit up in the light of the verandah lamp as the voice gained excitement in its vivid reflection.

"Yes, money! He told me it would grow. And I believed him. God knows how many pennies I was given or earned by some good deed. In spite of my age I was very patient. I tilled the soil with my fingers. When the money tree refused to sprout he told me the budding treasure was thirsty. So I watered it every day. In fact, I kept it so moist I got into trouble with Mama. There was another reason, too: the money seed was competing with the household for drinking water. One day I finally grew suspicious. Actually it was because Sammy laughed at me. So I dug out the soil and you know, all my pennies were gone. Papa Edema reassured me that I had dug out the wrong place, so I tried again, but Mama, realizing that I would dig up the whole compound until I found my pennies, suggested to the sweet old chief that he had to come up with some better story or else be prepared to assume full responsibility for the destruction of her soil."

The voice was completely lost in the trance of sweet memory. It was like watching a midnight movie of one's past played back on the screen of one's innermost mind. Vivid, lucid, alive. And to have as narrator none other than one's own voice.

"So, one night, he quietly explained the mystery to me," it continued.

By this time Edema, seated on the stool, was holding Onieyone, who must have now changed his mind. His old wrinkled face brushed on the little boy's delicate skin.

"*'Weri-Ogho re-gun, Ururo jo kan ren ni ale keke ren ogba to be to ri die lefum quale. Weri?'*" That's what he said to me. "You see, your money has actually germinated. But the root travels a great distance underground before coming to the surface in a very distant place, far, far from here, you see?"

Of course, I said. How could I doubt the sage? So I ran up to Sammy, who was just then walking down the steps towards the kitchen. I knew I was too wise to be fooled, I said to him. After all, I was born with my head in my hand, so they told me, like a meditating philosopher. But I did not end there. There could possibly be no harm in rubbing it in, just a little bit. So I added, "He who laughs last, laughs best."

"Oh?" Sammy asked mockingly.

"My money has grown." I ignored his effort. "The root is travelling underground."

"And where will it surface?" he inquired.

That was a good question. In order to find a good answer, I held my head in my hand, as I always did when I needed to think seriously.

"Hm, let me see." Then it came like a flash. "I know," I declared. "He said in a far away place. Very far away."

Sammy looked at me as if I disgusted or at least bored him—or was it pity for me? Finally, as he walked off, he said simply, "You are a fool," and went his way.

Grandma and Edema shared a piece of kola nut. Edema rose from the stool and went to sit near Grandma's pillow while all the children shifted towards the foot of the mat where there was more space. From here they could see both Grandma's and Edema's faces. Their attentive faces beamed their tale through the shadow. The outside lamp behind them cast light upon their front view. The evening was well on its way, but the children were not close to being impatient as yet. They knew what they wanted and knew the best way to get the best of it. What was it they so calmly awaited in disciplined anticipation? Perhaps the voice knew.

"From as far back as I could remember until I went away to boarding school at eleven, like the others had done before me, never a night went by when Edema and Mama did not tell us stories, unless we didn't deserve it, or when Edema was too sick to join us. Even then, we would go with Grandma to visit him."

It stopped. All was very calm and quiet. Far away in the distance a lonely wind howled. As it drew nearer, a mood of delicate sadness pervaded the atmosphere. The voice started to speak, stammered, stopped, hesitated for a brief excruciating moment, quivered, sighed and then continued.

"He is dead now, dead and gone, but his stories live on, tales of childhood, tales you never forget, how could you? But Mama is still alive—wonderful Grandmother—and I'll see her some day. She told us stories, too, as often as Edema did. They alternated most of the time, but sometimes they each told us a story or two each night. They told of the tortoise, the wisest being alive, and how he cracked his shell and sewed it back together. They told of the hare—how swift. And of the snail—slow but calculating. The snail always managed somehow to win the race against the greedy dog. Yes, they also told tales of the dog—how he acquired a nose that's never clean, no matter how much he washed it. There where also stories of human beings, intriguing stories that explained many mysteries to us. Like that one night when they told us of how man came to have the grooves that run down their backs."

The voice, telling the naked tale of a longing, lonesome heart, yearning to grip a fast dwindling humanism, clinging to a dissipating sensibility.

Several records had since played themselves out. The Ovaltine, forgotten in the heat of creative passion, had now grown cold. The man continued to write furiously, almost frantically. And with no moment's pause, as if afraid that the slightest pause would break that rare momen-

tous gift of boundless imagination that took him for a creative cruise down
the hitherto inaccessible river of his past. Skipping words, leaving t's
uncrossed and i's undotted, and momentarily blocking out punctuation,
he drove his pen across the pages, left to right, back to left and then down
again, in an almost hopeless relay race to keep up with his fleeing
imagination.

"Tales of poor men," continued the voice, "tales of rich men. They
told of Kings and Princes. They told of common people. They told of
peasant girls—yes—yes." The voice slowed down as if yielding respectfully
to an older. "And of royal maids—of Princesses."

IV

"Mo kpa ghereghere mo kpa ni origo olaja okan." That was the moment the children had been waiting for. "I tell—tell—tell, I tell on the
head of a certain king."

*"Olaja woy kah ni ome onibiren okan. Ome wey kan jono sengua a
tey ri. Owaro ka kpay, 'Aramikpojohele.' Oma okan naka oloja wey ne.*
This king had a daughter, as beautiful as you ever saw. The king called
her 'Aramikpojehele. She was an only child."

But before any story was told, an offering, at least a verbal one, had to
be made to the spirits of our forefathers.

"Mo gbi obi gbi ata gba su okan," Grandma served. "I take kola nut
and some alligator pepper and throw them at the canoe." Grandma did
not need to share her kola nut with the spirits. As higher than human
forms, they existed in the non-material. They dwelt in metaphysical symbolism and Grandma was not one to begrudge them the sacrificial offering
of symbolic kola nut and alligator pepper. Having thus settled with the
gods, Grandma could now begin her story.

"This king had many slaves. At least thirty of them, not counting
their children and their children's children. Among the slaves was one
old man called Uya. Much had happened in his lifetime, and his countenance told his tale. Everyday when the sun stood vertically above and
the rest of the household was busy inside the palace, he would quietly
walk away out to the solitude of the backyard. There, all alone and deeply
engrossed in his recollections, he would hiss, shake his head and say to
himself 'Eyi Uya!'—'What suffering!'—and shake his head some more as

the thoughts of uncomfortable sorrows of a distant past revisited him with painful memories of long ago.

"Uya had only two friends: Aramikpojehele, his fifteen year old princess-pet whom he raised on folk tales and innumerable little anecdotes, and Onejuwa, the most faithful companion you ever knew. Day after day Aramikpojehele listened unnoticed to the lamentations of her precious old guardian. Finally she could no longer hold back her curiosity. She decided to find out what all this was about.

"So one day, when the sun was again directly overhead, Aramik-pojehele found her way to the palace backyard. There, as usual, she found the old slave sitting on the ledge of the base of the huge pillar. He hissed, shook his melancholy head, sighed and murmured to himself, 'Eyi Uya.' Aramikpojehele stole up quietly behind the dejected man and hid herself unnoticed at the back of the pillar which Uya used as a back rest. After a while, Onejuwa, who had accompanied Aramikpojehele, strolled in-differently into the open space in front of the slave. Though still deeply absorbed in his recollection, Uya gradually became aware of Onejuwa's presence. He unconsciously followed him with his eyes as Onejuwa walked back towards Aramikpojehele. When Uya discovered the girl, he was not startled but rather became actually conscious of her some moments after his eyes fell on her.

"Having thus been discovered, Aramikpojehele turned slowly and faced him. 'Kind one, what is Uya?' she asked.

" 'What? Why do you want to know?'

" 'Every day at noon you sit here alone, hiss, shake your head and say, "Eyi Uya!" '

"Embarrassed by this discovery by one so dear to him of what he had always held as the last little privacy of his inner life, Uya tried to brush the issue aside. Not that he believed she would understand if he were to encourage a dialogue on it, though he knew how meaningful it would be to both of them to share the feeling—the feeling, not the fact,—and there was some dialogue.

"Taking her in his hands he tried to change the subject. 'What did you do with your loose tooth?' he asked.

" 'I held it tight in my fist, ran round the kitchen three times and then threw it on the thatch roof. I did everything just like you told me.'

" 'Good girl. It will now grow back very quickly. You'll see.'

"He smiled at her. Something he had since forgotten how to do, except, of course, in those few moments every day when he, Onejuwa, and the girl were alone, all by themselves in the shade, deep in the forest, under the Iroko tree.

" 'But tell me, why do you always say, "Eyi Uya" ' Aramikpojehele seemed insistent.

" 'Because I am a slave.' Flat, matter-of-fact, painful.

" 'You are not a slave to me,' the girl protested. 'You are my friend.'

"He looked at her affectionately. Tears began to dangle and sway, suspended in his eyes.

" 'I don't care what the Queen says, I'll always be fond of you,' she said, as she put her arms around him and her face, in profile, against his body. 'Please tell me what it is.'

" 'You will never need to know Uya,' he declared like one who had the power of seeing the end of everything, no matter how blurred it might now seem. To him, much of the present was just in time, a passing phase. Deep in the invisible depths, was the solid strand of human life, imperturbable, indestructible. That was what mattered. That was what he saw. 'Suffering is for slaves, servants and common people, not for Kings or Queens or their sons and daughters.'

" 'Why?' " Aramikpojehele asked.

"The old slave paused. He hesitated. How he wished he had been more private with his inner passions, not that he regretted them. No. Not for Aramikpojehele. But he had a curious foreboding, a feeling, not a fact. But a feeling as valid as the fact, if not more so. And it was for her sake that he feared. Not for himself. What more could happen to that eighty year old slave that was not already part of him? Perhaps one: death. 'But death,' he would laugh to himself, 'why, what can that do to me?' But there was a question before him, and the child he loved waited to be answered.

" 'But why can't I taste of it, too?'

" 'Taste of it?' he laughed, but not in such a way as to embarrass her. 'What do you think it is, food?'

" 'Well!' She gathered her forces for a debate with her old tutor, 'You say *"Eyiuya ta je"* and *"ta je"* means *"that one eats,"* doesn't it?'

" 'O, yes, it is a food,' he seemed to capitulate. 'But not meant for kings.' He waited, his face drawn out like the tale of the past eighty years while she struggled to change her line of attack.

" 'By that look on your face I can tell you're deceiving me. It is not food. Please tell me what it is.'

" 'All right. It is not food. But it is not something one tells another. No words can tell a person what suffering is.'

" 'What is it, an object?'

"The foreboding under which he suffered took greater hold of him. 'I must stop this before it goes too far,' he said to himself. And taking her hands and looking straight into her eyes, very sincerely, very dearly, he said, 'Listen, child, this is not the sort of thing I should talk to you about. Your mother will be angry if she finds out what you now ask. The King may send me away, far, far away.'

" 'No, kind one, please?' Not that she was stubborn. No. But curious, perhaps.

" 'Why don't you go ask your mother?' he suggested.

" 'She won't tell me.'

" 'You won't know until you have tried.'

" 'And if she refuses to, will you tell me?'

" 'Go ask her first.'

"The princess began to withdraw, but turned around and walked back to the old slave. 'But how would she know? You said it is not something that king's wives know.'

"Uya was embarrassed. 'No, no, eh . . .'

" 'Isn't my mother my father's wife?'

" 'Of course. She . . .'

" 'Or is father not a real king?'

" 'Why, he is!'

" 'Then my mother does not know what Uya is.' Perhaps the old tutor should never have taught her logic.

" 'These things do backfire, don't they?' he said to himself. And after much reflection, he turned to her. 'Listen, just go ask her. If she won't tell you—hm . . .'

" 'I will come back to you.' She helped him come through.

" 'Hm . . . yes.'

" 'And you will tell me.'

" 'Just come back,' he said, 'and we shall see. You know, I'm getting old and can't think too well.' Weak. That was the smile he gave to her.

" 'You can never be too old.' She held him and played with him. 'Besides, I like you better than all the other slaves, even when you stand here all alone, talking to yourself and saying *"Eyi Uya ta je"* over and over again.'

"Uya smiled mildly and held out his hands for her. She ran into them and they embraced each other.

" 'Only the sweet little one remembers old Uya,' Uya whispered. 'I raised your father when he was a little boy.'

" 'He used to tell me that,' Aramikpojehele confirmed.

" 'Yes, but no more. He has forgotten me. A great King has no head for an old guardian. There are more important things to think of. I am now like a worn out dress. When I was bright and full of colour, I was worn all over the place and given the greatest care. Now I am old and withered, and who wants to wear a tattered rag?' He paused and pressed the Princess closer to him.

" 'Tell me, sweet one, what were you talking about?'

"He quickly tried to collect himself. 'Who? Me? When?'

"Aramikpojehele released her embrace and looked up at him. 'Just now.'

" 'Oh.' He hesitated. 'Nothing. Listen, why don't you run off and go ask your mother what Uya is?'

" 'All right.' She started to run off; but before she had gone very far, Uya called out to her, 'And listen.' She stopped. 'If your mother won't tell you, ask your father.'

" 'All right.' She resumed her exit. 'And if my father won't tell me I'll come back to you and you'll tell me.'

" 'Go try your parents first.' Uya struggled to hold off any commitment on his part, for he feared. He feared he knew not exactly what.

"The Princess turned and continued to hurry off. At the door that led into the palace, she turned, stopped, and called out to her aged friend, 'Kind One, I will never turn away from you, even when I become as old as you.'

"Uya smiled warmly at her through the tears in his eyes. As she finally disappeared, Onejuwa walked slowly in her direction, leaving Uya alone to come to terms with his wretched, yet noble, solitude. He dropped his head down into the interlocked hands that waited patiently on his lap and tried momentarily to go blank on the life that held him prey. He gave way to a few soothing sobs, something he, the proudest of men, would hardly have dreamt of doing even a few years before. But it felt good. It released, at least slightly, the dangerous pressure that had inflated his big indestructible soul. But there was no self-pity. No, just sorrow and anger. For self-pity was anathema, destructive to the self. And he, as nature, in being one with it, was indestructible.

"Uya was quite a man. Never was there any other like him. Never will there ever be. 'Self-pity,' he used to say, 'leads ultimately to self-

destruction. But sorrowful anger, to the exultation of the self. At its mean-
est and lowest, it precipitates only vengeance.'

"He heaved a sigh, the first since Aramikpojehele brought in the
only external joy to a heart that had since learned to suckle solely on its
inexhaustible peace of mind. 'The highest duty of the pagan,' he used
to add, 'is to enrich the humanism of the tribe, not to destroy it, and in so
doing, to enrich his joy and indestructibility, in the natural and irrevocable
commitment of the clan.' He raised his head and gazed through the filter
of his tears at the distance that stood naked before him. 'In the tribe,' he
once said, 'a man may wander and go his own way, as indeed he must.
But at the back of his mind, even when all seems to forsake him, is the
profound and deep knowledge that he belongs. He belongs to the tribe,
the tribe that is by nature irrevocably committed to care. And if and when
he chooses to return home, or simply drop by, he will find the entrance
to the hut always open; for the clan has never learned to build a door
with which to either shut themselves in or lock their own out. It is that
knowledge, always present, though he might be unconscious of it, that
sustains him even if he decides not to return. That is the source of his
indestructibility.'

"That afternoon, Uya's mind was laden with forebodings of the ills
that threatened to be, all because of the simple curiosity of a little girl.
Not that he had any reason to be uneasy, but he felt it nonetheless. And
for a man like him, that was as good as anything logic or reason could
suggest.

" 'There's no telling what trouble may arise from this innocent question,' he warned himself. 'I had better stay away from it. She must not
find me here when she returns.' Slowly and with difficulty, he bent down,
picked up his walking stick and stood up. As he began to walk away towards the forest that surrounded the palace, towards a path that was
barely more than a foot wide, he confided to himself what might have
seemed obvious to any who knew him well. 'I'd rather wait until the
spirits call than die disgraced, not that I have much longer to live.'

"And so Aramikpojehele took her question first to her mother and
then to her father. Neither of them would tell her, not that either of them
knew. So she ran back to the pillar and found the old slave gone. She
looked around for him, stopping now and then to think where he could
possibly be. Then she brightened up. 'I know where to find him,' she
said as she turned and started to walk down the path into the forest. But
all of a sudden she stopped. From the look on her face it was obvious that
she was very disturbed. As she stood there at the mouth of the forest path,

struggling to master the conflicting passions that raged within her, we could hear a voice from afar off. It was very faint at first, but it grew more audible as we become more conscious of it. The voice said, the same voice as before: 'But she also knew something else, her father, the King, had said she was never to enter the forest alone or in the company of any of the slaves.' Aramikpojehele paced up and down the entrance to the forest as she struggled to make up her mind.

"Once she had been unhappy and cried all morning because the Queen had insulted the sweet old slave. It had all started when one morning, after playing in the rain, she danced her way back within the walls. As she approached home, she saw Uya coming out of the palace, dejected, tears in his eyes. Supported by his walking stick, he walked past her, shaking his head in sorrow. As she turned to follow him, she looked up and saw her mother standing in the doorway. Her first thought was to defy her and follow him. But she knew he would not approve. Besides, she could not go too far anyway, not with her mother standing there in the doorway and looking sternly at her as if to say, 'Let me see you follow him, if you have three heads.' So angry that she had decided to obey, she walked slowly past her mother into the palace as if there were nobody in the doorway. All the time she kept her eyes on the old slave until he had disappeared.

"Aramikpojehele went to her room, you would have thought, to cry. But she was too proud for that, too proud to shed a tear for what she detested. She was angry. And in that mood, she waited for the right moment. It would come, she knew, since her mother was bound to keep the King company sometime in the early afternoon.

"Then, accompanied by Onejuwa, Aramikpojehele set out in search of their mutual friend. They looked everywhere around the palace walls, even in the backyard, by his favourite pillar. They could not find him. Finally Onejuwa sniffed the air, called Aramikpojehele's attention and started to go towards the forest path."

"The voice faded out. And as it did, Aramikpojehele slowly turned, having made up her mind, and resumed her search, followed by Onejuwa. Farther and farther away from us they trotted playfully down the winding path that zig-zagged through the forest.

Uya was sitting under the Iroko tree, lost in thought. A blade of grass hung loosely from between his lips. He sat like he had done for the past several hours. His hands on his knees, he looked straight before him—lost. Lost to a reality that was beyond our experience. He was in that same position when Aramikpojehele and her companion approached along the forest path. Onejuwa ran ahead into Uya's hands while the Princess tip-toed noiselessly up and hid behind the tree, behind Uya, behind the solidity that had so far sheltered her from the devastating forces of the wind.

"Onejuwa," the old slave said, "you must be very thankful for what you are."

Puzzled, that was the way to describe the look on Onejuwa's face as he tried to figure out the implication of the—compliment? It was very quiet, except for the faint sound of a distant nomad serenading his flock to a mid-afternoon siesta. The wind that bore the delicate tune blew gently by with no further message from the lonely cowherd except that it was cool where he was, lying down beneath a flame of the forest tree at the edge of an open field on which the cows had just finished grazing them-selves to sleep. As the wind caressed Uya's withered face, it enlivened the innumerable microscopic holes that life had dug on it—the indelible marks of unforgettable times. They had hitherto been invisible, to us at least, perhaps because they were lost in the shadow of the two large grooves that ran down his face, one on each side, unique emblems of life's untiring sculpture.

The old slave lifted his hands to his face. He rubbed his tired eyes. Burying his face in his hands, it was like submerging the pangs of an impossible pain in the symbolic gesture of lying flat, face down on one's pillow after a gruelling communion with an experience so excruciating as to make one wish simply to scream. "Eyi Uya," he sighed, shook his head and hissed. "Eyi Uya."

As he rose with difficulty, turning on his right side, he looked slightly upwards and discovered Aramikpojehele just as she herself began to move round towards him. He stopped briefly and then continued to rise, Aramikpojehele lending a helping hand. "Your father told you . . . ," he started to ask, his voice barely audible over the crackling sound of his grinding joints.

"No," Aramikpojehele cut in politely. But she was not pressing the issue; not for the moment. Him, that was all she cared about at that moment. Still slightly bent, Uya turned around facing forward as he looked for Onejuwa, stretching his hand out to him. Onejuwa, carrying his master's walking stick in his mouth, walked up to Aramikpojehele, who took the walking stick and put it into Uya's right hand. A bird whistled briefly a tune up in the branches of the Iroko tree. Then all remained quiet as the three began to walk back along the forest path, back towards the palace walls.

An owl cooed, seemingly half mockingly, but surely half frightened. Perhaps. And the woodpecker continued her tap, tap, apparently indifferent to the passing episodes of time. The voice was clear and audible from the start this time. Inspired perhaps by the woodpecker's nonchalance.

As they walked back to the palace, happy in their mutual sorrow, Aramikpojehele felt happy enough to raise the question again. But Uya would not tell—not that it was something one could tell. In vain she implored the old slave to explain "suffering" to her. Still as sweet as ever, for he loved her very much, he tried to make her understand that there were certain things one knew by experience alone, not by words. At that, she modified her request and, instead, now asked him to give her the experience of "suffering."

But this is Grandma's story.

It was much later in the night. The children were still very bright-eyed as they listened attentively to Grandma tell her tale. First Angie's face, then Sammy's. They shone through the darkness, lit more by the excitement of the story than by the weak light of the electric lamp that kept melancholy watch over the enshrouded seven-piece compound.

One other face, Onieyone's, was covered with the sweater he was mischievously trying to pull off. Two hands reached over and pulled the sweater back down, revealing the rascal's face with a look of puerile anger. Eyes upwards, he traced the intruding hands to their owner, Edema.

Grandma's voice was still clear, strong and compelling in spite of what by then must have been some two hours of story-telling. Meanwhile the voice faded out as it came to. *"Kekerem ojo okan, tegba nemi gba juwere, Uya ka gin gba . . ."* So, one day, when he could no longer hold out against the endless pleas of the little Princess, Uya capitulated, much against his will.

In eager expectation the children leaned forward, all except Onieyone, who was involved in thinking up yet another futile plan for getting rid of the sweater.

"First thing tomorrow morning," it was apparent from his voice that Uya was yielding only to an inevitable pressure of a supernatural force that was beyond his control. A force far beyond the little girl and him. Yielding and wishing painfully that he did not have to yield. "When the cock crows," he said, "put on your best clothes of silk and damask, wear your jewelry of gold and silver and meet me at the pillar."

So the next morning, long before the appointed time, Aramikpojehele, richly dressed in damask and silk, and wearing coral beads round her ankles, gold and silver necklaces and gold earrings, leaned against the pillar and waited very patiently. She held a bundle tightly against her side. As a cock crowed in the distance, Uya appeared, walking with the aid of his walking stick. He came towards Aramikpojehele from behind her. As he approached, she could hear the tap tap of his walking stick. She turned to him, standing upright as she did so.

"Hm," moaned the old slave as she helped him to his seat on the base of the pillar. "An old man like me shouldn't be up so early. Hm. My poor waist." And holding his waist as he sat, "Hm. Hm. There was a time when I was young and very strong."

Aramikpojehele looked down at Uya with intense feeling, her eyes fixed piercingly on him. "You are still young, Old One," she reassured him.

"I'm eighty years old, you know," Uya protested.

"That's not too old—if you think about it."

Uya laid his walking stick by his side. "The time has come," he announced, "for me to go begin my journey to the distant land where there is no suffering."

Tears filled Aramikpojehele's eyes. Uya finally settled down and looked up at the soulful girl who stood close to him. "You look so beautiful this morning, my sweet child, that it grieves me all the more to see you set out on such a difficult journey. But since you have persisted so long, and might seek worse ways if I continue to refuse, I feel compelled to show you the way."

"Thank you, sweet Old One. I know it is against your will, but I am grateful for it. The royalty of my birth has prevented me from an experience of life, so now I must shed my nobility and go experience what it is to live."

"What you have chosen to seek is a particularly difficult experience. Suffering may be the best teacher, but so also is it the most hurtful."

"For that reason I am all the more anxious to seek it. All I wait for is your instruction so that I can proceed."

Uya was eighty and Aramikpojehele, fifteen. And as they built up their philosophical exchange it was like two people, both armed with shovels, taking alternate turns as they dug earth's soil for water to quench their insatiable human thirst.

"Very well," Uya shrugged his aged shoulders, "so then may you." He looked deep into her eyes for a long time until he could no longer sustain it, not without letting a solitary tear escape his fast moistening eyes. The spirits forbid. Not before the little girl. So he looked away, down first and then, as he raised his head he looked fixedly at the distant sun that was beginning to crawl lazily and reluctantly over the deceptively well defined peaks of the horizon. He tried to raise his voice, but it failed him. It was the first time that solid voice had ever failed to find itself. But he was not ruffled. He seemed to have expected it. He kept his peace for a little while, swallowed, and then tried again with the confidence of one who had just come out of a choir rehearsal. His voice was low, clear, drawn out and vibrant. It took the whole range of feeling in its wavelength and pierced the early morning air with emotion that was as moving as it was controlled.

"You are setting out on a long endless journey," he said at last. "No one can predict the outcome. No one ever knows. But you will have a glimpse of it after you have gone a little way. If you are lucky, you will find out what suffering is. Although, perhaps, even then you may not recognise it since you're not one with it."

He paused and stared at her at length. "But the instruction is simple." His voice quickened. He was anxious to get it over with, anxious to finish before his throbbing heart could overcome his tried control. "Go out through the forest path until it brings you to a wide and less winding road." As he poured out the instructions he shut his eyes as if he thought that in so doing he would prevent the sight of the painful event from registering in his memory. "Turn on your mother's hand and continue on this until you come to Itameta. Here one road goes on your mother's hand and the other on your father's hand. Take the one that is on your mother's hand."

But he should have known, and perhaps he did, that the mind that for eighty vital years had kept record of even the tiniest bit of experience was not one that would now cease to function. No, not by the simple act of shutting his eyes. But, perhaps that was his one misfortune. He was not capable of forgetting anything. He remembered everything, everything except the moment of his birth. "And," like he used to say, "that was because he was too busy supervising the delicate and complex transformation from the womb to the world."

"Keep on this path and," he dropped his head on his breast and lowered his voice until he was just barely audible. "May the spirits of our ancestors keep you."

Aramikpojehele's eyes filled with tears as she dropped her bundle and took his hands. "Thank you, sweet Old One, and may the spirits keep you, too."

Uya folded her in his embrace and after a few unspeakable moments of silence, said, "Farewell." He tried to smile. "Farewell, sweet child. Farewell." Then, as he tried to look up at her, he added, "We may never meet again."

"I won't be long," she assured him. "I'm coming right back."

Uya laughed, a mixture of mirth and pain. He knew how silly she sounded. But he missed it, that sweet uncorrupted silliness of youth. "You may never return," he tried to caution her. "But even if you do I shall be gone by then." He paused. "But my spirit will always be with you. Besides, you will at least have one friend when you return, if he too has not started on that final journey by then."

Another cock crowed. Then a dog barked in the distance. In their exchange that early morning, the animals seemed to take the world in their strides. At least so it seemed. And by now the sun had almost negotiated the top of the horizon.

"I shall have you then," Aramikpojehele said, "as I have you now." She gave him one last hug and then, letting go of him, said, "Farewell, sweet Old One. I shall miss you very much."

That he also would miss her very much, there was no doubt. How much? It was more than words could tell. So he simply said, "Farewell, child, the spirits of our forefathers guide you."

Aramikpojehele picked up her bundle, turned and began to walk towards the forest path. She stopped and turned back. "Can I take Onejuwa with me?" she asked.

"No," Uya said. "This is one journey one must make alone. But go take good leave of him and remember his face well. If he lives long enough to witness your return, he might be the only one who would remember you."

"Can't he keep me company for just part of the way? Please." Onejuwa came strolling in along the wall that ran the full perimeter of the palace.

"Let him keep you company until you reach the parting of the roads. There send him back home. For beyond there may lie suffering. Just let go of him and he will find his way back, better than any of us could." He paused. "Child, one companion you can have with you all the way. Take my walking stick." He handed it to her. "Let it keep you company. It is so old and worthless, no robber would care to steal it."

It was a situation that had great potential for sentimentality. But neither of them desired to descend to that depth. It meant too much for that, and they seemed to know it.

"Thank you, Old One. I shall treasure it." And as she felt the longing creep back in, she rushed to take her leave with, "We may not delay our parting." And turning to Onejuwa, "Come, let's go."

As they turned to leave, Uya held his hands to her, "How about one last embrace before we part—forever."

Aramikpojehele walked up to him and embraced him. "One last embrace, sweet Old One," she said, "but not forever." She turned and slowly walked off along the forest path. Onejuwa by her side, and the walking stick in her free hand, she soon disappeared at the first bend of the path. After a while, the old slave, his head bowed in sorrow, slowly walked off in their direction as if he were going after them.

The early morning sun was now clear of the peak and as if hung seductively in space against the faultless background of the cloudless sky, the fresh breeze drifted in from the East, and with it the enlightenment of the voice, soft, delicate and vaguely weak.

And so, Aramikpojehele went on her way, searching for suffering, something she did not quite know. How was she to tell if she found it, that that was what suffering was? This, we shall see. But meanwhile, let our story continue. The beautiful Princess, accompanied by her faithful Onejuwa, followed the directions as she was given them by Uya, the old slave, her good friend and companion.

Meanwhile, Uya's eyes filled freely with tears.

VI

Here, in the forest, the path along which Aramikpojehele and Onejuwa had been travelling, divided into two endless looking roads, one on the left and the other on the right. We followed the traveller and escort from behind as they arrived at the cross-roads. Aramikpojehele slowed down until she came to a standstill. She looked at both paths, one after the other. She got down on her knees, dropped her bundle and took Onejuwa in both hands. It was like the old slave had said. This was the intersection. Beyond here Aramikpojehele must go alone. Beyond here might lay suffering. Aramikpojehele bent over her little pet and pressed him against her breast. We could see her eyes fill with tears in overwhelming detail, as if it were a cinematic close-up. Slowly the liquid formed into a pair of droplets which fell on Onejuwa's back.

Aramikpojehcle was barely audible as she squeezed Onejuwa tightly and sobbed, "You'll be here when I return. It won't be long. O." She squeezed him tighter still. "O . . . I'll miss you. You'll think of me everyday, won't you?" Silence. She took his chin in her hand and turned his sad face to hers as we walked closer. It was a perfectly moving sight of both faces lost in each other. "You'll think of me, won't you?" Onejuwa looked at her. Another silence. "And you'll recognise me when I return?"

Aramikpojehele was overcome with grief. She inattentively let go of Onejuwa's chin, allowing the head to drop back down on her lap. Finally, she got up, picked up her bundle, looked down at him, and, while he quietly looked up at her as he stood very close, she turned and once more looked up the two paths; first briefly up the one on the left and then that on the right. And as she turned back to look at that on the left, we were standing right behind, close but not close enough to touch her. We seemed to be at a slight depression and so we raised ourselves on the balls of our feet in order to see above her, for Aramikpojehele was a tall girl. When we finally achieved a clear view, we found ourselves peering into the long narrow path, lined with forests on either side, their branches and leaves overhanging the path. We held our breath for a moment for no apparent reason. All was perfectly serene. Hardly anything moved, except the leaves swaying peacefully in the gentle breeze. No one was in sight. Far away, at what seemed like infinity to us, we could hear the distant sound of a woodpecker at work. But that was only momentarily. All was soon quiet again. Then, very close to us, almost behind us, we heard a bird singing. We looked very quickly upwards, simultaneously throwing our heads back over our shoulders. Before our eyes lay the branches and leaves above with the clouds beyond them, beyond everything. Slowly our eyes focused on the bird. It was quiet by now. It simply looked down calmly at us. It seemed to see right through us. It made us feel naked. And there was more in its cold passionless gaze, enough to ring a deep hollow echo in our shallow insides.

Aramikpojehele stood and, by twisting her head around, looked back at Onejuwa as he slowly and sorrowfully walked back along the forest path towards the palace. She took a last look down that path towards the palace. Then she turned her face to the path on the left. She hesitated and then began to walk away from us, slowly at first and then at an increasing speed; away down the path.

Onejuwa on his part also stopped, turned and looked back at Aramikpojehele as she disappeared. All this time the sound of the old tune, the pastoral music, crept into our ears. It was slow at first as the girl started out slowly, and increased its speed as she in turn increased her pace.

It was in the country and Aramikpojehele had been travelling all day as she now emerged from the forest into a wide open field. She crossed the open field, still looking straight before her. It was beautiful country, flat and green. The sun was just going down over the horizon to her left. Some birds were flying around and in the distance could be seen a flock of them flying straight towards the slowly dropping sun.

"Aramikpojehele travelled for several days." That was Grandma's voice. "Nothing happened. There was no one to talk to. No one to play with. Many times she wondered if suffering was not, after all, the loneliness of having to journey alone."

Aramikpojehele stopped, put her left palm to her face as a shade and looked into the distant forest ahead, across the field, then at the setting sun. She looked rather weary. She rubbed her eyes and as she looked again into the forest ahead, Grandma's voice continued to be heard.

"No, the journey must continue. A little rest, perhaps, but there's no turning back."

Aramikpojehele bit her lips in determination. "There's no hiding in an open field," she said to herself. "Perhaps suffering lies only a few miles ahead, within easy grasp, who knows?" There was a troubled look on her face as she searched the distance. Finally she gave up and began to drop down on the grass to rest. "Every road leads to it, somehow, it doesn't really matter how one goes." All was silent, except for a lone chirp from a tiny grasshopper nearby. "A little rest won't hurt," she concluded.

Aramikpojehele sat down, set her bundle as a pillow, stretched out, put her elbows on the bundle, her chin on her knuckles, and looked straight before her at the last rays of the setting sun as the flock of birds slowly disappeared over the horizon. All remained silent. For a while it seemed as if even the grasshopper had finally yielded to the prevailing mood. Then suddenly it gave another chirp. But that was the last, the last for that peaceful, deceptive day.

As Aramikpojehele stared at the fast disappearing sun and awaited, with seeming indifference, the approach of another enshrouding night, the voice, the man's voice, crept upon our sensibilities once more.

"How much farther? Is it really worth the suffering? Perhaps. Perhaps. Maybe it is in the journey itself. Who knows?"

All remained very quiet. Then, Aramikpojehele's voice, soft and very subdued, said, "Life."

It seemed like a dialogue between two voices, separated perpetually by time and distance; both audible, both unreal. And it was more than words. They also conversed in mood and pathos.

"Life," sighed Aramikpojehele's voice.

"How much like travelling to that distant horizon," was the commentary of the other voice, the man's. "We must continue this endless journey until we can go no further. Then and only then, when our breath is spent will our search end."

The sun heaved a sigh and finally dropped out of sight behind the distant horizon. As the shadow of the night began to enshroud Aramikpojehele, her voice continued to echo the loneliness that hummed a melancholy tune deep inside her.

"Night is beginning to fall," her voice said, "marking the end of another day on this hidden trail."

Our vision blurred in unconscious response to the droplets that began to form in the corners of her eyes. Through the liquid filter that resulted, her sombre face, neither wrinkled by effort nor staled by despair, filled the entire scope of our vision, like a blown up close-up on the screen of our minds.

Aramikpojehele's voice continued, "I've come a few more miles, taking me that much farther along the way." Her elbows still rested on her bundle. Her chin lay pensively on her knuckles as she continued to stare straight in front of her at some infinite unknown. "Perhaps it's not how far I am from an endless destination, but how far I can go."

All remained silent and the darkness continued to creep upon the overshadowed night. Her eyes were tired. So was she. She rubbed her face with both hands and bent her head down as she yawned solemnly. Finally she laid her head on the pillow to sleep. We moved slowly to the side and looked down at the calmness and resolve of the proud and beautiful face of humanity that not even the most violent storms of our times could ruffle or disfigure. No. Not even with the potent terror of the impending rages.

As the girl shut her eyes, the last of the early night moved in to take over from where the day left off its watch, and in the distance, far, far away, we could hear the sound of a cock crowing. Aramikpojehele slept that night as she had done for several days, out in the midst of nature, unsheltered from the chill of the early morning dew. The birds sang her only lullaby, while the hyraxes and the grasshoppers kept the night awake as they kept vigil over nature's ward for yet another breathing spell.

VII

Early morning. The sun was streaming in through the wet leaves, leaving a general effect of steam as the dew evaporated. Uya was still

sleeping at the foot of the Iroko tree. Onejuwa walked about very restlessly. At one point, he looked up—nothing. He turned, walked slowly
back around Uya and then resumed his restless pacing up and down. The
sound of the Moslem cowherd singing to the accompaniment of his Kora
(or was it the shepherd boy on his flute?) dominated the atmosphere.
Now, very slow, soft and sad, it was clearly audible, enough to complement the excruciating passions that scorched the insides of Uya and
Onejuwa as they kept their endless vigil, waiting for the—well, it was a
gruelling and devastating conflict of eternal hope and eternal futility—a
conflict of eternity.

Onejuwa scratched the now rather brown fallen leaves. He stopped.
His face revealed the sadness in his soul as he turned to look down the
forest path once again. Slowly he walked up the path yet another time.
The sound of the music stopped abruptly as suddenly there was a brief
indistinguishable sound in the forest not too far away in the direction of
the path. Onejuwa stopped and listened. His eyes seemed to bulge out of
their sockets. His ears turned over and swung into position. Uya sat up.
The sound was heard once again, a little closer this time, but from a
slightly different direction in the same general area. Onejuwa repositioned
his head and ears accordingly. Uya started turning his face in the same
direction and listened carefully, with as much excitement as was still possible for a man of his age. The whole atmosphere was one of keen expectation. All was serene as a beautiful butterfly flew into view and settled
gently on Onejuwa's left ear. He twitched his ear by reflex, but otherwise
did not seem to notice or care.

It was much later in the night. Sammy, Angie and Onieyone were all
attention and in identically keen expectation. Grandma continued to tell
her story. She was audible but not loud enough to be understood save by
those she told it to. The lamp of a passing bicycle cast its light on
Onieyone's face. Grandma had prohibited all cycling within the compound for the safety of the children. But there are always those who refuse
to understand and Grandma had her way of handling things. But it was a
special story she was telling that night and she hated to interrupt the
children's involvement in it. So she let the cyclist carry his "suffer head"
elsewhere.

There was a plate on the table with a fork and some left over food.
The man was still at his desk, his pen poised on the paper. Several sheets
were spread not too carelessly on the table. On his face he wore a look of

keen expectation. He held his head with his free hand as if to think. Then he stretched and tried to resume his writing. But he hesitated, gave up, and began to rise, putting the completed pages together. He stacked the pile beside that of the unused paper, employing a book to hold down one batch. He looked around. There was a bookcase along the wall to the left but it was not within the reaching length of his arms, so he took off one of his slippers, shook the dust off it and used it to hold down the other pile, first putting a discarded sheet of paper on it to keep the pile from being dirtied by the sand from his feet. Finally he walked away from the table, stopped, stretched, and looked at the clock on the wall. It read 8:37. Then with only one slipper on, he crossed the parlour into the bedroom.

Shortly afterwards, he came out of the bedroom. He was now dressed in a black mohair suit, holding by the collar a medium weight dress coat in one hand. His hair was uncombed and still slightly moist. In the middle of the living room he dropped the dresscoat on the sofa. He took a book from the bookcase and walked up to the combination dining and writing table. There he replaced the slipper with the book and then took a comb from beside the plate. As he combed his hair, he walked back towards the sofa. Dropping the comb on the end table by the sofa, he picked up the coat, took the car keys from an abalone shell on the end table and walked out into the night that waited outside.

He checked the door to make sure it was locked and then, putting on the dress coat, he turned right and walked a few yards down the corridor to the covered walkway dividing the first floor apartment. He turned right into the corridor, walked past a washing machine and dryer and stopped at a black Volvo two door sedan. He opened the door, looked over the top as he entered and started the car. It backed out into the driveway, stopped, straightened out, moved forward to the street, turned right and drove into the night.

About 9:00 p.m. all the cars had their lights on. The black Swedish car, stained with white patches on the right forward mudguard and the trunk cover, was now crossing an overpass from right to left while several cars sped past on the expressway below. There were many more cars driving away towards the North than were going South. This could be seen from the far greater number of red tail lights as compared with white headlights. Of course, to the north throbbed the pulsating heart of the city. And it was Saturday night. The radio was on, providing a background of cool Dollar Brand jazz. The traffic was not too heavy. The slightly winding street was lined with trees. From the back seat one would have had an interesting view of the man's head and the road from his point of view. His watch on the traffic, though relaxed, was attentive. As he began to look steadily in front of him, he saw first the scene of Uya and Onejuwa still waiting under the Iroko tree, and then the picture of Grandma and the children outside on the verandah. Sharing the dramatic mystery of the night, these scenes superimposed themselves on his vision, one after the other. The children were more relaxed and Grandma was drinking water from a glass which she then set aside, taking care to remove it from any limbs that might unintentionally hit and break it. The green light turned yellow, then red, and once again to green. Forward all the time, never in reverse.

After a brief flurry of mad, unintelligible gibberish that passes for news on American radio, the sound became the soft, delicate and piercing voice of Bea Benjamin singing, "You Don't Know."

Both sides of the little side street were lined with parked cars. The sound of music, dancing, chatting and noise-making all helped tell the tale. There was a line of two or three cars standing facing the black Volvo which waited in the foreground. Just ahead, a car pulled out of the hitherto completely occupied roadside parking. As the road was blocked in front by the three standing cars, the driver of the Volvo maneuvered a 180° turn, backing up once. The parked car backed up to allow the Volvo to park in its former place and then drove off. There were protests from the drivers of the standing cars, but they were unintelligible.

The man opened his door slowly to avoid an accident. He stood with his back against his car as one of the standing cars suddenly sped past him. Then, slowly and cautiously, he crossed the street, his silhouette sharpened by the headlight, and walked towards the open doors of a house which, unlike others, was very well lighted. There was all the evidence of a swinging party with silhouettes and shadows dancing and couples standing outside. It was soul music and the dancing, the buguloo. He put his hand to his eyes to shut out the music while he watched the dancing and got the desired effect. It was the most vivid dramatization of the animal in human beings.

It was still early in the party so many were fairly sober and most of the lights still on. As the man entered, several people, some dancing, called out their greetings. One girl called out his name but, though audible, somehow it was just slightly indistinguishable, perhaps because it was said unexpectedly and in such a way that it could have been any one of several names. He smiled back, shook a couple hands and walked round towards the right. A slim, beautiful girl came up to him from the opposite direction. They exchanged a few words which were drowned in the prevailing raucousness. But from their facial gymnastics and the dance of their heads and eyes, it was obvious that a conversation was underway.

"May I take your coat?" the girl offered.

As she helped him out of his coat, he started to say, "I hate to say it but—"

"I do look irresistible," she interrupted. They both laughed.

"Is he here tonight?" he asked, looking about.

As she walked off with the coat, "I'll tell you about it," she said. "Be right back."

He was friendly but not particularly affectionate, polite but neither formal nor cold. It was apparent that he was admired in the group. But he did not make a big deal of it. His eyes followed the girl as she entered one of the rooms. Then, pocketing his hands, he looked around slowly. As some other girl walked towards him from the left, the first girl, who was now returning, hurried up just fast enough not to be distasteful, forestalling the other girl, but not ungracefully.

All the behavior in the little pantomime was smooth. There was not a trace of unsophistication, or worse still, of pseudo-sophistication. There was nothing which would have reduced the effect to some sort of sex thing. There was little affectation.

"How about something to drink?" she asked.

He stepped aside to signify, "after you," then walked slightly behind her into the dining room.

They came out of the dining room, holding their drinks, and sat together on an empty sofa. The party was still swinging but with soft, slow music which did not intrude into their conversation. He was staring straight ahead while listening to the girl who was turned towards him.

Softly, first looking at the man, then down, she started to say, "I find it very difficult to understand. But really it no longer bothers me, not since that day." She paused and sipped her drink. "You see, that's why I always want to talk to you. You're the only one who understands." They exchanged brief smiles. "You know, I find it very easy to talk to you frankly. I don't feel like I'm exposing any part of my intimate self. It's as if I'm just talking to myself."

She was now looking in front of her, like he was, beside her. They both sipped their drinks in silence. Now there was rock 'n' roll on the dance floor. Before their eyes others wriggled and flopped mechanically all over the place. Nothing like the grace and elegance of the sensibility to rhythm back home.

"You see," the girl continued, "on the surface everybody takes me for a pretty, easy going, perfectly satisfied person."

"So you seriously don't think you're beautiful?" He smiled a soft, friendly smile.

Her head hung downwards, giving her neck a chance to tell its own tale. "Not that," she said. "You see, you are the only one who really knows me. I can't put up a front for you. You see through every smile. You understand me." She paused. "And eh . . ." she hesitated.

They sipped their drinks in silence looking at the dancing savages. They exchanged a brief smile and he returned his face to the frenzied Caucasian orgy while her eyes lingered on him.

"I like you," brief laugh, "very much." And after a pause she continued. "You know what I like most about you?" He turned his head, but she was now looking down, turned towards him. "You listen. You can listen to me talk for a long time without feeling compelled to say something."

He continued to look straight in front of him. His view of the dancing in the background gradually became blurred. The girl's voice was still distinctly audible and the man seemed to listen attentively. But the view before his eyes became liquid and as the dancing faded from his sight, he began to see the forest and the clearing under the Iroko tree.

"Some people don't care to listen," the girl continued. "Others feel they must say something, perhaps something profound. But not you."

Onejuwa and Uya held their breath and Uya managed to stand up, leaning against the tree, waiting anxiously. All remained silent and expectant.

"And something else I like about you is that just as you can deeply feel for me, so also you can ignore me and tell me to go lie down when you think I'm just being silly."

The noise approached the path from the forest.

"But at all times you listen."

A warthog appeared on the path.

"You pay attention to what I say. And you don't pose that air that often makes one feel as if one is addressing a psychiatrist."

Onejuwa, disappointed, shook the innocent butterfly off his ear, turned around and began to walk slowly back to the Iroko tree.

Her voice began to drop slowly, "When you listen, it is not as if you are condescending or else trying confidently to find out some crazy illness in a patient. It's like talking to a perfect equal, to oneself."

Uya, also disappointed, permitted a hiss to escape his lips and turned as if to go back to sleep. But he changed his mind and tried to walk up to meet Onejuwa.

The girl's voice became faint and finally faded out. In the forest, the pastoral tune was audible all of a sudden, sharp and pointed, opening with a single note, then continuing a little softly. And as the girl's voice faded away it was succeeded by that ubiquitous masculine voice that for sometime had receded to the background.

"As Onejuwa walked back to Uya," the voice could be heard as it started yet another dialogue. "Everyone needs someone to talk to. Someone who listens. But once in a while, even those who care cannot listen, not when their minds are far, far away. And they must listen to the sounds from somewhere else, from another reality, from deep within them."

VIII

The path was wider than the others. Actually, it was a road and a fairly straight one. It looked like it ought to be a safe one to travel on, or rather, that if it was not safe, nothing else could be. Suddenly a batch of freshly cut bushes appeared up the road from the forest. The stem of this stalking shrub seemed to consist of six legs, like the wheels of a locomotive. The pieces of bush settled down together, slightly off the road, to give the appearance of a shrub that was naturally growing there.

"There were those who missed Aramikpojehele," Grandma said. "Her disappearance naturally caused a commotion in the palace. But, well, Uya and Onejuwa waited endlessly in vain on the forest path, under the Iroko tree. They used to listen for the slightest sound. They still do."

The highway robbers crouched behind the heap of freshly unrooted brush, laying in wait for whoever would be their victim. They settled into such positions as offered all three of them cover from any unsuspecting traveller. Rather impatiently one of them rose and looked greedily down the road, only to be pulled down by another.

"Get down, you greedy rogue," said the second robber to the first. "If you carry on in that manner everyone will discover us and go another way."

"Wait," said the first, struggling to rise and take another look up the road. "Yes, I was sure."

The second rose greedily in the midst of pulling the first robber down. "What?"

The sudden change of intention by the second robber and his sudden rise resulted in both of them falling back, hitting their heads on the hard roadside. A little quarrel ensued, but it was quickly brushed over as they resumed their wait.

"What did you see?" asked the second robber.

"Look for yourself," replied the first.

So he did. "Now here comes a rich traveller. Look at those beads and all that silver and gold."

As the third robber slowly took a peep from the side of the bush, the first joined in chorus with the second, "See those gorgeous clothes. Hee, hee." He rubbed his hands enthusiastically and danced about. "Thank God for all his tender mercies. Just think how much we will make from selling all that."

Speaking for the first time, the third robber cut in slowly and coldly as he withdrew his gaze from the road, "We won't be selling anything. That's just a little girl. Let's leave the poor thing alone."

"Poor thing? With all that jewelry?" That, of course, was the first robber. "You must be joking."

"Don't you have a conscience?"

"A thief with a conscience?"

Aramikpojehele staggered up the road, very exhausted, just barely keeping upright. Her eyes were partially closed. Her beautiful clothes were quite rumpled by now and she clung to the bundle under her right arm. On her left shoulder she carried Uya's walking stick. She approached the robbers, all the time biting her lower lip as a sign of determination. Her face clearly told her pain and weariness.

"Must you listen to everything?" the second robber scolded the first. "You might save your energy for the business at hand." It was certain that he lent honest advice.

"Your energy for this helpless little thing?" mocked the third. "You heartless rogues." He threw down his wing of the hitherto mysterious moving shrub. "Count me out."

The second robber was quite understanding. He said to the third mate, "See you at the mission." Then he turned to the first, "Come, let's go."

Just then Aramikpojehele was staggering past the bush. The first and second robbers jumped her. She screamed and struck out viciously with her stick, donating each of the two at least a pair of solid blows.

"Let go of me. What do you think you are doing? Rogues! Here!," she hit out again.

"My God," screamed the second robber, holding his head. "She has broken my head."

The first mate laughed, still trying to hold her. "Hee, hee. That should make you think better. Hee, hee. The little girl does not have a conscience! She . . ." Aramikpojehele politely interrupted him with a hard conscientious blow to his nose. "My nose! Jesus Christ . . ."

Aramikpojehele continued her search up the road, running as fast as she could considering her exhaustion.

This time it was the turn of the third robber, standing by the now fallen pieces of the fake bush. "Hee, hee, hee." He filled his lungs. "You might have saved your energy for some more honest business at hand! Hee, hee."

The first and second robbers remained standing in the middle of the road. The second was holding his head, which had a huge bump, and the first held his bleeding nose. They looked very angrily at their third companion.

"Hee, hee," he continued his religious torment. "Perhaps even thieves should have a conscience?" As he turned and began to walk away down the path, he added, "See you at the mission."

He walked away down the road along which Aramikpojehele had come. His head drooped dejectedly in front of him. The others watched him go. They looked at each other for a while. Meanwhile, Aramikpojehele continued to run fast away, her walking stick swinging in the air. Her bundle was scattered on the road with some of her broken trinkets.

"Come, let's catch her before she escapes," the first robber was the first to wake up from his daze and unconsciousness, inflicted as much by the surprise of Aramikpojehele's furious courage as by the actual devastating drumming of her swinging walking stick.

The second stopped shortly after they started to run after the poor girl. "The bundle. The bundle!" He returned to get the bundle and bent down to pick up the scattered jewelry, still holding onto the bump on his head.

"You rogue." One thing could be said for the robbers, they chose the most appropriate and honest names whenever they addressed each other. "By the time you are through getting that bundle she'll be gone."

"Isn't it the bundle we want?" asked the second.

"No, fool." It seemed as if the first robber was beginning to lose his temper. "The jewelry is more expensive."

The second mate picked up some of the jewelry. Holding one piece up, he proclaimed, like the half-baked minister in the oven of his pulpit on yet another Sunday, "This is real gold."

The first robber rushed madly to him. "Let me see."

"By the time you're through picking that up," the second robber said as he ran after Aramikpojehele, "she'll be gone."

The first robber hurried to pick up some of the jewelry in one hand. He ended up with a handful of dirt, as he ran after the second. Both of them ran as fast as they could up the road. The situation was precisely like this: the first robber was running with one hand to his bleeding nose and the other hand was full of sand, grass and what not, with perhaps a few pieces of jewelry. The second robber carried the bundle in one hand and held the other hand against his bumped head. But that was the same hand in which he tried to hold some of the fragments of jewelry he has taken pains to pick up. Most of them fell. The overall result was the apparent difficulty in holding on to all that and yet run very fast. After still some more.

The panoramic view from the point of view of the third robber, including him in the foreground as he looked on, was a perfect irony and contradiction. The birds sang sweetly in the nearby branches. The early morning sun lingered caressingly over the seemingly peaceful road. In the distance, Aramikpojehele continued to run away, stumbling, falling, rising and running once more. The robbers were hot on her heels. The sound of the pastoral tune rose once more to lend its soothing and peaceful music to accompany an all but soothing and peaceful episode. The robbers steadily gained on Aramikpojehele and as they came very close to her, they approached the vanishing point of the third robber's vivid perspective and passed out of our weary sight.

The third robber's face. His eyes rather filled with tears. Briefly superimposed upon his now blurring vision was a ghost impression of Aramikpojehele struggling with, striking, biting and scratching, her captors as they carried her off. He turned around and resumed his walk back down the road in the direction Aramikpojehele had only recently come from.

"What a shame!" He sighed and shook his head. "What suffering!," he hissed.

All seemed serene. It was a beautiful picture, the very peaceful road, and the forest on either side and the whole endless length of the path. The third robber walked away, dejected, along the left hand side of the road.

And from above we heard a bird whistle and shortly after, a woodpecker at work indifferently marked our passing times with his tap, tap, tap.

IX

And so Aramikpojehele became a captive, long before she even had a chance to find suffering. That was what hurt her most. The robbers stripped her of all her beautiful clothes and jewelry and sold her into slavery. But even those rogues had a little conscience. They left her her most prized possession, the walking stick the old slave had given her. It was old, of course, and certainly worthless. Perhaps that also was on their minds.

From one place to another the beautiful princess, in search of suffering, was hawked throughout the land. Finally, she was sold to Egin Aka, King of Essor, the land where one blew fire, not with a fan, but with one's mouth.

The royal kitchen at Egin Aka's palace was an outdoor circular open shed made of wood poles and roofed with thatch. It had a low circular wall about two feet high. Among other things there was a fireplace in the centre above which was a drying shed. The fireplace was simply a large tripod with some pieces of firewood properly arranged beneath it. Aramikpojehele's hands were tied behind her back. She was in rags. Her hair was dishevelled. But though her situation was extremely pitiable, her countenance was brave and determined, almost mocking. There was no trace of self-pity. Just anger and defiance.

Yes, Essor is a tripod. Egin Aka, the wood of the drying shed, thoroughly dried by the heat and smoke. The King was very slim and dry with a cruel countenance. You couldn't say his name was an exaggeration.

"Now let us see how useful you can be." Those were Egin Aka's first words, very sweet, kind and as dry as nothing else but himself. "I have no patience for laziness. I can't stand mistakes. So the first error you make I shall sell you back into slavery." The Princess looked around her, weary and exhausted. "Your first task is to make a fire and boil me some water. Akpa!" he called out.

A slave of about thirty-five years old appeared, panting breathlessly. "Olojo Massa?"

"Show the slave where the firewood and pot are."

"Yes, Most Worthy King."

Then the King turned to the Princess, "Now hurry and boil the water quickly." He looked her up and down. "You look very lean and hungry."

You would have thought he looked better. "But you won't have anything to eat until you have boiled the water." Perhaps similar treatment had left its permanent physical impression on him. Turning to Akpa, "Make sure she boils the water properly. I shall be back shortly." And he walked away.

"Ningen Ningen," that's how Grandma used to describe people like that. "Ogbe shishi egin aka," as dry as the wood of the fireplace shed.

Ekpa untied Aramikpojehele's hands, "Come, slave," he said. "Let me show you where everything is." He led her out. Shortly she returned carrying a pot of water which she set down near the tripod. She went out again and returned with a bunch of firewood which she arranged under the tripod. She went out once more, this time in order to get hot coal with which to try to light the firewood.

"Oh spirits," she cried. "This firewood is all wet and will never catch fire."

As she looked around for dry wood, Akpa entered. "What are you looking for, slave?"

"Who? Me?" Aramikpojehele was deeply hurt. "I am a Princess in search of suffering."

"A Princess in search of suffering." The fool laughed mockingly. "Pooh. Aren't we all? . . ." He paused, "Now, what are you looking for?"

Aramikpojehele was almost in tears. "Dry firewood," she said. "This here is all wet."

Akpa was alarmed. "Listen, fool," he said. "You are supposed to make that fire with wet firewood."

"What!" The poor girl was astounded. "But it won't catch fire."

Akpa looked at her in amazement for some time and then as he walked out, "Use your head." That was all the advice he had to give.

Aramikpojehele stood dazed. Finally she took the pieces of firewood one by one and tried to clean them dry with the rag that was her dress.

"What are you doing?" asked the Fool who could not possibly have been usefully engaged elsewhere. "If you are not careful, you won't last long in this palace. Now use your head," and he walked off again. Nothing like a slave playing the boss to a new slave in the absence of the master.

"Oh, sweet Old One, where are you?" Aramikpojehele was alone and could give vent to her pent-up emotions. She cried softly. "Why can't you hear me cry? O spirits, O Old One. She paused. "What suffering!"

Aramikpojehele applied fresh hot coal and the wood began to smoke. She looked around for a fan, finally found one and started to use it to blow the fire. Just then the King returned.

"What!" he exploded, just barely escaping bursting his scant body.

"Are you using a fan to blow a fire in this land? What is the meaning of it? You must have evil spirits in you."

She cried weakly. She was exhausted.

"Of course, see how you shed witch's tears."

"I only wanted to make the fire catch faster," she tried to explain.

But he pounced on her and started to beat her. "Shut up. Everybody knows that in this land you blow the fire only with your mouth."

The Princess' tears were most unbearable.

"Akpa!" The fool rushed in. "See what evil spirit is in our land. Tie her up immediately and I'll sell her back into her miserable slavery."

Akpa tied her up as she continued to sob bitterly.

"Come on, let's go." Egin Aka pushed her out and as he followed her, turned and said to Akpa, "Slave, clean up that fireplace before I return."

"Yes, great King."

"And throw that contaminated fan into the river."

While the King led her away, Akpa started to clean out the fire. "Why did he call me a slave?" he wondered in foolish anger. "Especially in the presence of that slave?"

Egin Aka led Aramikpojehele, her hands tied behind her back, into the not too crowded open air slave market. Her face showed how much she had been beaten. There were several groups of tradesmen with their human commodity. King Dry-as Bonga Fsh (that was another of Grandma's matter-of-fact nomenclatures) pulled Aramikpojehele by the hand towards one of the groups and proceeded to demonstrate her qualities as much by gesticulation as by words.

In another slave market Aramikpojehele was offered for sale by someone else. Sold.

At least she had one thing to be thankful for, that she was "hot" on the market.

X

And so, once again, Aramikpojehele was sold into slavery and hawked throughout all the lands. Several times she was bought and then sold once more, always because she either did not know the customs of the land or found them impossible to abide by. For example, in one land where she was bought, it was the custom that slaves did the cooking on their heads instead of on tripods. This she could not do. She struggled to avoid it with tears and pleas. Finally she was forced to attempt it and in so doing most of her beautiful hair was burned in the fire. Of course she was beaten mercilessly, tied up and once again sold back into servitude. So she continued from one slavery to another, sustained by only one hope, that someday, when all this was over, she could again resume her search for suffering. Meanwhile her hair grew back in again.

Once she was bought by a wealthy merchant. From the front of the merchant's big, very attractive house, one could see one of two other smaller houses from the centre of the compound. There were a few reasonably well-dressed (considering their position) slaves doing different chores around the compound. Aramikpojehele, her hands tied in front of her this time could be seen walking behind the merchant, a rather fat, pleasant looking, kind, jolly fellow of about fifty. He was dressed in an expensive flowing wrapper, the extra six yards of which were carried in a train behind him by a little well-dressed page of about six years of age. The merchant wore a collarless, flannel, long sleeved shirt, and had an ostrich feather in his hat. His walking stick was elegant. Before him walked a pair of adult slaves carrying some other purchases in baskets on their heads.

Aramikpojehele, looking really bad, walked alongside the little page who every now and then looked up at her in innocent curiosity. A girl ran up to Aramikpojehele. Oti was the merchant's daughter. She was about the same age as Aramikpojehele and looked fairly like Aramikpojehele might have looked had her sad experiences not been. Oti was beautiful and well-dressed with jewelry and other decorations, and looked strikingly like the Princess did when she left her father's palace.

"Won't you let me untie your hands?" Oti asked. But she got no answer. "Listen, we can be friends." Silence.

Oti ran up to her father and stopped him as they approached the steps of the house. "Father, please untie her hands."

"Why?"

"Please."

"Very well, why don't you do it yourself?"

"She won't let me. I mean, I'm sure she won't let me do it."

Too late. Her little slip was enough to rouse the suspicion of the good-natured, chubby man.

"What's going on?"

Without answering, Oti took her father's hand and guided it to Aramikpojehele's tied hands. She smiled at the girl as Oti's father undid the knot, glancing inquisitively but not harshly at her. Meanwhile, the servants entered the house with their load. As the merchant began to ascend the few steps that led up to the verandah, Aramikpojehele and Oti stood looking at each other. Oti was trying to be—is not the word, "friendly"?

"Utienyi," the merchant called out to his daughter. "Take her to Imele. Let her have a thorough scrubbing. See that she's given some clothes. Those rags on her should be burnt."

Oti led Aramikpojehele away to one of the small houses. On the way she started to take her hand but was afraid that it might offend rather than reassure Aramikpojehele of her intentions to be friends.

The merchant stopped at the threshold and, turning around, called out to Oti.

She ran up to him, leaving Aramikpojehele standing. He lowered his voice and in an amusing combination of affection, jest and threat, warned, "No special favors now. Don't tell me somehow she ran away."

They looked at each other for a moment, then Oti looked down. Still looking down she said, "Father, I like her. She probably hates me already because she is your slave, and I am your daughter." She paused and then looking up at her father, "Do you think I'd want to let her go?" The merchant looked at her in silence. They turned to leave but Oti stopped and turned around, "One thing, Father, can she wear some of my clothes?"

They stared at each other, then the merchant turned, and as he entered the house said, "We'll talk about that later."

"Come this way," she said as she walked past Aramikpojehele.

"My father is a King." The voice was Aramikpojehele's voice. "My friend was an old slave. I miss him now. And Onejuwa, too. But I still intend to continue my search. I'm just waiting for the time when all this will be over and I will be free again."

Oti's bedroom was neatly decorated with the kinds of presents a child in those days got from a father who travelled a lot. Some animal skins were on the wall, bow and a quiver. In the quiver were arrows with brightly coloured feather quills. There was a little cane straight back chair by the bed.

They were both fairly well-dressed in Oti's clothes, but Oti had a necklace on. Though simple, it made the slight distinction between daughter and slave. They were both sewing with ebony needles and talking.

"And this is a search for suffering?" Oti took great care not to show how ridiculous she thought Aramikpojehele sounded, so much care in fact, that she gradually started to accept it as valid, if not true.

"Otherwise I'd stay with you," Aramikpojehele said. They exchanged a brief smile. "Besides, I miss Onejuwa and the old slave."

Oti was looking at her sewing as she started to say, "Isn't Onejuwa . . ." She stopped short, but perhaps a little too late.

Aramikpojehele, slightly offended, looked at Oti who, unsuspecting, continued her sewing as she tried hard to find a new subject, though there was nothing else she wanted more to talk about than Aramikpojehele's search. When nothing turned up, she looked right into Aramikpojehele's full gaze.

"O, I'm sorry," she said. "I forgot you don't like referring to him—" She stopped before she slipped again. She smiled as Aramikpojehele's softened her look. "Okay?"

"Hm, hm," Aramikpojehele said, and they both resumed their sewing. "Perhaps after I have found it, I—"

"Aramikpojehele!" interrupted the merchant's voice from the centre of the compound. The girls looked at each other. Aramikpojehele placed her sewing on the bed and as she went out, "I'll be back," she said.

Oti continued to sew but soon slowed down to a stop as she lost her concentration. She dropped her sewing and rested her head on the pillow, her legs still on the floor. She interlocked her fingers under her head and looked at the ceiling, absorbed in thought.

The merchant was sitting on a large, luxuriously embroidered chair, apparently a treasure. Behind him stood the little page, fanning him with a large fan made of hide, leather and red felt. Aramikpojehele came out of the house and prostrated herself before the merchant who placed his right hand on her head, signaling her to rise.

"You have been a very good girl," he said, "and I am considering setting you free and maybe helping you go prove your story, which I find difficult to believe. But before that, I want you to do me a small service."

Excited, Aramikpojehele knelt before him. "Thank you very much," she said. "I shall do anything you ask. Anything. You see, I even kneel down to thank you, something royalty must never do, especially to a commoner, even one as wealthy as you."

"There goes your sick mind again," the merchant said without any harm. "Maybe the medicine man can help you before you leave, but this is something else. Right now, all I want you to do is this. Go look in my room and on my bed, by the pillow, you will find a red and yellow wrapper. Go bring it and wash it for me."

"I'll do it right away." She got up and ran back into the house.

"Poor child," the merchant said to himself. "I'm beginning to love her like my own daughter. I wonder how people like this ever get sold into slavery."

"It is bec—" the little page quickly shut his mouth as the big man turned towards him. Luckily for him, Aramikpojehele returned just then.

"Is is this?" she asked, holding up a calico handwoven wrapper.

"Yes," he said, and pointing at a calabash on the verandah, a foot or two from him. "There is the soap."

She took the calabash full of soap and stepped down into the compound, a few yards from the verandah. She placed it on a step and began to walk towards one of the small buildings.

"Where are you going?" he asked.

"To get another stool on which to do the washing," Aramikpojehele answered.

"No, no, child." He laughed his jolly heart full. "In this land you do not wash clothes on benches. You use your knee."

Bewildered, but willing to try yet another feat, Aramikpojehele sat on the bench and brought her feet up to her seat, making a platform of her two knees. She placed the wrapper on her knee, looked around, then rose and began again to walk towards the small house.

"What now?" asked the merchant as he continued to enjoy the early afternoon breeze which was partly created by the little page and his fan.

"I'm just going to get some water," she answered.

"Water!" His apparent melodrama was too much for the poor Princess. "Now child," he was still being pleasant. "It is not really a job. I want that wrapper washed immediately." There was a stern note in his voice, enough to make Aramikpojehele confused and cause her to stammer.

"But . . . but . . ." It was hopeless. She was doomed (actually that is rather a fatalistic way of putting it) to the frustration and pain of an inability to accomplish trivial but impossible tasks.

"Don't you know that you do not wash clothes with water in this land?"

"What then does one use?" Doomed, so it seemed, by that strength and wisdom which made her inadequate to operate in an endless chain of silly situations that could be commanded only the frailties of the mind.

"I'll tell you," the merchant replied. "You spit on the cloth until it is wet and then you wash it." He arose and went towards the house. "Now I must go have a nap. Let that wrapper be washed and dried when I wake up."

And so the Princess sat down as before and began to spit on the wrapper. "What suffering!" she hissed. Indeed, what suffering. It might have been some dangerous feat that demanded supernatural powers and a courage beyond the normal lot of even the bravest mortal. But as trivial a joke as washing a bloody wrapper with sputum, a joke silly and yet impossible. And to think that her life depended on it and that not all her courage, strength or wisdom could save her from so stupid and ridiculous a dilemma.

"To wash this wrapper with my sputum," she laughed. She laughed so loud and long that it was no longer quite so funny. Not that it had ever been. Her loud laughter gradually rose into quiet sobs that rent her already battered soul. "What suffering! O, Old One, what suffering!" And so she spat on the wrapper all afternoon until her throat cracked and blistered with dryness.

Much later on that same day—it is evening now—Aramikpojehele sat in the same position on the stool except that her feet were now no longer pulled up against the stool but flat on the ground. The wrapper, still dry, lay hopelessly on her lap. She had fallen asleep and her head lay on her knees.

He was dressed in evening clothes, the merchant was, as he came out of the house. He stopped on seeing the Princess sleeping, then walked slowly up to her. As they say, he could not believe his eyes.

Oti appeared unnoticed at the doorway of the house, lavishly framed by the fast enshrouding darkness of yet another night.

"You haven't washed the wrapper yet?" The merchant shook Aramikpojehele's head in anger. She woke up, startled out of her sustaining dream. "This is the smallest task I've given you since I bought you."

"Father, you promised not to talk to her like that." Oti seemed to have expected it. She rushed down to her friend's aid, rather to Aramikpojehele's aid.

"I told her I would soon set her free," he informed his daughter. "After she did just this little job, and now see." He paused as if to master the disappointment of not being able to carry off the charitable act he had so readily allowed himself only several hours before. "And all this time she has been the most hard working of them all." That was what hurt him most, perhaps. "I'll beat some sense into her." Which, of course, was rather an illogical conclusion, yet very human.

Oti stopped him, standing between them as Aramikpojehele rose. "You promised not to beat her," Oti insisted. "But if you must, you will have to beat me, too."

The merchant stood still, stupefied by the earnestness and novelty of his daughter's defiant confrontation. It was a premiere performance for her, but her unmistakable commitment wielded enough force to cripple her father's good natured rashness.

Aramikpojehele sobbed softly but bitterly at the stool, struggling to wake up once again to the rude realities she no longer seemed able to avoid for any reasonable length of time. "Eyi Uya, Eyi, Uya," she said to herself. But whether it was the pain of yet another devastating blow dealt to her weakening indestructibility or the humiliation of the glaring realisation that it was Oti, her persecutor's daughter, who was now commiting herself to bear her burden, it was difficult to tell what made Aramikpojehele sob that evening. And there was, of course, the longing, deep down at the bottom of it all, the dual longing to resume her search and with that to return to the warmth of the company of her old tutor slave and Onejuwa. Not that this warmth had completely deserted her, for in fact, this dual longing, this ceaseless yearning and expectation was the strength that kept her from collapsing under the ravaging forces of the silly trivia of her present existence.

"Aramikpojehele, don't cry." Oti wiped her tears with her pretty dress, to her father's horror.

"O spirits of my fathers," the Princess sobbed, "all this because I am searching for suffering. And even that search I can no longer resume. O, Onejuwa, where are you? Uya, where are you?"

Tears filled Oti's eyes. "It's all right." She pleaded with her friend, yes, her friend. "Cry no more." She took the wrapper from her, threw it down on the stool and led Aramikpojehele away. "Let's go. Come to my room and there we can both talk, or cry together, if you prefer."

Oti led the Princess away as her father looked on. He stood there watching them disappear into the house and remained in that position looking in their direction long after they had entered. Finally he called out to his little page as he turned and walked across the compound and away into the fields somewhere. "Omimi," he called, "get my walking stick. I'm going for a walk."

And so her sufferings continued. But in spite of them she did not yet know, so she thought, what suffering was. She still longed for that day when she would be free once more to resume her search. All this time, as she continued to be sold from one slavery into another, no moment went by when she did not think of her dearest and closest friends, Uya and Onejuwa, and above all, her vital and exciting search for suffering.

XI

The slave markets were not the most stimulating experience, not for one who was the commodity up for sale. But they were much worse for those who went through them day after day without succeeding in being sold. Besides the pain and torment of the experience, it irritated the frustrated master who took it out on his poor selling commodity. Ironically, it was a humiliating fact for a sensitive slave to face, that he or she was doing poorly on the market! This at least, Aramikpojehele did not have to face, and for this she was thankful. For, like they say, "she was hot on the slave-market!"

"Uya, the old slave, and Onejuwa," the voice was as mellow and melancholy as it was masculine.

She also thought of Oti, the merchant's daughter who had been good to her and had done all she could to help her. Once in a while, she also thought of her parents, the King and Queen. But she knew they must have given her up for lost. She feared they might accuse the old slave of having killed her in the forest or sold her into slavery.

"You know what the King would do in that case?" Grandma was expert at telling these stories. With little pauses here and there, and voice variations skillfully arranged to form one musical and dramatic whole, she could never bore the children. No, there was not a single night when, at the end of her story we were not left yearning for more. That was long ago, long, long ago. But my soul still longs for it now—not for the fact, but the feeling—rich in its subtle joy, and for the mind at peace with itself; that humanism, I feel, is now threatened in the blindness of false progress. But it is indestructible, I know, and some day Grandma, I'm coming home—home to those innumerable little cares, concerns and natural, hence unchangeable, affections that are the heart of my existence, the essence of my humanism, solid, supreme and indestructible.

But back to Aramikpojehele and what the King would do to the old slave. It frightened her each time she considered it, but she could not keep it out of her mind. The thought haunted her everyday.

Once again, Aramikpojehele was led through the crowds in yet another slave market. She was very haggard. Her neck and shoulders were bare and her face showed evidence of her indescribable—well—

"There were many who still bought Aramikpojehele." The male voice rang in our ears with the shepherd boy's unrelenting pastoral faintly in the background. "And many now who felt she was not worth a cowrie. But with all those who did buy her, there was always something, some little trivial taboo, which made it impossible for her to perform what would otherwise have been an easy task. But she persevered, waiting, waiting, just waiting for that moment when she could again resume her search for suffering."

A circular house was in the process of being built at the edge of a clearing in the forest. The brick wall was only about two feet at its highest point. The grass was green as it always was at that time of the year, and there were several patches of different brightly coloured flowers. Outside the building a middle-aged man of average size stood by a mixing board on which there was some clay and soil. Aramikpojehele, looking a little better stood by the builder. From the mud on her two feet it was apparent she had been mixing mud by walking up and down in it. Bricks were piled up on the side, and on either side of them also mounds of clay and soil.

"We need to mix some more mud," said the builder as he mixed equal parts of soil and clay on the board. "Go fetch some water."

"Where from?" Aramikpojehele asked.

"The stream over there," the builder pointed towards the forest to the right of him.

"Where shall I find a pail?"

"A pail?" The builder seemed surprised at so simple and justifiable a question. "You must be out of your mind, slave. Nobody fetches water from that stream with a container without invoking the curse of the spirits."

Aramikpojehele picked up a cup lying nearby on the ground. "But it will take endless trips to fetch enough water using this," she said.

"I just told you one does not use anything to fetch water from that stream." There was a tinge of anger in his voice. But he was willing to be helpful to her, to offer advice. "Use your mouth." And the way he resumed his mixing one would have thought, and rightly so, that he considered his a simple and justifiable answer.

"My mouth?" Why did her sense of humour have to be so completely vanquished? "O spirits of my father, what is all this?" She struggled to hold back her upsurging sobs.

"Get going!" He also had lost his sense of humour, if he ever had one. "And be sure the mud is completely soaked when I return." And he walked away.

Aramikpojehele stood there for a while. She hissed and shook her head sorrowfully. What suffering. Then finally she dropped the cup and began to walk towards the river as we followed her to the accompaniment of the cowherd and his Kora, with the soothing rhythm of the singing birds high up on the nearby trees for a persistent chorus. It was only a short walk to the edge of the forest. She entered and soon came to the stream. We looked up and down the stream which curved away at both sides, and then turned to look at Aramikpojehele as she stepped a few feet into the stream, bent down and had a drink. Then she took a mouthful for the builder's mud and headed back through the forest. But before she had gone a few feet, she swallowed inadvertently and lost her load. She returned to the stream for another mouthful which she took back to the building. Aramikpojehele emptied the mouthful of water onto the dry soil and clay mixture and then began to return to the stream.

Back at the stream, she took another mouthful and carried it back to the building site. She repeated this many times, often accidentally swallowing as much of her load as she ever got back to the mud heap. A hiccough, a hiss, a silent murmur, a reflex muscular twitch, just about anything made her lose the water she was transporting. Meanwhile her stomach gurgled with unwanted water.

The sun was now beginning to set and evening fast approached. No impression was made on the essentially still dry mud mixture. Another last time at the stream. She was very tired and she staggered towards the forest to the stream. Located at the stream we could see the building through the not too thick stems. When Aramikpojehele reached the stream our eyes followed her profile as she staggered onto the bank, collapsed and passed out. When she finally woke up and stepped again onto the stream evening had arrived and the birds and beasts that spent the night along the banks of the stream had now returned home and were keeping an empathetic watch on the seemingly homeless girl as they got ready to go to bed.

While she prepared to take another mouthful we heard a bird singing up in the tall trees across and down the stream away from us. We swung our heads up fast to the bird's position as our Princess turned in the same direction. Then she looked down and tried to take another mouthful and started back towards the building as we followed her. It was evening now. The builder, very angry, was standing by the mixing board as we emerged with Aramikpojehele from the forest into the clearing.

"You good for nothing ass." He stamped his feet. "The mud is as dry as I left it." He paced about threateningly. Aramikpojehele, unperturbed and indifferent, awaited the end with exceeding clam. "I have owned many lazy slaves before, but none as lazy as you." He whipped her furiously and savagely, but she neither moved nor cried. "You do not even cry." His stupid ego was hurt. "You'll see." He dropped the whip and began to beat her with his hands.

"No use," Grandma said. "She'd been beaten so much that she had grown to live with it. As for crying, there are only so many tears each of us has to shed before our quotas run out."

"Such suffering," Aramikpojehele said so calmly. She almost smiled. And in the background, the builder's ruthless blows fell menacingly on a cold and indifferent body. Aramikpojehele hissed.

"Do you dare hiss?"

She had built a calm centre deep in her inner depths and in this haven nothing could touch her soul but what she permitted. Behind that barricade lay the essence of her indestructibility.

"Please builder," she remarked with a devastating casualness, "don't beat me anymore. Don't you see how you bruise me? It's useless, no one can make me cry anymore." She seemed like an impartial observer of her own life.

The builder summoned the full strength of his futility to strike her. "I'll—" he started to say. But he was choked by the cold indifference that flowed out of Aramikpojehele's heart.

As he poised for what had all the makings of a death blow, Aramikpojehele calmly picked up a heavy stick nearby. "Don't touch me," she said. "If you do, I'll break your head."

"What?" He slowly dropped his crippled hands as Aramikpojehele's cold indifferent eyes, sparkling like the water of the stream in the forest beyond the clearing, burnt out whatever was left of his inflamed inside.

"Before you say it," she even took the wind from his weakly parting lips, "let me suggest it. Sell me back into slavery." And as she slowly walked away into the solemn triumph of the black night, she added, "I've grown used to that, too."

The builder stood still with hardly enough consciousness to follow her exit with his eyes. A long time later, when the hyraxes began to bark in the distant forest, beyond the stream, he picked up his whip and walked off after her.

XII

It was much later in the night in Grandma's compound. Grandma was absent from the verandah, and in her absence Edema took on the telling of the story from where she had left off. His weakening voice was just barely audible. Shortly after, Grandma, now wearing a heavy velvet shawl over her shoulder, came out of the house and rejoined the group. She handed Edema a kola-nut, briefly interrupting the story. While the children looked on, he broke the nut into its three cotyledons, and this he accomplished by taking it in his fingers and pulling the pieces apart from the top, all the time applying pressure through both thumbs. He arranged the pieces on his right palm and held them before Grandma. Just then Auntie joined the others from the direction of the house. She sat down between Grandma and Onieyone, carried Onieyone onto her lap and held him to her by means of her fingers which were interlocked on his chest. That must have been one thing he liked for it was the only time he did not put up a struggle to free himself.

Meanwhile Grandma took one of the pieces of kola-nut. Edema offered the rest to Auntie but she yielded to him, sure he was the older. He took one of the pieces and gave the rest to Auntie. Reaching for a knot at the edge of that white wrapper which gave him the frightful appearance of a ghost, he untied it to reveal a shell of dried hot alligator pepper. He broke it and shared the seeds first among the older people. He then gave a few to each of the children. Angie ate hers without any unusual effects while Sammy tried to camouflage his discomfort with a smile successively at Auntie, Edema and Grandma. Then, as he looked at Onieyone, he began to laugh as the latter threw his seeds in his mouth, bit them and immediately spat everything out. The others laughed at him as he continued to spit out and blow his mouth, but they were sufficiently mild to bring him only to the verge of tears but not beyond. Grandma picked up the glass of water that stood beside her and held it to his burning mouth. As Onieyone gulped the water down, Auntie relieved Grandma of her hold. While she turned to Edema who began to resume the story but hesitated and turned towards her. "It is your story," he said.

So Grandma once again took over her story to the pleasure of the children who were most anxious to know what became of the princess; and to the relief of the little rascal who was glad to have the group's attention diverted away from his burning mouth scorched by a few harmless seeds of alligator peppers. By the looks on his angry face, it seemed certain that he had sworn never to take the silly little things again. Not that he had not sworn the same thing before. For him, it was a test of manly perseverance. If the others could chew and swallow these seeds without apparent discomfort, why not he? In particular, if Sammy could,

he himself certainly could; in fact, he could do better. He could . . . crunch
a mouthful with ease? . . . or two handfuls? . . . do it all, and swallow, of
course, all in one minute? . . . in one second? . . . why, certainly . . . he
could do it all with one big, broad beaming smile . . . an everlasting smile
of . . . pain? . . . never mind.

All that mattered was that he would show them. Not that he quite
knew what. But that really did not matter. Just wait until the next time
around, and at that time . . . well . . .

"And so our princess was sold into slavery once more. She became so
used to all her cruel sufferings that she no longer cared. In one instance,
she lost an eye, poked out by the rather affectionate wife of one of her
countless masters, and, of course, the loving mother of what passed for
children. But Aramikpojhele continued. She held her head high and above
the waves that stormed and buffeted against her delicate but indestructible
skin as they tumbled recklessly downstream to the pulsating rhythm of
their incessant beat. Aramikpojhele continued. She knew that someday
it would all end, that is, if she did not allow herself be sacrificed for that
end, if she did not . . ." Grandma paused. The night continued to flow in,
in the footsteps of the long retiring day.

"In spite of everything, she clung to one treasured hope, that someday she would be free again, free to resume her search for suffering.

"So, sold from slavery to slavery, Aramikpojehele went through all
the land. Finally, she was bought by a certain traveller who liked her
person, in spite of her bruises, and admired her beauty, in spite of her
rags. This traveller treated her more as a companion than as a slave or
servant. He took her through several lands until one day they came into
a certain forest. Shortly after entering the woods, Aramikpojhele began to
feel a curious sensation. She wondered what it could possibly be. But it
did not take too long before her recollections came back to her and she
seemed to sense the sprouting of a vague in-growth of realisation. She
knew it. She was certain she did."

It was very sunny that morning, along the road in the forest.
Aramkipojehele was neatly dressed. She looked the perfect match, perfect
companion for a perfect traveller. Except that she was now blind in her
left eye, she was very well and apparently quite happy with her new
"master," as she insisted on calling him. He was a fairly young man, the
traveller was, about twenty-five, not at all bad looking, pleasant, gay,
cheerful, and one might add, rather talkative; "bent on communicating"

was his proffered phraseology. They walked at a fairly fast pace, like perpetual hikers just starting out on yet another day's trek. He was talking, but slowly and inadvertently, Aramikpojhele grew inattentive as her senses toyed with the particularities of the place.

"It isn't too bad," the traveller was saying. "You get lonesome sometimes. But then it isn't always that you want company, anyway. At certain times, you are thankful to be alone." Like a shy lover who could get going once he got enough encouragement to spur him on, he paused and waited for her to say something, just anything, no matter how irrelevant. That he would pause for someone else was quite out of character with him. But what is there in the behaviour of a fledging and sprouting lover that is in character with his normal self?

"But it has been different since I met you . . ."

"Since you bought me." She interrupted, without seeming any more attentive than she had been.

A silent dialogue flashed between their faces. The traveller, still smiling in spite of his embarrassment, again turned to look at her. But he found her looking about her and away from him as if trying to recollect something. He imposed a voluntary silence on himself, in an affectionate gesture, at least so it seemed, not to interrupt her lovers' dream. Rebellious, true. But still . . .

"Go on." She was still looking about her.

"No. That's all right." It must be confessed that that was awfully sweet of him. For her part, she conceded a brief oblique glance at him.

"What's the matter?"

""Ho . . . eh . . . I shouldn't disturb your . . . oh . . . deep thought?" He smiled with a not unpleasant mischief.

"I'm listening."

It was obvious that they enjoyed each other. Each one seemed to have a great talent specifically for teasing the other. She wielded a sophisticated wit, with a good and well-blended flavour of biting sarcasm. On his part, he matched this feminine excess and extravagance with a masterful command of no less equal wit and an inexhaustible store of carefully controlled misleading and ego-deflating remarks.

They walked in silence, the traveller looking straight before him. Aramikpojehele was still exploring the surroundings for what seemed like the missing link to a past that was struggling to manifest itself in her consciousness.

"I thought you promised not to refer to . . ."

"Hmp . . ."

"Then why did you . . ."

"I'm sorry." It was this quality which they both shared that kept them so close to each other and allowed for the maximum communion between them. "You were talking about travelling alone and . . ."

"Yes. Yes. Sometimes one prefers to travel alone. In fact, ultimately it is inevitable. But since I met you . . ."

"You know, this place feels very familiar."

"What do you mean?" he asked. "This is a far off land." He laughed softly.

"You couldn't have been anywhere near here at anytime in your . . . eh . . . interesting . . . life? Not too many people come this way."

He paused, rubbed his hands together and said, "Of course, anyone can recall having been any place, sometime," and as he looked straight into her eyes, "at least in a dream perhaps."

As he spoke, Ara saw a walking stick lying by the roadside. She stopped, while the unsuspecting traveller continued talking, in effect, to himself. She stooped down and scrutinized the lonely walking stick.

"I wonder how it got here," she muttered to herself. Tears glided stealthily out of the angulated edges of her still delicate eyes as she picked it up. She hurried to catch up with her fellow traveller who had already stopped, turned, and was now waiting for her only a few steps away.

"This is the walking stick the old slave gave me," she said, showing it to him.

Anire, after a brief pause, turned to follow the princess who had begun to continue down the road.

"Trvavelling with you is a different thing." He seemed bent on carrying right through to its blasted end, his philosophising, the sentiment of which secretly amused them both, "It is . . ."

"It was exactly here that they waylaid me."

As she interrupted him, she stood pointing with the walking stick at the roadside to the left of her.

"That was a long time ago. I've lost count of the years."

They walked on in silence.

"There are those who . . ." But Aramikpojehele interrupted him again. It was as if he was doomed never to carry off this sober and apparently most crucial contemplation. Perhaps it was out of place in a relationship that did not need verbalisation, which, at its best, could only detract from its sublimity. Words, it seemed, were superfluous. Worse than that, they were incapable of expressing the essence, since they were less than the essence itself.

They had now emerged from the forest into the open field. The sun was beginning to rise in the east. It was shortly after dawn. The scene was a grand panorama, the sunrise in the east, and Ara and Anirejuoritse standing at the spot where the princess once spent the night on a lonely bewildering emptiness. In the foreground of this life painting, they stood looking at the landscape, with their hands above their brows to shade the brilliance of the early morning sun from the sensitive lenses of their imperfect eyes. Dew laid thinly upon the grass. There were birds in the air. Birds on the open field. Afar off, a flock of birds seemed to be flying towards the jolly traveller and her royal companion. They were coming, so it seemed, from the distant horizon, from far behind the reddish orange glow of the lazily awaking sun.

"I once spent the night at this very spot," Ara said, interrupting the traveller. He followed her as she made a complete right about turn, and she pointed straight west with her walking stick. It was vividly reminiscent of the shepherd on the open field pointing out the limits of his boundless kingdom; some scenic ancedote from the Bible tales.

"You see that horizon over there?" she paused. "I remember looking steadily at it for a long time and debating whether I should not have journeyed there instead of pursuing my ill-fated search."

It was one integral beauty of man and nature as they wandered about casually that morning in the freshness of the rustic air, perfumed by the fragrance of the leaves and flowers, and bathed in the pool of the invigorating sunshine. Two separate souls at peace with their individual selves; two separate souls at peace with each other. And as she continued to reminisce in the soothing warmth of that bubbling piece of nature's earth, the sound of the little shepherd boy, playing solo on his loneliness-inspiring flute filled the air with its mystical music—soft, piercing, rather sweet, touching and profound in its evasive simplicity.

Yet another morning. And the sound of the Moslem cowherd was rather excited as it came on loud and clear and filled the forest with its potent non-descript symbolism. They walked in silence along the deserted path; Aramikpojehele and Anirejuoritse did. The music soon fell to the background, yielding the air to a tireless woodpecker at his endless work. Then it was the turn of another bird, but this time it sang a brief sweet melodious song. Finally a dog rendered the finale, barking at his loudest.

Gradually revealing itself, the long path stretched out before them, bounded on both sides and overhead by the forest. In the distance, the Iroko tree towered way above the rest of the vegetation. He came dashing fast down the road towards Aramikpojehele. Sobbing, she ran towards him. She bent down on her knees, embraced him and, resting her head on his back, wept bitterly. Onejuwa remained in the princess's embrace as the traveller arrived on the scene. He stood, very moved, and watched them for a long time as their thoughts melted into each other, intermingled with their tears. All was silent except for the birds singing in the canopy of the branches above, the branches that kept perpetual watch over all the earth-bound creatures it sheltered beneath its outstretched arms. Finally, Aramikpojhele arose carrying Onejuwa in her arms. On his part Onejuwa tried to wipe off the remnants of tears on her sad face, all the time gazing inquiringly at the wound of her blinded left eye.

"He seems to know you well," Anire remarked as casually as he could to hide his utter confusion.

"He is mine." She pressed him tightly against her bosom. "Onejuwa, Onejuwa, if only you knew all that has happened to your friend."

"How could you possibly know him?" This certainly was more than a joke, so Anirejuoritse thought.

"You didn't believe my story, did you?" she asked.

There was another period of peaceful silence as they continued towards the huge tree. Anire shook his head slowly.

"No, I didn't, but now I don't know what to think." For a while he seemed speechless as he stared at her for a long time. "You know, I admire you a lot." But it was not easy for him to resist a humour, not even for once. Not that he ever tried. "A princess, and you have allowed yourself to suffer so."

But she took him seriously, not that she did not know that he had intended to tease.

"Suffering," she seemed to be talking to herself now. "Suffering. That's what I originally set out to find . . . Now that I'm almost home perhaps I shall be free once more to resume my search again."

In the history of so sublime a relationship, neither of them allowed the incompetence of words to intrude upon their implicit communion which was above verbalisation, which it seemed to scorn. No. Much as they played with words, they kept them away from their deep mutual sentiments. And now, not even for the extreme emotion that the situation potentially had, they were not about to diminish the profundity of their communion with the empty profusion of unnecessary articulation.

"From this moment," Anire said, "you are your own master." He smiled mildly and a trickle of laughter escaped his lips. "You are welcome to travel with me, as a partner . . . like the companions we have grown to be. "He paused and looked up at her. "Will you come?"

No word was said. They looked into each other's eyes for a long time as Ara debated her alternatives and Anire weighed his chances. Ara looked down at the face that stared at her, Onejuwa's.

"Thank you very much," she said at last, "you are very kind. But no . . . no for both offers. I am your slave. You paid twenty cowries for me, and that, at least, you must get back. Sell me to my parents and you will be more than repaid."

Anire struggled to hide his disappoinment. But as a perpetual traveller, he had come to learn the truth of his own words: "Sometimes one prefers to travel alone. In fact, ultimately it is inevitable." Ultimately, he fought hard to get used to the idea that this was it. At other times in his life he had practised the rare art of blending the mind and the emotion into one, two in one, each serving as a buoy for the other, each backing up the other, each in fact leading the other.

"I will have no part of it." Anirejuoritse was definite on this point. "You are mine, and I am free to set you free."

"Caring for me as much as you, why don't you do as I request?" The princess was as adamant as she was calm. "Sell me to my parents. You can refuse to take the money after the bargain is made. If you like, you can share it amongst the household slaves."

"No, sweet, charming, wonderful, princess. By your elegance, no."

It was true that he could not isolate his keen humour and sharp wit from any situation for too long. Neither of them could; not even from what might have seemed so serious a circumstance as would have made a black man bleach.

"But you must, most gracious and bewitching . . . em . . . traveller? . . . you really must." She smiled back at him, a welcome soft mischievous smile. "Don't you see how it would show me how much my parents will pay for me?"

The expression on Anire's face betrayed the simple fact that he really had not expected that. But it was too late. He was one down and he had to admit that she had a foresight that had the potential for superceding his; or rather, being a woman, that she had the potential for almost equalling his, and that by that same vice of being a woman, that potential would never be fully realised anyway.

"Well, in that case," he said, "if it is just for the fun of it, I'm a sport. Come let's go."

As they hurried off towards the palace, Onejuwa cut a funny caper behind them as he attempted the dual movement of gracefully dancing his joy for Ara's return and at the same time running fast to keep up with the tired feet of the experienced travellers. Meanwhile, Aramikpojehele sought and obtained an agreement regarding her costume for the impending drama.

"I will change into old rags," she said. "I can hardly wait."

XIII

A few minutes later the traveller stood waiting, alone, in front of the king's palace. It was a beautiful sunny day and all was fresh and bright. It was rather quiet, no slaves bustling around. The huge door parted, each half guided to its lock by an elegantly attired palace page. The king, he must have been about fifty-five years old, tall and imposing, and draped in regal robes, emerged from within, taking his time as he measured his elegance in the calculated paces he took along the damask-carpeted aisle. Anirejuoritse bowed respectfully, dramatic in his equally calculated emphasis.

"Are you the traveller who has come to sell me a slave?" His Eternity asked.

"Truly, King, I am the very same he." Anire did not find it too easy to overpower the scornful sarcasm that threatened to explode within his suppressed disdain.

"The slave is a girl, very beautiful and most intelligent; all these in spite of the rags ... I mean rags she wears."

"Very well," said the king. Actually, he was a rather likeable fellow. "Bring her in."

Anire turned and beckoned; and Aramikpojehele entered, Onejuwa in her hand.

"Here she is." Presenting his commodity with the flair of a neo-pagan pantomimist. "What do you think?"

"You travellers from distant lands have a peculiar insolence in the way you talk."

One thing had to be said for the king; subtle intimations were not wasted on him.

"It is our pagan pride, Mr. King," replied Anire who, for a brief moment, seemed to have forgotten the possible consequences of arousing the monarch's displeasure.

"No more," the king said. "As for the slave girl, she looks interesting," which, I suppose, said an awful lot. "What is your name, child?"

Aramikpojehele did not answer.

"She is called Aramikpojehele," the traveller explained, encouraged by what seemed like early signs of the success of the joke he and Ara were bent on carrying out. "And the name means . . ."

"That is a strange name. Where did she get it from?"

"From her father, who is a King." The "rascal" coughed mischievously. "The slave, Sir, is a princess."

"Interesting." His Highness seemed also to be in the mood for a battle of wits. "A princess and a slave. Tell me, slave . . ."

"Do you call me a slave?" Aramikpojehele interrupted angrily, threatening to spoil the fun for which she was the very architect. It seemed as if the realisation of her expectation was too much for her to take. Suddenly, it all did not seem quite so funny after all.

"Shh," cautioned the traveller, and turning to the king, "You must excuse her, Mr. King, it has been a rather long day, even though it all seems like late morning. Besides, she does not like being called a slave, no princess does, and especially by you," and the rest he muttered to himself, "who should know better." He was very careful to drop his voice on those last words, but not low enough for them to go unnoticed.

"Watch your tongue, traveller," the king cautioned. "If you hope to have your head on your shoulders when you leave this land."

Just then the Queen appeared through the open doors. She was about fifty and must have once been beautiful. She also was regally attired, and the bright morning sunshine duly complimented her with an extra brilliance.

"Which is the slave?" she asked, as if she thought the traveller could possibly have been one, which he in turn did not take too kindly.

"By your ignorance," this much he essentially kept to himself, "you must be the Queen."

"What did he say?" Her Royal Femininity inquired of the king.

"There she is whom you seek." Anire pointed at the princess.

"What use have we for a thing like this? A slave who . . ." For a while it seemed like she addressed herself only to the king as if that was the lowest she was willing to go.

Aramikpojehele burst out with fury, "And you too! . . ."

"Shh," Anire cautioned again.

"She is rather sensitive and touchy about being called a slave," the king announced knowingly to the Queen.

"Well," she heaved a sigh, "that's a new one." She made no attempt to disguise her angered and disdainful mockery.

"Well, traveller," the king continued, "how much are you asking for her?"

"Why would you even consider buying her?" That, of course, was the Queen.

"How much would you offer?" The traveller tried to ignore the Queen.

Turning to the Queen, the king intoned, "At least she can look after Onejuwa. He seems to like her."

"Her stench will suffocate him in no time."

"Onejuwa will keep her clean, and happy," Anire was confident, "better than any of you can." He was growing expert in his new art of differentiating between his audience by tonal variations. Not that he did not need it, since he knew the king and took his earlier advice to heart, and that in spite of his nonchalant and care-free attitude which might have led one to believe otherwise.

"He . . ."

"Stop talking about my Onejuwa like that," Aramikpojehele interrupted the king.

"The slave is rather hot-tempered," it was now the Queen's turn to announce, confidently, her profound discovery to the king.

"What did you call him, yours?" asked the king.

"Onejuwa is mine." Ara placed it in such a matter-of-fact manner that it almost sounded neither here nor there.

"Isn't he our daughter's?" And for the first time, the Queen addressed herself to someone less than the King, perhaps because the person she chose probably thought otherwise about his rank. "Tell me, traveller, where did she steal him from?"

"That is for you to ask your daughter."

"Slave," she turned to her, "where did you steal him from?"

But Aramikpojehele was silent.

"If you want her to speak with you," the traveller always liked to volunteer useful hints and advice whenever he could, "you must stop calling her a slave. I am afraid there is no other way."

"Tell me, child," only the king was willing to compromise, "where did you find him?"

Aramikpojehele might have lost her temper then, had she not considered it no longer becoming of her, in the circumstances. After all, she had handled more shocking and brutal situations before, and she had survived them all.

"Uya told me so," she sighed, addressing herself.

"Where did she pick up all these names?" Madame Queen was apparently quite upset. "The slave dares . . ."

"Control yourself." The king restrained her.

"Yes, Mrs. Queen," concurred the traveller, "please control yourself."

"Child, the slave you refer to is dead," explained the King in a fatherly way. The Princess screamed and then cried but soon struggled to control herself. "That is one point whoever taught you all these stories left out." He continued triumphantly, "But that does not matter. Now, traveller, I am taking a liking to this girl. How much did you want for her?"

"How much does the great Queen think she is worth?"

"Let's see." (At least she was willing to consider.) "If she were perfect and well behaved, I would say ten cowries. But she is ill-mannered, which makes her worth five cowries. Then she has only one eye, that is two and a half cowries. She is a thief, one and three-quarter cowries, and a liar, seven-eighths cowry. Besides, I do not like her, so . . ."

Anirejuoritse could no longer hold back his biting sarcasm. It was his sharpest weapon for revenge. "Sweet Madam," he said, "Sweet Madam, I actually would take nothing, if she's worth that much to you."

"Traveller," said the King, "I'll give you five hundred cowries for her."

"What? This good-for-nothing slave?" One hardly needs to say the Queen was rather flabbergasted and overwhelmed.

The King patted Aramikpojehele on the shoulder. "I know you're worth more than that, but you'll be worth any amount I offer."

"This rat who impersonates our beloved daughter?" Perhaps the recollection of her daughter prevented her from being violent.

"In fact," mused the good natured King, "she reminds me of her. O, maybe I'm getting old."

"Perhaps! Perhaps!" Anire disguised his mockery with a fitting smile.

"The two of you make me sick the way you trifle with the precious memory of my daughter." Exasperated, the kind old lady stormed back into the palace which quickly swallowed her up.

"The precious memory of her daughter," Anire repeated to himself. "Not the memory of her precious daughter."

"The offer is fine with me, Your Highness," he announced to the

King, bowing with such great respect that he almost toppled over, "and your latent goodness impresses me."

"Mene!" the King called out. A servant of about thirty years came running out and prostrated before him. "Go to the guardian of my treasury and bring me a bag of five hundred cowries." The servant ran back in without having given the not uninquisitive traveller the benefit of the sound of his voice.

"Take the greatest care of her," Anire, one could not say, "pleaded" with the king. "She is dear to me."

"If she is a good child," he replied, "you will have nothing to fear."

"A child, of course," Anire quibbled as Mene returned with the money.

Taking the money from Mene and handing it to the traveller, the King philosophised, "Here is your money. Let us call it a token payment."

"Of course," the traveller approved, taking the money. "It's just a token." He went over to the princess, embraced her and as he turned to leave, "Farewell, Aramikpojehele, and have a good stay."

"Farewell, Anire," she said, hating to see him go. "And thanks for the trade."

"Farewell." He turned to leave, stopped and returned. "By the way, Aramikpojehele, here is the money for which yours bought you. Throw it away or share it amongst the slaves."

Anirejuoritse turned and walked away through the arched entrance to the palace walls and along the very straight walkway in front of the palace. The walkway was lined with flowers on both sides. Aramikpojehele watched him go. When he had gone a long way, he stopped, turned, waved to her and then continued on until he disappeared into the bright beautiful morning sunlight.

"Mene, take her away," the King said when he finally turned away from the rascally traveller who had fired his imagination and somehow impressed him with his daring rudeness and audacious sense of humour. "Let them clean and dress her wounds and give her clean clothes to wear."

Mene began to lead her away. "Mene." He returned to the King who whispered into his ears, "Watch how she spends the day and report to me. Let her keep Onejuwa as long as she wants."

He stood there, the King did, in the warmth of the brilliant sunshine, and watched them go round the side of the palace. Finally, when they had disappeared round the corner, he turned and entered the palace.

XIV

And so Mene kept close watch on the Princess, how she spent her time, what she did, and as much as he could deduce from external manifestations, what she thought. Everyday she would go to the forest, accompanied by Onejuwa and sit under the Iroko tree and sing.

It was mid-afternoon on one such day. Aramikpojehele, tears in her eyes, sat under the Iroko tree, singing. Onejuwa was playing passively around. Now and then he walked up to ther, stared into her tear-filled eyes and whimpered. She pulled him up to her, still singing, held him between her legs and stroked him. Finally he walked away from her and resumed his slow, disinterested play. A butterfly flew teasingly in front of him. He started to pursue her, but stopped and let her go. Aramikpojehele's singing was very slow, sad and soft. It was intermingled with tears.

> *Eyi mi Aramikpojehele rey*
> *No gbese mi ren ra fi Uya*
> *Owa mi re mi, esi mami*
> *Iye mi ri mi, esi mami*
> *Odi Onejuwa mi naka*
> *Onejuwa owun naka e mami*

Here she sobbed and hissed. *Eyi Uya, Eyi Uya.*

> This is me, Aramikpojehele
> Who used my own feet to set out in search of suffering.
> My father sees me, he doesn't recognise me.
> My mother sees me, she doesn't recognise me.
> Only my Onejuwa alone
> Onejuwa alone still recognises me.
> Such suffering! Such suffering!

As she stirred Mene's back quickly disappeared in the bush along the path that led to the palace behind the Iroko tree.

And so she would sit out there and sing and weep day after day without stopping come rain, come sunshine, in the heat or in the cold. Never a day went by when Aramikpojehele did not spend the afternoon in the forest under the Iroko tree singing and weeping. Never an occasion went by when Onejuwa did not keep her company.

One day the slave, Mene, finally reported this to the King who told the Queen. But she didn't believe him and dissuaded him from finding out. But one day, when he could no longer resist it, the King arranged to go listen to her. On the appointed afternoon an unusual thing happened. The sun was shining brightly while it rained and as the people say, that meant that the elephant was giving birth in the forest. Just as the sun began to set, the King stole away quietly from the Queen.

Led by Mene, he walked up gently from the palace to the forest and hid just where the path opened until the clearing around the Iroko tree. There, he listened.

Aramikpojehele's voice was now not distinguishable from that of Grandma, Edema, Auntie and the children. As the voice sang to the accompaniment of drums, the King and Mene moved up behind the Iroko tree. Tears were beginning to be visible in the King's eyes, something that was never known to happen to royalty in that land. They sang:

> *Eyi Aramikpojehele rey*
> *To gbese mi ren ra fi Uya*
> *Owa mi re mi, esi mami*
> *Iye mi ri mi, esi mami*
> *Odi Onejuwa mi naka*
> *Onejuwa owun naka e mami*
> *Eyi Uya, Eyi Uya.*

As the voices continued the song, the Queen who had followed the King at a reasonable distance, joined him unnoticed and listened.

> *Eyi Aramikpojehele rey*
> *To gbese mi ren ra fi Uya*

This time it was Grandma's voice, vibrant, delicate, piercing and touching.

The Princess wailed while the others hummed the chorus, *Eyi Uya, Eyi Uya.* Such suffering. Such suffering.

The Queen rushed to embrace her daughter, weeping all over her. "My child, my child—o spirits of my father, what have they done to you? Who poked out your eye?"

The King and the slave joined them. The King went down on one knee and took her hands in his.

"Child, you must forgive us."

"A slave who is worth less than a cowry," Aramikpojehele said, "is incapable of forgiving."

"You must forgive me," her mother pleaded. "I didn't know it was you," and she sobbed.

"You must forgive us both," her father entreated. And turning to the slave, "Go proclaim the return of our Princess. Bid them—"

"Stop," the Princess ordered the slave. "No one proclaims the return of one who did not go anywhere. I have been amongst you all these days but you did not notice. There's no reason to celebrate now." Quite frankly, one might have thought she read the Bible.

"Child," the King took her by the shoulder. "I ask for forgiveness, not as a King, but as a father."

"First answer me this," she said, still indifferent, "then I will consider your plea."

"But before that, tell me who plucked out your eye."

"I went out into the world to search in vain for suffering," she said, more to herself than to any of those who listened. "Then finally, I found that," she hesitated. "Never mind. Now that you are answered, answer me this. What happened to the Old One?"

They all looked down. Mene walked away back towards the palace.

"We thought he had killed you or sold you into slavery," her father answered.

"So you killed him." Frozen with pain, Aramikpojehele's words were chilling and cold.

Mene returned with a large red coral bead which he held out to her. "He left this for you, if you ever returned." Her parents looked up again. "It was stolen but Onejuwa snatched it from some traveller one day, biting him all over until he almost died. Then he took it to the place where the Old One was buried, there." He pointed in front of her at a mound still in the shade of the Iroko tree. "And he left it lying on the grave!"

As she followed his fingers with her eye, a hitherto unnoticed mound was revealed six feet away, fairly higher than the rest of the ground. The grass about it had been freshly trimmed. Onejuwa was quietly lying on it as if embracing it. The sun shone particularly brightly on the mound as if descending in a shaft through the branches of the Iroko tree. The drizzle fell in a few single, scattered strokes. All was perfectly silent except for the sound of the falling rainstrokes. From the branches above, a bird looked down silently at the slave, the Princess and the royal couple with Onejuwa six feet away, completely oblivious to the living world. The King and Queen remained down on their knees on either side of their daughter. Mene stood behind her, still holding out the coral bead.

Aramikpojehele, as if stunned, slowly arose, her parents' hands gradually falling off her as they slowly followed her with their eyes, tormented by the painful realisation of their seemingly irreparable damage.

Her eyes fixed on the grave, Aramikpojehele slowly staggered towards it while the others looked on. As she neared the grave, the sound of Grandma, Edema, Auntie, and the children, accompanied by drums, could be heard singing the same immortal song.

> *Eyi mi Aramikpojehele rey*
> *To gbese mi ren ra fi Uya*
> *Owa mi re mi, esi mami*
> *Iye mi ri me, esi mami*
> *Odi Onejuwa mi naka*
> *Onejuwa owun naka e mami*
> *Eyi Uya, Eyi Uya.*

Aramikpojehele finally arrived at the mound. As the singing continued she slowly collapsed on the grave holding Onejuwa who hardly moved and they both embraced the final resting place of their old friend. She sobbed quietly and he whimpered. The rain slowly stopped falling. The sun still shone brightly. And the singing continued, softly.

As the voices died out, the bird sang ill-ominously, high up in the branches. And in a nearby tree, a woodpecker resumed his relentless tap-tap as he menacingly kept track of our times. And from afar off, from the inaccesssible distance of a past long gone, a gentle breeze blew calmly by and on the crest of its waves, poised delicately in the threatened splendour of the yet unravaged nature, in the fragrance of the yet unpolluted forest air, the solemn sound of the lonely shepherd boy on his enchanting flute, or was it the voice of a Moslem cowherd, singing to the accompaniment of his bewitching Kora, was carried delicately to where we stood in the chilling warmth of the African sun.

The sound came through to soothe our ears and pierce our hearts as we left the sunshine and the rain, the colours in the sky and the elephant delivering its baby in the forest on yet another sunny late afternoon. The soft and touching sounds came through to us all right, as we walked away and left behind us the forest, the woodpecker, the little bird and the forest path. We left behind us the Princess and Onejuwa at Uya's grave in the shelter of the indestructible old canopy, under the Iroko tree.

XV

Through all of this came Aramikpojehele's voice, clear, soft and distinct. "Yes, Onejuwa," it whispered, "come, let's weep at his grave."

It is very late at night in Grandma's compound. We could see old papa Edema's back as he walked home alone in the same white wrapper that made him look like a ghost. On the verandah, Auntie was lifting up Onieyone who was now asleep on Grandma's pillow on the raffia mat. She carried him in her hands as she stepped off the mat and waited. Sammy picked up the pillow and Angie rolled up the mat and carried it away. Grandma, for her part, carried the drinking glass, pouring the water away onto the open ground of the compound. As they withdrew into the house for the night, papa Edema disappeared into the night.

And the voice, the man's voice, the same as in old times, rose once more for what seemed like a would-be *nune dimitus*.

"Edema is dead now, Sweet Old Man," it said. "But Grandma lives and is waiting for me to come back." By now everybody had completely retired into the house and the voice struggled to hold back a sob as it began to grow faint, "Soon . . . soon . . . soon I'll be back . . ." And as the single outside light was switched off, plunging Grandma's compound into pitch darkness, the last faint word could be heard ringing in the night, "Someday."

It is very late at night, in his living room. In fact, it is almost two o'clock in the morning. He is exhausted from writing all day. As he stands up from the chair and collects the manuscript together, he still has on the same old shirt. His suit jacket is lying on the sofa, his tie hanging from the bookcase. His shirt sleeves are unbuttoned as they must have been for I don't know how long. His shirt tails are flying, his shoes are under the table. As he arranges the paper together, stretching intermittently, the sound of the pastoral song comes on clear as if from the record playing on the old turntable. He looks up at the clock on the wall. It reads 3:45 A.M. As he puts away the manuscript and begins to walk towards the bedroom the record slowly ends and he hears faintly, Aramikpojehele singing.

> *Eyi mi Aramikpojehele rey*
> *To gbese mi ren ra fi Uya*
> *Owa mi re mi, esi mami*
> *Iye mi ri mi, esi mami*
> *Odi Onejuwa mi naka*
> *Onejuwa owun naka e mami*
> *Eyi Uya, Eyi Uya*

This is me, Aramikpojehele
Who used my own feet to set out in search of suffering
My father sees me, he doesn't recognise me.
My mother sees me, she doesn't recognise me.
Only my Onejuwa alone
Onejuwa alone still recognises me
Such suffering, such suffering.

At the entrance into the bedroom, he stopped, turned off the switch and plunged the room into total darkness. All was calm and quiet against the background of Aramikpojehele singing and Grandma humming one of her old favourite songs to her little rascal. The man's voice whispered to itself in the bedroom as it faded out and he began to fall asleep.

"I'll be back home soon, Mama. Much sooner than I thought. And you will wait for me, Mama. You promised you'd wait. You'll wait, Mama, won't you?"

SEATED WOMAN HOLDING BOWL LUBA CONGO

Biographical Notes

AMA ATA AIDOO, a young Ghanian dramatist, is a former research assistant with the School of Drama at the University of Ghana. Her first play, *Dilemma of a Ghost*, was published in London, and her short stories have appeared in many journals. She has recently completed a new play.

SAMSON O. O. AMALI is a research assistant with the Department of Linguistics at Ibadan University in Nigeria.

GEORGE AWOONOR-WILLIAMS has been called Ghana's best contemporary poet. His works, which have been widely published, include a collection titled *Rediscovery*. Formerly with the National Television Service of Ghana, he is presently attached to the Ghanian Embassy in London.

JIM CHAPLIN was a student in the African Studies Center at Makerere College in Uganda. His recent death in an automobile accident was a loss both to poetry and to his numerous friends.

JOE DE GRAFT has been an important influence in the development of the theatre in Ghana. His play *Sons and Daughters* has been published in London and has been produced with great success several times in Africa. He is also known for his poetry.

SOLOMON DERESSA is an Ethiopian writer. He writes poems and short stories in both English and Amharic. He has studied in France and is at present Head of Production in Radio Ethiopia.

R. SHARIF EASMON is a well known doctor in Freetown, Sierra Leone. He is also well known as a writer. His play *Dear Parent and Ogre* has been regularly performed in Africa, and *The New Patriots* received critical acclaim. The stories are from a new collection which are expected to be published in the States.

ROMANUS N. EGUDU is a Nigerian who until the present civil war had been on the faculty of Nsukka University. His poetry has appeared in *Black Orpheus* and *The Journal of the New African Literature*.

R. A. FREEMAN is a young Nigerian who is doing research work in linguistics at the University of Ibadan.

RASHEED GBADAMOSSI was born in Lagos, Nigeria, and educated in England where he took a bachelor's degree in economics at Manchester University. He is at present doing graduate studies at the University of New Hampshire.

Dr. Eldred Jones is professor of English at Fourah Bay College of the University of Sierra Leone. He is well known as a distinguished critic and his study of Shakespeare *Othello's Countrymen* is a highly regarded work.

Sadru Kassam was born in Mombasa in 1941, and he attended the Aga Khan High School there. He received an honors degree in English at the University of East Africa, and now teaches at a high school in Nairobi.

Taban Lo Liyong is a young Ugandan poet and critic. He has done graduate studies at the writers workshop in the University of Iowa and is at present connected with the Cultural Division of the Institute for Development Studies in Nairobi, Kenya.

Matei Markwei is from Sierra Leone and is now Dean of Students at Freetown Teachers' College. He attended Lincoln and Yales Universities in the United States. His poems have been read over the BBC, and have appeared in several anthologies.

Steven Moyo is a Zambian born in Luanshya. He is editor of the Zambian literary journal *Jewel of Africa*. His poetry has been published in *Presence* in Paris and in *Transatlantic* in London.

S. Nair is a young writer who studied English under David Cook at Makerere. He is associated with the *Penpoint* group in Kampala.

Matthias Njoku was born in Eastern Nigeria, at a town called Ovoro-Owerri. He lived in England for a period and then studied in the States at Howard and the New School for Social Research. He claims a major influence on his work is Sterling Brown. He is at present on the faculty of the new Federal City College in Washington, D.C.

Nathaniel Obudo is a Kenyan from the Kisumu area. He trained as a teacher at Siriba College, and is presently pursuing higher studies.

Joseph O. O. Okpaku of Nigeria is editor of the journal *New African Literature* (Stanford University). He is a doctoral student in the Department of Theatre Arts at Stanford. He has written two plays, one of which won a prize in a BBC competition.

John Roberts is a former journalist on the *East African Standard* in Nairobi. He is now in London, where he works with the African Service of the BBC.

John M. Ruganda is a young East African poet who formerly studied at Makerere. He has been connected with the magazine *Penpoint*.

PETER RUORO is a young Kenyan writer whose work has appeared in the important African journal *Transition*. He is presently studying in the United States at Wheaton College, Illinois.

PROSCOVIA RWAKYAKA is from Uganda. She attended Gayaza Secondary School and the Makerere University, where she received a B.Ed. She now teaches at Tororo Girls' School in Uganda.

PAUL SITATI is a young Kenyan writer at present completing his studies in English at Nairobi University College.

JOHN SSEMUWANGA of Uganda was educated at missionary schools before attending Makerere College. His work has appeared in magazines and anthologies.

OKOGUBLE WONODI recently finished his studies in the United States, and returned to assume a position as a lecturer at Nsukka University. His poems have appeared in *Transition*, and he is at work on an anthology at the present time.

BOEVI ZANKLI—Prince Bibby Boevi Body-Lawson was born in Lagos but of Togolese parents. He is an actor as well as a writer. He performed in the Lagos Theatre Workshop and has been in both TV and film. He is at present a student at Howard University.

UCHE OKEKE is a distinguished Biafran artist who has won several prizes while he was working at the University of Zaria. A selection of his drawings have been published by the Mbari press in Ibadan. He is at present in Germany.

OTHER MANYLAND BOOKS PUBLICATIONS

"Manyland Books, a house which as its name implies, tries to bring us some of the best of writing from other countries."
—The Kansas City Star

NOVELS

HOUSE UPON THE SAND, by *Jurgis Gliauda.* 168 pages. L.C. Cat. Card No.: 63-17248. Cloth. $3.95.
"*House Upon the Sand,* a novel of savage ironies, belongs with the best of the literature on Nazidom . . . it tells of a decent German aristocrat who turns into a Nazi killer with chilling ease."—*Time.*
". . . this novel . . . pictures the 'crime and punishment' of a German landowner just before Hitler's empire crumbled. . . . Recommended for larger collections."—*Library Journal.*

•

THE SONATA OF ICARUS, by *Jurgis Gliauda.* 169 pages. L.C. Cat. Card No.: 67-31646. Cloth. $5.00.
"Good fictional biography is rare and *The Sonata of Icarus* is one of those rare occasions. It delves deeply into the innermost being of one of the greatest artists of Lithuania, Mikalojus Konstantinas Čiurlionis (1875-1911), a composer and a painter, and a master in both worlds. . . . It is adult, it is fresh, it is filled with arresting aperçus; its men and women breathe and leap across the pages—and there emerges a person and an artistic philosophy that the world must reckon with."—*Charles Angoff.*
". . . Mr. Gliauda can hammer in his theme with an almost biblical style of simplicity and spirituality. The whole work, it seems, is a metaphor based on the Greek myth of Daedalus and Icarus."—*Sunday Advocate,* Baton Rouge, La.

•

REJUVENATION OF SIEGFRIED IMMERSELBE, by *Ignas Šeinius.* 247 pages. L.C. Cat. Card No.: 65-17034. Cloth. $5.00.
"There are three kinds of satire. The first may be called negative and destructive, depending for its excellence upon the genuineness and justification of the satirist's venom. The splendid satires of Juvenal belong to this category. The second type of satire is benevolent and innocuous; it makes a pleasant mockery of human foibles without malice. In this category we may include the works of Horace, La Fontaine, and Voltaire. The third kind of satire may be called dynamic and constructive. It aims at stigmatizing human wrongdoing,

striking at the root of the evil. . . . It is in this third category that *Rejuvenation of Siegfried Immerselbe* belongs—a brilliant novel by a brilliant Lithuanian writer who has written many fine works in both Lithuanian and Swedish."— *King Features Syndicate.*

"Mr. Šeinius' tale is intellectual spoofing in the grand manner, but it also reveals vast knowledge of many of the lunacies that have plagued our times."— *The Chicago Tribune.*

•

FOOTBRIDGES AND ABYSSES, by *Aloyzas Baronas.* 229 pages. L.C. Cat. Card No.: 65-28126. Cloth. $5.00.

This prolific author sees World War II through the eyes of a young man who is seized by the retreating Germans and forced to join front-line labor unit. This anti-hero is dragged through the "twilight zone" of devastation in Lithuania and East Prussia, and toward the heart of Germany—always one step ahead of the advancing Red Army.

An international flotsam of characters is swept together with the narrator of the novel, who records in swift sketches the trail of total war. Beyond their fate and the constant rumbling of the big engines of destruction, the reader can discern the tragic fate of a small nation caught between two totalitarian giants.

"(The author) here successfully fused lyrical poetry with savage realism to create a prose that conveys with elegiac power the recent tragic history of his nation . . . impressive book."—*Saturday Review.*

•

THE THIRD WOMAN, by *Aloyzas Baronas.* 169 pages. L.C. Cat. Card No.: 68-54593. Cloth. $5.00.

The third woman of the title is more than a lovely young girl ordained by fate to share the life of a waif of history. She is also a symbol of the Other Person who is the eventual victor in all plans and in all the proposals of man. "In truth, the third woman always wins. Death is the third woman. She deprives wives as well as mothers. She is patient and ever waiting. You can rely on her."

"It is astonishing how much Mr. Baronas says in so little space. Like all fine works of literary art, *The Third Woman* can be enjoyed on many levels: as sheer story, as history, as philosophical commentary, and as prose poetry."— *Charles Angoff.*

•

THE DELUGE, by *Mykolas Vaitkus.* 178 pages. L.C. Cat. Card No.: 65-27473. Cloth. $3.95.

The Bible continues to be an unending source of ideas for all art forms—

literary, musical, sculptural, architectural, pictorial. Two recent Nobel Prize winners in literature have borrowed heavily from the Bible.

Mykolas Vaitkus' triumph, in the present novel, is that he may properly be discussed in this company. His artistic obsession, apparently, is the story of the Flood as told in the Old Testament. It is truly one of the greatest concepts in world literature.

Mykolas Vaitkus retells this story in the form of a conflict between two peoples, the Shimites and the Sunnarians, and in terms of the two opposing leaders, Itnah and Sinth.

". . . his descriptions have a power which in its mystical splendor is truly Biblical. As this weird tale proceeds, it holds the imagination of the reader paralyzed in its grip."—*King Features Syndicate.*

•

THE WINNOWING WINDS, by *Gerald E. Bailey.* 135 pages. L.C. Cat. Card No.: 67-28549. Cloth. $4.00.

This work attempts to define revolution by a momentary focussing upon the microcosm of a fictional North African country in which Arabs, French, and Americans die or survive to enter a new world.

Says Mr. Bailey of *The Winnowing Winds:* "I toured Algeria briefly before the outbreak of revolt there. I was in Morocco, as a member of the Strategic Air Command, during the year that saw the victory of the revolution in that nation. I knew that one day I would have to tell a story of people great and small; of Arab, French, and American people caught for a moment in this new age of revolutions."

Mr. Bailey, in his knowledgeable novel, has caught this dichotomy in an arresting story, brimming with living men and women and exciting situations.

SHORT STORIES

SELECTED LITHUANIAN SHORT STORIES. Edited by *Stepas Zobarskas.* 279 pages. L.C. Cat. Card No.: 59-15934. Cloth. $4.00.

"Twenty-one stories are printed, the last four under the general heading 'Legends and Tales.' In these one would expect to find a strong element of folklore, and one is not disappointed. . . .

"Freshness, simplicity, vigour—these are the qualities one hopes for and plentifully finds."—*The Times Literary Supplement.*

". . . The authors range from figures prominent in the national and cultural revival at the turn of the century to contemporary writers living in exile. . . . They all provide interesting insight into the cultural history and political tribulations of the Lithuanian people. And since American readers are almost completely ignorant of Lithuanian literature, the appearance of such a book is to be welcomed."—*Library Journal.*

•

THE HERDSMAN AND THE LINDEN TREE, by *Vincas Krėvė*. 128 pages. L.C. Cat. Card No.: 64-23673. Cloth. $3.95.

This collection of stories is but a small part of the whole treasure created by the foremost Lithuanian author, Vincas Krėvė, whose versatility has enabled him to produce short stories, dramas, Biblical narratives, and oriental tales, with equal success. He was the first, and probably the only, figure in Lithuanian literature who applied the style of folklore to some of his stories, using legends and songs of lamentation filled with musical and recitative elements.

". . . *The Herdsman and the Linden Tree* digs deep into the dark abyss of the human heart. . . . It is a gem of insight and evocation of mood and of the atmosphere of a locale. But its value transcends all boundaries of space. It alone places Vincas Krėvė in the front rank of modern writers."—*Charles Angoff* (From the Introduction).

"Krėvė is a giant of Lithuanian literature who has much to offer to lovers of literature everywhere."—*The Slavic and East European Journal*.

•

NOON AT A COUNTRY INN, by Antanas Vaičiulaitis. L.C. Cat. Card No.: 65-21429. Cloth. $3.95.

Author of novels and short stories, poems, criticism, and translations from the literatures of the West, Antanas Vaičiulaitis ranks as a distinguished man of letters in the broad European tradition.

Some of Antanas Vaičiulaitis works have already been translated into French, German, Italian, Spanish, Estonian, and Latvian. *Noon at a Country Inn* is the first volume of his fiction to appear in English.

All but two of the stories in this collection are set in the author's native Baltic land. Yet against this background, so exotic and remote to Westerners, his narrative range is astonishing and perfectly comprehensible.

"*Noon at a Country Inn* introduces a European writer of genuine value and stature. . . . Few with his qualities are extant today."—*Clark Mills*.

"We hope more of Vaičiulaitis's stories will be translated into English."—*Books Abroad*.

POETRY

ALOHA: POLYNESIA, by *Joseph Joel Keith*. 60 pages. Cloth. $4.00.

The poems celebrate the landscape, the flowers, the doves, the children and older people of Hawaii, and many a poem in these pages has the impact of "the white plumeria lei" that the poet lifts "from the still water, the gift that someone cast from a passing ship."—*The Capital Times*.

"Keith is a very good example of the modern poet as a creator of mood."—*The Indian P.E.N.*

•

AMENS IN AMBER, by *Leonardas Andriekus*. 85 pages. L.C. Cat. Card No.: 67-31645. Cloth. $4.00.

Leonardas Andriekus, a priest, poet, and editor, is at present the provincial superior of Lithuanian Franciscans in the United States and Canada. His verses bear out the observation that "some of the most glorious poetry is instinct with religious passion." The book is lovely. The illustrations are black-and-white plates showing insects in cocoon stages; the verses are uncrowded on glossy paper so that each page—glowing white—is like a special container for a gem. The poems are light, as a rapier is light. The style is modern. The mood is Christian. Recommended for public libraries, primarily."—*Library Journal*.

•

THE BELL OF TIME, by *Charles Angoff*. 74 pages. L.C. Cat. Card No.: 66-30065. Cloth. $4.00.

"Charles Angoff is one of America's literary jewels. For nearly forty years, he has been an unassuming but creative force in the field of letters, during which time he has given an excellent account of himself in every genre. Although his poems, legion in number, have appeared in periodicals at home and abroad, *The Bell of Time* is his first book of poetry.

"The poet is deeply involved with a dynamic appreciation for the human condition. With a few strokes of his pen, we are treated to wit, pathos, and laughter, always with imagination and rare understanding."—*Books Abroad*.

•

TO REGIONS OF NO ADMITTANCE, by *Danguolė Sealey*. 86 pages. L.C. Cat. Card No.: 68-56020. Cloth. $4.00.

Danguolė Sealey's verse, as many-layered as her experience, blends the ancient modes of the Lithuanian folk song with the modern idiom. Contemporary in their interiority and individualism, these poems are not encased in solitude, but offer themselves to nature in a manner that is not typical of the Western poetic tradition. They are fragments of communion with plant and beast, lover and God.

Her translations of Lithuanian imaginative prose have appeared in several American magazines and have been presented over the BBC in London.

FOLKLORE

LITHUANIAN FOLK TALES, compiled and edited by *Stepas Zobarskas*. 240 pages. L.C. Cat. Card No.: 58-13716. Cloth. $4.50.

". . . 36 classic tales . . . and each as interesting as many Grimm's tales. Each tale is beautifully illustrated by Ada Korsakaitė, a well known Lithuanian artist . . . *Lithuanian Folk Tales* is a book for both the young and old."—*The Chicago American*.

•

THE MOUNTAIN DOVES and Other African Folk Tales, edited by *Nola M. Zobarskas*. Illustrated by Pranas Lapė. 137 pages. L.C. Cat. Card No.: 64-16986. Cloth. $3.50.

A collection of 22 folk tales from the African continent, ranging from the simple nature-myths of the Bushmen to sophisticated Ethiopian morality tales.

The stories in *The Mountain Doves* are English translations of various African versions of still earlier language and dialect accounts of oral legends. . . . Individually, they are enjoyable fiction that provides convincing spiritual truth. Collectively, they provide a useful addition to the growing body of texts in English of this most ancient, most enduring, and most revealing form of artful human expression.

"Different teachers will probably want to approach retelling these stories to their classes in different ways, but, however retold, they offer a sensing of the mood and soul of Africa rarely captured."—*American Junior Red Cross News*.

•

TUNDRA TALES, edited by *Nola M. Zobarskas*. Illustrated by Pranas Lapė. 175 pages. L.C. Cat. Card No.: 66-30066. Cloth. $5.00.

As a people the Eskimos comprise only a small segment of the world's population, yet their folklore is rich in customs and traditions which have remained intact for nearly two thousand years.

"Interesting to adults who study and collect folk literature from various parts of the world, these tales might have a special attraction for children."— *Sunday Advocate*.

"The (pre-Christian?) earthiness and absence of sermons are refreshing: fantasy wedded to the harsh terms of life in the tundras."—*Books Abroad*.

•

HISTORY

ESSAYS IN GREEK POLITICS, by *Raphael Sealey*. 199 pages. L.C. Cat. Card No.: 67-28844. Cloth. $6.00.

These ten essays, of which nine have appeared previously in journals, offer a new analysis of Athenian internal politics. The author, a member of the faculty of the University of California, rejects the usual view that Athenian political conflicts stemmed from differences of class-interest, and that two relatively constant bodies of opinion diverged on large issues of constitutional principle and foreign policy. Instead, he believes that the conflicts existed between numerous small groups of politically active families, each group bound together more by the personalities of the leaders than by a distinctive policy. The essays attempt to establish this thesis by examining a series of crucial problems from the time of the Peisistratids in the sixth century B.C. until the the age of Alexander.